THE MORON'S GUIDE

TO

GLOBAL COLLAPSE

*A thumbnail sketch of how we got into this mess with
sardonic observations on the passing,
or rather the crumbling, scene*

*Including "Dubya's Lament,"
from Best of 2005 in Cynic Magazine*

Jenna Orkin

D1411990

Jenna Orkin deserves, and now has, an immortalized place in [From the Wilderness] history...

[She also] has a fierce and unyielding sense of humor... She wields it with precision to open our eyes to some of the funnier and some of the less palatable and deeper aspects of human life...

Michael C. Ruppert,
Author, "Crossing the Rubicon: The Decline of
the American Empire at the End of the Age of Oil"
and "Confronting Collapse."
Founder, www.Fromthewilderness.com, www.CollapseNet.com

On one of the articles in this book:

...excellent. [It] should also be a cautionary tale for Peak Oil organizations which risk becoming captive to the oil, financial and business-as-usual industries which they work to scrutinize...

Jim Baldauf,
Association for the Study of Peak Oil and Gas,
ASPO-USA

To Jenna Orkin:

...Without your work with the blog, [from which many articles in this book are drawn] Michaels [sic] book Crossing the Rubicon that helped me connect the issues of Peak Oil etc., I think I would have ended up believing that I really had lost my mind. Instead I have been given the tools to inform the people close to me. Thank you for that. I'm getting carried away here... Just wanted to tell you that you are an inspiration and a true hero in my world. —*A.*

I've been discussing Peak Oil with friends and co-workers for seven years. For seven years, I've correctly identified numerous economic patterns, political and social impacts. Called the crash of 2008 and the real estate crash. All largely based on the research and insight found here at this blog. *[Note: The blog was established in 2006. The writer is probably conflating it with the website with which it was originally linked, From the Wilderness.]* I keep coming back to this blog because it is the ONLY place I have found were [sic] peak oil is acknowledged and discussed in a civilized way. —*Peaked Out*

This blog opened a lot of new eyes. —*V*

Thanks for all the hard work and great info. —*Vic-chick*

From us, all the best is felt towards Mr. Mike Ruppert and Jena [sic], too. For without their genius and relentless stick-to-it-tiveness all this time, many of us just wouldn't be here anyway. We were drawn to the light. —*Mrs. P.*

Never before has man had such capacity to control his own environment, to end thirst and hunger, to conquer poverty and disease, to banish illiteracy and massive human misery. We have the power to make this the best generation of mankind in the history of the world—or to make it the last.

John F. Kennedy,
speech to the UN calling for an end to the Cold War
and converting the Moon Race into an international
cooperative effort, Sept 20, 1963, two months and two days
before he was removed from office.
www.oilempire.us/moonrace.html

The Earth in Eight Verses

"This is your garden," God told Man,
"to cultivate." (Was that Voltaire?)
Man looked and said, "In my opinion,
it is good, this, my dominion."

But Paradise soon lost its charm
as Man grew restless and ambitious.
Striking out, exploratory,
he sought ever greater glory.

And it was also good as he
plumbed sea, tamed forest, so he thought
they partook of Infinity
and having been, must always be.

His cities grew and towers rose.
Man was fruitful, multiplied.
He said, "In order to stay Master,
I must build more, higher, faster."

The prophets railed, those wild-eyed fools,
"What about the Pygmy Owl?
Arroyo Toad? Blue-crested tit?"
Man shrugged, said, "Never heard of it.

Eat, drink, be merry. Seize the day
for it is yours. The time is Now.
Can't you see the only thing
that matters is that I am king?"

While far away, beneath the seas,
the fish were gone. In desert, wood,
without a sound, a word or tear,
ten thousand species died each year.

The earth grew warm and oceans rose.
Birds and plants died off till, as
in tales of Midas told of yore,
there was no kingdom anymore.

Acknowledgments

To Mike Ruppert, who introduced me to Peak Oil and whose website, www.fromthewilderness.com, educated me in how the world works; to Mark Robinowitz whose website, www.oilempire.us, is a goldmine of enlightenment in separating real information from its evil twin, disinformation; to the staff at Collapsenet.com and to Carolyn Baker whose wit and insights have kept the rest of us at Fromthewilderness.com and Collapsenet.com going.

To my students, whose openness and intelligence have helped shape the message of this book.

To the contributors to the comments section of the World News Desk at www.CollapseNet.com and www.mikeruppert.blogspot.com whose experience and insight educate our growing band in the Peak Oil and Permaculture movements.

To 9/11 Environmental Action, Congresspersons Nadler and Maloney and their staff, the workers at Ground Zero, the New York Environmental Law and Justice Project, Dr. Cate Jenkins of the U.S. Environmental Protection Agency, Hugh Kaufman and Robert Martin at the now abolished USEPA Ombudsman's office, Community Board One, Suzanne Mattei and the parents, students and staff of Stuyvesant High School who fought for cleanup after 9/11.

To Phil Botwinick for his ass-saving computer savvy and to All Ivy Writing Services, J.C. Louis, Michele Farbman, Charlotte LoBuono and Brian Calavan for their invaluable help with the footnotes. To Ash Chang for her incisive observations, Veronika Lyubenko and Djasur Asliev for their practical insights and Felipe for his ideas on marketing strategy.

To my mother, my son and Adele

Contents

INTRODUCTION

As this introduction is being written, Japan is under siege from the Fukushima nuclear disaster—a man-made volcano spewing radioactive elements into the air and soil while levels near the site have attained to 7.5 million times the norm;[1] the two Koreas hover on the brink of war, a situation of global import since they could draw in China and the U.S.; the governments of Portugal and Ireland have collapsed, the latter, several times and already the European Union is out of money with which to bail out Spain, the next in line and largest domino of the PIIGS to fall. The financial debacle in the U.S. has led to criminal investigations of fifty bankers and directors to date while the "fraudclosure" crisis is a hybrid creature with the face of a farce and the body of a tragedy.

But even as the mayhem picks up speed around the world, a phenomenon is taking place which seems curiously at odds with expectations. At first, the public protests their own particular piece of the collapse (the residents of the Gulf Coast railing against BP,) but as the cause of their outrage grinds ahead full force regardless, they eventually lapse into mute despair. An acceptance of impending apocalypse has emerged and spread without even being discussed.

The media, even such apparently venerable sources as the History Channel, have nudged this zeitgeist along with doom-porn by way of Nostradamus (Google that name in conjunction with "schizophrenic" and you get 136,000 hits) or the Book of Revelation (which Ken's Guide to the Bible describes as, "St John on Acid.") Thus is the public's attention neatly deflected away from the magician's sleight of hand as he picks their pocket yet again.

These circus sideshows are intended to instill terror which, in one form or another, has become the lightning rod of our discontent—rendering us helpless—as opposed to rage which could actually get us somewhere. Whenever too many people organize to audit the Federal Reserve or investigate insider trading, a fresh, though invariably unsmiling young face turns up from a country few Americans can locate on a map with, say, an explosive in his boxers and a father who's unusually well connected in that country's energy, banking and communications sectors. Or, in anticipation of a hurricane, New York City shuts down the transportation system for over 36 hours and supermarket shelves are swept as bare as any seen in the former Soviet Union. Or Nobel Prize economist Paul Krugman suggests that the economy could benefit from a faked alien invasion.[2]

An axiom of this book is that there are indeed forces that benefit from the sort of disasters we are currently witnessing. How could there not be when many of those disasters are manmade? The economy, with its glories and its attendant downsides, is not an act of God; nor is Fukushima, although the earthquake that instigated the meltdown was. But earthquakes are not so freakish that the engineers who designed the plant could afford to overlook the risk. And even some earthquakes themselves, or at least their level on the Richter scale, are intensified by manmade climate change.

So who is to blame for this abysmal state of affairs?

You are. I am. We may not be as deeply implicated as the biggest fish in the cycle but chances are that if you're reading this, you have taken more from the earth than you have given back since it is virtually impossible not to do so in modern society.

However, there are even bigger fish to fry, as you are no doubt aware. Since the purpose of this book is to elucidate how the system really works, in so doing, some of those perps will be identified.

Meanwhile, how did we get here? How did the system get so out of control?

Until recently, Everyman has not asked these questions because he was sufficiently content. He made a good enough living and, more importantly, he had hope it could get even better. It's only when his life falls apart that Everyman becomes a philosopher.

The second reason is the apparent opposite of the first: Everyman has been too busy earning a living to notice that his pocket was being picked.

But every so often, an incipient question would insinuate itself into Everyman's thoughts, while he was driving to his second job, say; something about some vague, faceless bastards somewhere. But what can you do? You'll just have to take out another mortgage. As our economic crisis has proceeded, perhaps when Everyman lost one or both of his jobs, the questions have multiplied.

This book is for that person entertaining those first half-formed questions; who is just waking up to the idea that maybe the world does not work the way he always thought it did. It is intended to be merely a primer, the first step for the poor schmuck who sits bolt upright in bed one night gasping, "Fuck!" A whole new awareness lies packed in the exclamation, bringing with it questions that threaten to rent apart the fabric of beliefs that Everyman has always lived by. To those, this book attempts to provide some initial, thumbnail answers. Readers who are interested in further pursuing the subjects discussed here can investigate among the array of superb books that delve into greater detail. They are by experts in their fields. I am but an Every [wo]man like the reader herself, coming by my information via an ad hoc education in the trenches.

A number of subjects treated in these pages are controversial, such as the actions of the United States government surrounding the attacks of 9/11. Beyond presenting some salient pieces of evidence, I do not lay out a detailed case proving complicity although when one goes against the grain, one bears a hefty burden of proof. Others have already performed that service superbly on such websites as www.fromthewilderness.com and www.oilempire.us as well as in such books as Michael C. Ruppert's Crossing the Rubicon. Were I to undertake the same project, this would be a far more cumbersome book than the "Moron's Guide" status to which it aspires.

ঙ   ঙ

My own baptism into the world as it really works came courtesy of 9/11.   Trying to acquire accurate information about the environmental conditions downtown turned into a crash course in government cover-ups and bureaucratic chicanery.   Like the few other activists who worked on the issue from the beginning, I had to learn science—a subject that had lagged behind the others at the girls' high school I'd attended—in order to confront the U.S. Environmental Protection Agency on their own turf.   And in so doing, I learned how officials lie without incurring liability and how the media acquiesce in the process.

Since 9/11, disasters in housing or the economy have forced other laymen to obtain analogous expertise.   We are Judy Holliday in Born Yesterday ("*A cartel!*")   But once the process begins, it never ends; each question leads to a deeper question as you trace the thread to its source.

And what is that source?

The first answer is, "Money."   But delving further still, one finds that the heart of the problem is not only money which is a human construct created for convenience—a symbol—but resources, the real stuff which money symbolizes, the elements of life—water, food—which we in our spoiled culture take for granted.   In fact, so hubristic have we become that often people in the developed world, when asked for solutions to the energy or food crisis, will blithely respond, "Human ingenuity," as though if a person is smart enough and you throw enough money his way, all our problems will be dispelled.

Money would not be the root of our evils if resources were infinite.   It's those pesky laws of nature that get in the way.   The way money works requires infinite growth.   The earth is finite. There's the rub; where the rubber meets the road.

And of those finite resources, the grease on which the engine of global commerce runs is oil.   Thus, the Rosetta stone to which we must turn is Peak Oil.

PEAK OIL 101

Introduction to Peak Oil 101

There are two kinds of people in the world and they're not the usual dichotomies: Hunters vs. hunted, doers vs. thinkers or patients vs. nurses, etc. It's those who think, "It can't happen to me," (whatever horror the "it" of the moment refers to, usually a natural disaster in a country where nature is a more active participant than it is in the U.S.) and those who have always known their day would come: The gods would realize they'd been overlooked; reality would hit and it would be their turn to suffer like all those people they'd only read about in the newspaper or the history book.

Peak Oil is the "it" we've been dreading; the monster we always knew was in the closet or the shadowy corner. For me, it was the crevice between the bed and the wall. In the space between familiar objects lay the unknown. Nature abhors a vacuum and so did I—it was filled with demons waiting.

Peak Oil is also the monster in the attic mirror for what we who harbor secret fears secretly know is that we've been getting away with murder. That is why we gravitate towards horror stories at the safe distance of literature or movies. They're mesmerizingly familiar but when the story is over, we can close the book or walk out of the theater.

Peak Oil will also provide the answer to those fleeting questions: How would I have fared two hundred years ago before electricity, gas and plumbing? With 6.8 billion people on earth all using water, food and energy, can this last forever? What's wrong with this picture?

It is horrific and yet home at the same time; the hell we have to endure before earning a place in Heaven or even back on earth (albeit an earth transformed to its natural state, probably minus a few billion of us). We have indeed been living on borrowed time and borrowed land and now it's the day we always knew would come, the Day of Reckoning, payback time.

ᥰ   ᥱ

Most of the following articles have been written over the course of the last seven years since I first heard of Peak Oil in a talk given by Mike Ruppert at a conference commemorating the third anniversary of 9/11. I'd been invited to speak on the environmental disaster that had ensued after the attacks, largely as a result of the U.S. government's lies about the air quality downtown. My son had been a junior in high school there; hence my immersion in the issue which continued and grew even after—several months later than I would have liked—I was able to withdraw him from the school.

What the environmental disaster of 9/11 had taught me was that we were up against a monster. You can't fight City Hall, particularly on a national scale. Yet fight we did—"we" being a handful of activists and scientists—for the alternative, giving up, was not an option. We would save what or whom we could. Disheartening as the battle was, we did help secure $20 million from Congress to clean the seven schools in the vicinity of Ground Zero, albeit in the summer of 2002 after the kids at Stuyvesant High School, which my son attended, had been exposed to extraordinary levels of contamination not only from Ground Zero but also from the waste transfer station located at their north doorstep.

This was perhaps our greatest concrete achievement apart from getting the issue into the national and international press and thus educating a public who had initially been gulled by the government's lies.

After those fraught first few years, the Law of Diminishing Returns kicked in. While programs were set up to treat Ground Zero workers and Lower Manhattan residents, office workers and students, their emphasis was on symptoms rather than root causes of illness. (This impression is gleaned from conversations with some doctors participating in the programs as well as patients.) Treatment seemed to focus on steroids whose long-term ill effects might arguably outweigh their short-term advantages.

Also, with the passage of time, more people were manifesting such obvious symptoms that the activists who worked on the issue had grown to a large cohort. The need to clamor for government action was being taken over by Ground Zero workers who were by now sick and dying and who, by virtue of this condition combined with their proven heroism, were extremely effective advocates.

Some truths are like Justice Potter's definition of pornography: "I know it when I see it." There's an involuntary, heartfelt, "A-ha!" after which life is never the same again.

Mike Ruppert's talk at that symposium on the third anniversary of the attacks was one of those moments for me. My focus shifted: I realized that the enemy was even more insidious and hell-bent than I'd understood. The environmental disaster of 9/11 was but one piece of a bigger and even uglier puzzle.

With my allies in the movement for government transparency and appropriate clean-up and healthcare, I'd been living the wrong movie. This was not some 70's tale of David vanquishing Goliath, the good guys triumphing albeit after a long, hard struggle. The enemy had a global plan and Peak Oil was its raison d'être.

It's ironic that the first question I asked Mike upon meeting him was one that had come to mind every so often over the course of my whole life: "They keep talking on the news about 'economic growth.' Can the economy keep growing forever?"

"No!" he exclaimed, bouncing a little on the balls of his feet. "That's the point!"

He hadn't mentioned the economy in his talk but it underpinned his argument that diminishing supplies of oil, on which the economy depended, would precipitate not just a muting of our lifestyle, a lapse into a sort of genteel poverty, but a collapse that would dwarf the Great Depression, resembling, more, the fall of the Roman Empire.

(That's one of two times when Mike has addressed a question that I've never been able to answer before. The other was at Petrocollapse, the Peak Oil conference I moderated in October of the following year. I'd always wondered, "During the Depression when everyone lost money, where did it go?"

"The Depression was not a loss of wealth," Mike said at the press conference that was held during the break. "It was a transfer of wealth.")

Einstein spent much of his life looking for a Unified Field Theory to explain how the universe worked. When theories presented themselves, he would often reject them on the grounds that they were too complicated. He believed that the answer, when it was found, would be simple. It seemed to me that Peak Oil offered a Unified Field Theory for how the world works, at least these days. It tied up loose ends, explaining 9/11, the Iraq War and the then impending, but now in progress, collapse of the economy. Within that Unified Field Theory, Peak Oil itself was the Prime Mover.

In the course of the struggle over the government's lies about the air quality after 9/11, I'd become an Internet junkie, researching whatever leads and links could help my cohorts. Now I shifted the subject of my research to Peak Oil, sending articles from the media to Mike's website, www.fromthewilderness.com, and writing articles of my own. In 2005, Jan Lundberg of www.Culturechange.org and I invited Mike to speak at Petrocollapse, the first Peak Oil conference in New York City.

In February of the following year, Mike asked me to moderate the From the Wilderness blog, www.mikeruppert.blogspot.com, though it would not be fully launched until May. (Since then, it has undergone another incarnation as the World News Desk at Collapsenet.com.) Like the World News Desk, the blog mostly collected links from major international media as well as some specialized websites. But Mike and I also wrote for it regularly, particularly since the main FTW site folded in the chaos following a burglary of the offices while Mike and writer Stan Goff were investigating the death of Pat Tillman in Afghanistan by friendly fire. (From the Wilderness broke the story of the subsequent cover-up among high-ranking generals, also implicating Secretary of Defense Donald Rumsfeld.)

It's from this background that the following articles are adapted. They are intended to be user-friendly; comprehensible even to those who have only just encountered the concepts of Global Collapse and Peak Oil. It is not too late for such folk. And it is with them in mind that articles have been included concerning subjects that the Peak Oil movement might consider peripheral such as the background to 9/11 with its implications for and of the American government; or the myriad ways in which the government and media lie, particularly by omission and its sidekick, distraction. Such articles are necessary to present a more complete picture. The Peak Oil message is weakened if the reader is left with questions hanging like chads: "Yeah, but what if we don't fight those terrorists?" "Don't we have to restore economic growth?" or, "Spitzer? Wasn't he the guy who frequented $1000 an hour call girls?" For, as the South American revolutionary Simon Bolivar, said, "An ignorant people are the blind instrument of its own destruction."

Peak Oil 101

From the Introduction to Petrocollapse, the first Peak Oil Conference in New York City, October 5, 2005

There is a Chinese curse: May you live in interesting times.

You may have seen the New York Times Sunday Magazine article, the *Beginning of the End of the Age of Oil.* This is one of the first major articles in the mainstream media to acknowledge that we are indeed at the end of an era, even of life as we know it. But what are the implications of that end? Articles on the subject steer clear of that aspect of the impending disaster known as Peak Oil which expert Matthew Simmons has called "the single most important issue of the 21st century."[3]

What is Peak Oil?

First, let's talk about what it is not. It does not mean we're running out of oil completely. Recent articles have indignantly pointed out that we aren't and they're right, though they're attacking a straw man argument; the message of the Peak Oil movement is more subtle than that.

Peak Oil is the theory that Shell geologist M. King Hubbert first publicized in 1956, based on his observation of individual oil fields, that after discovery, oil production follows a bell-shaped curve. When a field is discovered, production rises until it reaches a peak after which it declines, whether commensurately or not.[4] (Most depictions of this phenomenon are symmetrical; the argument that the decline may be far more precipitous than the ascent will be addressed later.) Extrapolating from this, Hubbert predicted that the United States, seen as a sum of its oil fields, would reach its peak around 1971 and the world, in the 1990's.

1971 rolled around; we were awash in oil. People said, "Hubbert's an idiot, we're vindicated; party on."

Then came 1972. U.S. production was all downhill from there. Turns out Hubbert had been right.

Events in the Middle East extended the life of worldwide oil production by about ten years so that Hubbert's initial prediction of global peak in the 1990's is arriving right around now; Thanksgiving Day, to be exact, according to the wry prediction of expert Kenneth Deffeyes.

So what? There's still a lot left, right?

There is, but it's harder and more expensive to get as well as being of lower quality. At its peak, Saudi Arabia offered an average of thirty barrels of oil produced for every one invested. The Energy Returned on Energy Invested (EROEI) is far lower now.[5] At some point in the future, when the ratio is closer to 1:1, it will no longer be worth the time and money it takes to produce the oil. The oil will just be left in the ground. Thus the assurance that we have a trillion barrels or more left is largely irrelevant.

Well, then isn't this a great opportunity to transition to alternative energy, like renewables? To grow vegetables locally? Get more exercise riding bikes? And exercise our brains, too! Necessity is the mother of invention. "They" will come up with something. They always have.

Thus have Peak Oil prophets been dismissed as something between a party-pooper and a guy holding a sign that says, "The end is nigh."

But "they," on whom we're relying to save us, did not create oil in the first place. Nor earth, nor water which are also "endangered." The alternatives are dandy but they don't offer anything close to the EROEI (Energy Returned on Energy Invested) ratio of oil.[6] Scientist-turned-economist Chris Martenson calculates that to replace oil would require either more than 6,800 nuclear reactors (the US currently has 104); nearly 6 million 1 megawatt wind towers; 13 million acres [over 20,000 square miles] of land covered by solar photovoltaic panels; or more than 16 billion acres of farmland (about 135 percent of the total amount of agricultural land in the world) converted to soybean biofuel production.[7]

And that's only to achieve the level of oil we were using in 2009. If we want to increase our consumption at the rate of 1% a year as the EIA assumes we do, we'll need to raise those numbers by 26% by 2030.[8]

So what's the nitty gritty of the Peak Oil crisis? Long gas lines? A bad depression? Or some third thing, the likes of which have never been seen except perhaps in the wake of Hurricane Katrina?

Remember that it's not just cars that eat oil; it's people too. Oil and natural gas are used for pesticides and fertilizer. Without them, we won't be able to grow enough food to feed the global population of 6.8 billion people. Putting aside our knee-jerk liberal indignation about those chemicals polluting and depleting the soil and water, they account for how we got to this population level in the first place. The "Green Revolution" of the sixties was based on that decidedly un-green—in the eco-friendly sense—dirty secret. (Actually, it's even dirtier than that: Pesticides originally derived from nerve gas and other chemical weapons left over from World War II, having been manufactured by I.G. Farben, a German company with which the Rockefeller and Bush families did business even as the war proceeded.[9] I.G. Farben also participated in the experiments on human subjects in the concentration camps as well as in the development of Zyklon B, one of the gasses used in the gas chambers.[10])

An English professor I knew once pointed out the announcement in a deep, Godlike voice that opened each episode of an educational series called Life on Earth: "Life on Earth has been made possible by a grant from the Mobil Oil Corporation."

Whether or not the double entendre was intended, it was true on more levels than most of the audience at that time understood.

We're all aware of our own mortality though we may try not to think about it. Yet a bad diagnosis always comes as a shock.

How much more shocking to face a bad diagnosis not just for yourself or someone in your family, but for everyone you know and the world into which you were born and which you imagined would still be there, more or less the same, when you died.

But that is what we're talking about when we talk about Peak Oil.

**You Know Things Are Really Bad When Those in Charge
Don't Even Try to Hide Them Anymore**

(2005)

Like any disaster, Peak Oil makes strange bedfellows, from tree-hugging, gray-pony-tailed hippies to number crunchers from the most conservative government agencies. The main difference is language: With the bureaucrats, you have to read between the lines but their message is all the more powerful for the knowledge that it goes against their grain to say it. Case in point:

> *"The era of plentiful, low-cost petroleum is approaching an end," writes Robert Hirsch, Senior Energy Program Advisor for Science Applications International Corporation in "The Inevitable Peaking of World Oil Production," published in this month's bulletin of the Atlantic Council. "The good news is that commercially viable mitigation options are ready for implementation. The bad news is that unless mitigation is orchestrated on a timely basis, the economic damage to the world economy will be dire and long-lasting."*[11]

Explaining that reserves should not be confused with production since after a field arrives at peak, the reserves are harder to extract, Hirsch warns that worldwide demand for oil is expected to rise 50% by 2025. At the same time, production is in decline in 33 of the world's 48 largest oil-producing countries. Hirsch describes OPEC's position as changing from one of publicly projected confidence to warnings that are more in line with Matthew Simmons' recent book, *Twilight in the Desert: The Coming Saudi Oil Shock and the World Economy*. By way of illustration, he quotes Dr. Sadad Al-Husseini:

"[A] whole new Saudi Arabia [will have to be found and developed every couple of years] to satisfy current demand forecasts."

Hirsch points out that many of the alternative fuels being touted as replacements for oil are not liquid and can therefore not be used for transportation. And he explains why economists (sometimes referred to by exasperated Peak Oilists as "flat earth economists") fail to "get it" about the oncoming shortage of liquid fuel: They "are accustomed to dealing with hard minerals whose geology is different."

Referring to the study which Hirsch himself, along with Robert Wendling and Roger Bezdek, performed for the U.S. Department of Energy, he cites the oft-quoted section that lays out three scenarios:

    1. If mitigation began twenty years before the arrival of peak oil…

    2. If mitigation began ten years before the arrival of peak oil…

    3. If mitigation began with the arrival of peak oil…

"It became abundantly clear early in this study," he writes, *"that effective mitigation will be dependent on the implementation of mega-projects and mega-changes at the maximum possible rate…. If mitigation is too little, too late,* **world supply/demand balance will have to be achieved through massive demand destruction (shortages.)** *"* [12]

In other words, if supply cannot rise, the only choice is to reduce demand. With this equation in mind, reflect on the narrow escapes from "terror" over the last few years that have coincided with holidays, i.e. the height of the travel season. One of the results, in addition to the erosion of our civil liberties, has been heightened fear of flying. If that didn't work, an added layer of security hassled, humiliated and otherwise deterred would-be travelers from embarking on a trip. The airlines may have felt a blow to the bottom line but oil was conserved.

Contrary to the classic Platonic depiction of Peak Oil with a symmetrical slope on either side of the apex, Hirsch asserts that in the countries that are on their way down, the peaks were sharp, not gently varying or flat-topped, and that in some countries, such as the U.K., the descents were rapid. It is almost as though in the accurate graphs, gravity was at work: slow ascent, precipitous decline. If world peak follows the pattern of these countries, he says (and why would it not?), **the world will have less than a year's warning**.

At that point, welcome to No Man's Land:

>*"The trucks will no longer pull into Wal-Mart. Or Safeway or other food stores. The freighters bringing packaged techno-toys and whatnot from China will have no fuel. There will be fuel in many places, but hoarding and uncertainty will trigger outages, violence and chaos. For only a short time will the police and military be able to maintain order, if at all."*[13]

Peak Oilists differ on what happens next but hovering, largely unspoken in their vision, is what is uneuphemistically called Die-off.

How widespread this will be and how long it will take is where the differences come in. Also in the basic "how" of it: Violence? Disease (whether natural or manmade?) Starvation?

(Newcomers to these unsettling notions may object that the Soviet Union underwent collapse but emerged relatively intact, if smaller. However, Dmitriy Orlov points out that in the Soviet Union, there were few renters for landlords to throw out of their apartments.[14] Also, the United States has been methodically fashioned to be car dependent, with highways where once there were railroads.)

Peak Oilists also differ on who will survive but there's a consensus that the meek shall inherit: People in more primitive societies than ours should weather the storm better than the rest of us. They have less to lose, are already off the grid to a greater extent, are less reliant for essentials on the trappings of modern life and are accustomed to living in the simpler ways that will be required.

On the other hand, in our own society, Darwin's Survival of the Fittest will also come into play, giving priority to strong young thugs.

"This is the age of Big Men," asserts Orlov, "charismatic leaders, rabble-rousers, ruthless Machiavellian princes and war lords."[15]

As for the numbers, experts calculate how many people the earth can sustain without the artificial "steroid" effect of oil-derived pesticides and natural gas-derived fertilizer (which also, by the way, have the side effect of depleting the soil.) The estimates vary widely but two billion is often cited. However, some Permaculture practitioners believe it is possible to feed us all. And Rebecca Hoskings' film, "Farm for the Future," asserts that an appropriate forest garden can be five times as productive as a conventional farm.

But as the large scale implementation of such projects is not on the radar as yet, what we're looking at, given the current paradigm, is more likely to be saying good-bye to 4.8 billion of our closest fellow earthlings, very probably including ourselves and those we care about.

However this population reduction plays out, whether through prudent decision-making to husband resources and control growth (hard to imagine) or through more radical and violent "final solutions" including famine and ensuing diseases, this is the heart of Peak Oil darkness, the reason everyone is skittish of talking about it and so quick to write off those who do.

Yet it is not only these apocalyptic visions which keep those in the know from sharing their privileged information; it is also the responses they call for. These are at least as distasteful to the current power hierarchy as they involve relinquishing some of that power and enduring major sacrifices along with everyone else. Few cultures in the history of mankind have ever done such a thing unless they've been forced to.

For indeed, there *are* answers. This book does not attempt to explicate them in any depth; it is intended more as a primer for the newly awakened reader to get the lay of the land before delving into the nitty-gritty. For the next phase of research, some websites, books and films are recommended at the end.

What can be said here, however, is that surviving Peak Oil and its consequences requires an all-out Manhattan Project on a global scale. It requires understanding on the part not just of those in power but also of individuals. For "the center will not hold" and whether we like it or not, power is going to migrate centrifugally to the outer reaches of society. We see harbingers of this phenomenon already in towns like Ashtabula County, Ohio, where Judge Alfred Mackey told residents to arm themselves as the Sheriff's Department had been cut by more than 50%.[16] Meanwhile, for similar reasons, the police in Madison, Wisconsin recently stood down gun-toting citizens.[17]

Such a brave, new world requires brave citizens with new insight. Where will they get it?

Surviving the fallout of Peak Oil requires challenging every assumption we've grown up with about the status quo, about what is right and about whom we should look to for leadership and expertise. It requires independent research, independence of thought and in the release of the old paradigm, it requires a depth of honesty that is unfamiliar to most people who haven't put in their fair share of time on the psychologist's couch.

Say You Survive Die-Off: Then What?

January, 2006

Watching *The End of Suburbia*, you get the feeling that inside their buttoned-up suits and behind their measured explanations, those experts are scared out of their gourds.

Likewise when you read *The Peaking of World Oil Production: Impacts, Mitigation, and Risk Management*, also known as the *Hirsch Report*—commissioned by that nest of left-wing dissidents, the United States Department of Energy.[18]

The good experts of Science Applications International Corporation, one of the largest military contractors on the planet, know their way around writing a study for a federal agency. Most of the language is dry enough to delight the heart of the dreariest bureaucrat.

Then in a section called "Wildcards," while suggesting possible ways out of our predicament, they let the cat out of the bag. The cards are so wild, it's painfully obvious that in the interest of preserving hope, the bearers of unpleasant tidings have morphed into fantasists.

First comes the pipedream, touching in its whimsicality: "Huge new reserves of natural gas are discovered." (*Under the refrigerator.*)

Then, the vortiginous descent into ever more outlandish scenarios: "World economic and population growth slows and future demand is much less than anticipated..." (*Because people get tired of profits and sex.*)

"Middle East oil reserves are much higher than publicly stated."

That one might almost sound plausible if it weren't for that kill-joy, Matt Simmons, telling us that the public statements of Middle Eastern oilmen do indeed paint an inaccurate picture, only in the opposite direction.

Finally comes the grasping at straws: "Some kind of scientific breakthrough comes into commercial use, mitigating oil demand well before oil production peaks." (*Some kind of scientific breakthrough... any kind. Anybody got any ideas?*)

The members of the New York City Peak Oil Meet-up are only a little freer with their inner freak-out over the issue. I'm not naming names because I didn't announce at the meetings that I'd be writing about them, since the idea hadn't occurred to me yet. But some members, particularly those whose knowledge about the issue rivals that of the most renowned experts, betray more teeth-chattering helplessness than they intend. Or perhaps less—maybe they'd like to spill it all and have a catharsis. The trouble with Peak Oil is you can have your catharsis but it isn't going to change a damn thing about the problem.

"How can you stand knowing about this?" journalist Michael Kane says he is sometimes asked. It's a question Peak Oilists might all ask each other except that it's a little like asking an inmate how he feels about being on Death Row.

What the question means is: How can you know what's around the corner and not go crazy?

The answer is: Do I have a choice?

No, you don't, and the absoluteness of that is strangely comforting; it reduces the number of decisions you have to make. On a personal and local level, you can hit good ol' Google who's always there when you need it, find out which communities are preparing for the coming apocalypse that you could stand to move to, and learn about Permaculture, First Aid and whatever other skills seem applicable to your situation. But unless you're Messrs. Obama, Putin et al., there's not much you can do about Peak Oil on a global scale. (That may change as Collapse unfolds. When Congress is forced to face the truth, they may be more open to your outlook and the solutions it offers.)

Let's go back for a moment to the Edenesque days before anyone outside of a few wonks in the oil industry and arcane corners of the government had ever heard about Peak Oil. Back then, it was generally agreed that just about the worst moment in the average person's life came when he heard he was going to die. "How beautiful life is," he'd think miserably, "and I won't be around anymore to see it."

But here's what makes this disaster different from all other disasters. With Peak Oil, even if you survive, life as you know it won't.

According to the starkest of the Peak Oil paradigms, we each face two possible fates:

1. Die in the "die-off." (A friend complains that this phrase has the impersonal ring of "jerk off.")
2. Survive while everyone who refused to heed the warnings dies.

Either way, you're fucked:

1. You die.
2. You don't die; you're the Last Man Standing in your neck of the all-too-metaphorical woods.

The joy of crying, "I told you so!" to those bastards who called you "crazy" loses some of its appeal when you're also crying it to a bunch of dead loved ones. They may have called you "crazy," too, but they had their redeeming moments.

According to Elizabeth Kubler-Ross' well-known outline of how people come to terms with their own death, depression is followed by acceptance. Let's say the same sequence of attitudes applies in the case of Peak Oil; here's what acceptance might look like:

"The human race destroyed the planet anyway, so Mother Earth will be better off without so many of us."

Hmm... I'm all for the big picture but maybe this one's a little too cosmic? For all its blind, selfish destructiveness, isn't the human race, like old age, better than the alternative?

Of course there's always the bright side that Jan Lundberg, a rebel from the family that publishes the oil industry's Lundberg Letter, looks on. Lundberg, who coined the term "Petrocollapse," isn't what most people would call an optimist. He's the one Congressman Roscoe Bartlett quoted about the trucks not rolling into Safeway and all that.

His vision of the aftermath of Peak is of tribes of strong young men roasting vermin over furniture fires.

But he also sees post-Peak as an opportunity for a fresh start. Those who survive, whether or not it's because they're the fittest, will have learned their lesson: Mother Nature or Else.

This lesson will have been so hard won, it will be passed down from generation to generation so that our tragic yet absurdly avoidable end is never repeated. And if the moral gets diluted over time and mankind grows cocky again, there won't be any easy oil anyway for people to destroy such pockets of Mother Nature as remain.

That's not such a bad vision to live with: Sustainable living, at last. So what are we waiting for? Bring it on! It's just getting from here to there that looks like it could be a rocky ride.

When's Show-time?

Thanksgiving, 2006

Why is this Thanksgiving different from all other Thanksgivings?

In some ways, it isn't.

Thanksgiving three years ago, FEMA closed up shop for the residents of Lower Manhattan and Chinatown which had suffered catastrophic business losses after 9/11. (At Christmas, the EPA closed its hotline for cleanup.)

The fine tradition of pulling-the-rug-out-from-under-the-populace-while-they're-otherwise-engaged is alive and well. Today's article on how the government is preparing for Peak Oil announces: Court Backs Quick Permits for Mountain Coal Mines. The environmental impact, which the court considered "minor," includes blasting away hilltops to uncover coal seams and dumping the leftover rock and dirt in valleys, burying streams. About 1,200 miles of streams were thus buried from 1992 to 2002.[19]

That's what happens when the process of adhering to regulations gets overthrown in favor of "streamlining."

The moral? It pays to read the paper on holidays.

Meanwhile, as everyone heads off to their respective kitchens or in-laws', a few are thinking intently, if only to themselves, of one person: Ken Deffeyes, the standard-bearer for Hubbert's legacy and the author of *Beyond Oil—The View from Hubbert's Peak.*[20]

For according to his estimation—tongue-in-cheek but nonetheless close enough—today's the day Peak arrives. *Apres moi,* says this Thanksgiving, *le deluge.*

Let's hope we're all wrong; that by anticipating disaster we appease the wrathful gods who have in mind more just desserts than just pumpkin pie.

Double Whammy: What Happens When Population Growth Meets Resource Depletion

Based on correspondence with and research by David Pimentel, Professor of Ecology and Agriculture at Cornell University

(2006)

The population of the world currently stands at 6.5 billion people—with a quarter of a million added each day. Of these, 3.7 billion are malnourished and therefore more susceptible to disease. The U.S. population is projected to double in seventy years. In China, even after fifteen years of a one-child per couple policy, the population is still growing because of the sheer number of potential parents. For the same reason, world population would double in seventy years even if there was a limit imposed of two children per couple.

Food, Water, Energy

99.7% of our food comes from the land; the remaining .3%, from the ocean. Food production in the U.S. stands at 1.2 acres of cropland per person. World food production has been declining per capita over the last twenty years with 20% of per capita cropland lost over the last decade. **Topsoil is being lost at ten times the rate of replacement. It takes 500 years for nature to replace each inch. (Composting can expedite the process.) Genetically modified foods do not make any difference since their modifications have mostly to do with resistance to herbicides rather than increased crop yields.**

Each acre of corn and certain other crops requires 500,000 gallons of water during the three-month growing season. Thus it takes 250 gallons of water to make a one-pound loaf of bread.

Per capita use of oil is 3,000 gallons per year in the U.S. with 550 gallons going to food production. Peak Oil is expected to arrive within the next few years after which the oil will be harder to extract and of lesser quality. The transition to alternatives will not be simple. Ethanol, to cite just one example, takes 30% more fuel to create than the ethanol itself provides. And hydrogen is not the panacea the government would have us believe: 4.2 kWh of electricity are required to produce 1kWh of hydrogen; it is also a dangerous fuel.

So what do we do?

Replace annual grain crops with perennial grain crops, says Dr. David Pimentel of Cornell University.[21]

And stop using corn to produce ethanol; it's a waste of energy, cropland and water.

Val Stevens, Co-Chair of the Optimum Population Trust in the U.K., recommends growing crops suited to the local soil and climate, working with nature rather than against.[22]

What about conservation?

Andrew Ferguson, also of Optimum Population Trust, emails: **"It would be a mistake to reduce energy consumption per capita without also starting on the path of population reduction.** The reason is that the politicos [Politicians' plus economists as well as the Commercial world] would use the reduced energy consumption per capita to say that the population can go on expanding, with the end result that when fossil fuels really do become impossibly scarce, there will be an even larger population crash."

This is a version of the Jevons Paradox, which shows how trying to make a problem better can end up making it worse.[23] For instance, someone who conserves energy may also save some money; but if he or she puts that money in the bank, the bank will lend it out to six people or more (because of fractional reserve banking) who will invest in businesses which will in turn use more energy than was originally conserved. The paradox comes into play when one is engaged within a system whose operating principles are antithetical to one's own.

And that is the sort of system we're dealing with when it comes to population reduction by which, I should make clear, I do not mean anything more sinister than a gradual decrease brought about by a decline in the birthrate. Population reduction is not in the interest of the rich and powerful. A growing population is a win/win situation for corporations that get cheap labor and consumers, as well as for politicians who get cannon fodder to combat the Commie/terrorist bogeyman of the moment. In addition, various religious and ethnic groups may encourage their own populations to breed as a defense against a potential enemy. That's why scarce resources could paradoxically be seen as a reason to increase the population of one's own group rather than reduce it: "If there's not much left, we'd better be the ones getting it." Apart from certain religions' advocacy against birth control, other cultural factors militating against population reduction, says Val Stevens, are machismo, lack of education and the oppression of women.

Does this matter for the rest of the world? After all, when Peak Oil hits, globalization will largely cease. What will count most are the resources available locally, not on the other side of the planet.[24] (Many Peak Oil experts argue that we should prepare for this eventuality by starting to think locally now. This is actually taking place, though not on anywhere near the scale required to make a sizeable difference. It would be a mistake to be lulled into a sense of security by stickers at Whole Foods boasting that the product they adorn was "Locally Grown.") So population reduction may be enforced, albeit unevenly, by nature: What AIDS, drought and flooding have left undone may be accomplished by famine and ensuing diseases.

However, before that happens **we could take the reins by providing incentives to have fewer children or, as Dr. Pimentel prefers, placing burdens such as additional taxes on those who have more.** In addition, wrote Andrew Ferguson, governments should aim for more "balanced migration."

Instead, Val Stevens emailed, "we have 'perverse' subsidies, here in the UK at least, and also in France, whereby families get all kinds of financial help from Government with the cost of children, however many children there are. There is child-benefit, maternity benefit, paid maternity leave (and the right to extended unpaid leave for fathers.) There is also now a 'baby-bond' for every child born—a sort of bank account opened by the government for it.

"I believe that child benefit should taper after two, and stop altogether after three. Various groups campaign for more 'child-friendly' policies that make it easier and easier for couples to have children, and go to work, pursue a career, etc. So there will soon not even be the deterrent of more children meaning serious loss of income to a couple."

The Easter Islanders Weren't So Dumb After All

February 27, 2008

I've always harbored doubts about the Peak Oilists' perennial question of whether we will turn out to have been any smarter than the Easter Islanders—those sculptors of enormous heads on the most remote inhabited island in the world—who supposedly perished after chopping down their last tree: Did they really do that?

Surely it's more likely that they chopped down a number of trees while leaving others to germinate, if that's what trees do, but that by the time the tree population had gotten more fragile, some blight came along and did away with the remaining ones. In other words, rather than destroying their own sustenance, they probably miscalculated the need for a buffer, the likelihood of a "Black Swan" (an extremely unusual) event. For catastrophes may be rare but add them all together—fire, flood, epidemic, hurricane, tsunami, violence—accumulate enough years and the likelihood of one coming to a neighborhood near you escalates steeply.

A few nights ago, I talked to a woman who recently returned from Easter Island. She said the blight theory wasn't so far off. What actually did in the trees were rats from ships, possibly from Polynesia, who ate the trees' roots.

So the Easter Islanders weren't so dumb after all. But we still are: We haven't extrapolated from their example.

Are We Smarter Than Yeast?

February 2, 2009

We may be smarter than dinosaurs but we're still dumber than yeast.

Mathematician Albert Bartlett[25] and scientist-turned-economist Chris Martenson[26] underscore the insidious way in which exponents drive their underlying figures to creep up on you. In the end they're still moving at the same rate but my, how they've grown. And when a monster creeps, the world shakes.

Say you have a yeast culture that doubles in size every minute (not biologically possible but this is an abstract problem). It's 12:00 AM and the culture consists of a few unassuming cells in a Petri dish. In twenty-four hours the culture will fill the room.

Question: At what time will the culture fill only *half* the room?

Answer: 11:59 PM.

You can hardly blame yeast for getting caught by that one, especially when we're replicating their example, albeit with more subtle numbers than "double." Using rates closer to 4% or less, exponential growth is what's driving the population explosion, Peak Oil and the economy. But regardless of the number (provided that it's larger than one,) there's always a turning point when horizontal motion morphs into a vertical ascent.

Example: A couple of months ago, we observed that for the United States to create its first trillion dollars took its entire history of two hundred plus years. To create the next trillion took the last six months.

When will we start to notice? When we're creating a trillion dollars every six minutes?

The sword of Damocles settled overhead last week when the word "hyperinflation" found its way onto CNN.

Here in New York City is where a hefty per cent of the Smart Set lives. At least, that's our reputation and certainly some of us believe it ourselves; it's the reason we put up with the rats as well as each other on the subway.

We are the industrious ant; we work at what we've been told will bring us security and respect. And we're really good at it: "If you can make it there, you can make it anywhere."

But what if the ant had it all wrong? After all, grasshoppers aren't extinct either. Ants are busy little bees and look at what's happening to the bees.

In New York, we are in the eye of the storm. Indeed we are, at most, one degree of separation from the people who produced the storm, so we're the last to see it coming.

We feverishly forge ahead building our awe-inspiring edifices because it's all we know how to do. Meanwhile, we pray they'll be finished and we can get our fifteen seconds of fame before the laws of nature kick in and show everyone who's boss.

The old paradigm dies hardest here because the dream is most vivid and within grasp.

"What's the population of your country?" I once asked a student from Moldova.

"Four million," she said, "but half of them are here."

They come seeking a seat at the table of the American Dream.

What a surprise when I tell my students that the gurus of the not-so-distant future will be people like their grandparents whose hard-won understanding of gardening is precisely the sort of knowledge the students came here to escape.

Yet much as they have sacrificed in pursuit of a better life—some of the Latin Americans crawling through sewers or crossing the desert on foot—they are not rooted. They are more ready, willing and able to entertain the notion that the United States is not necessarily a force for good; they have lived under its boot.

It will take a while longer to wean the American people off their expectations. Time is measured by change. As long as the status quo is tolerable, there will be no incentive towards a paradigm shift in thinking. Only when the shit hits the fan will the layabout wake up to the realization that the party's over. At that point, evolution will speed up markedly.

HOW WE GOT INTO THIS MESS

The Original Sin of Economic Growth

It is well enough that the people of the nation do not understand our banking and monetary system, for if they did, I believe there would be a revolution before tomorrow morning.

Henry Ford

The study of money, above all other fields in economics, is one in which complexity is used to disguise truth or to evade truth, not to reveal it. The process by which banks create money is so simple the mind is repelled.

John Kenneth Galbraith[27]

Markets have a very safe way of predicting the future. They cause it.

George Soros[28]

The "repellently simple" process of money-creation to which Galbraith is referring is the old-fashioned way: They print it. Or, these days, they press a key on the computer. The mind is repelled not, initially, by disgust (that comes later), but by disbelief.

"But how can that be?" cries the voice of reason.

Because Congress said so. They bequeathed their birthright—and ours, via the Constitution—to the Federal Reserve in 1913, pursuant to a meeting in 1910 on Jekyll Island which was attended by the movers and shakers of the day, using first names only and dispatching their servants in favor of an ad hoc staff who didn't know who anybody was.[29]

In his 1930 book, *The Federal Reserve System: Its Origin and Growth*, Paul Warburg (one of the attendees of the meeting twenty years earlier) defended the secrecy thus: "It is well to remember that the period during which these discussions took place was the time of the struggle of the financial Titans- the period of big combinations [of businesses], with bitter fights for control. All over the country there was a deep feeling of fear and suspicion with regard to Wall Street's power and ambitions," an excuse to which a number of protests leap to mind along the lines of, "Didn't the meeting itself justify those suspicions?"

Officially, the merry band was on a duck-hunting holiday. (Perhaps Dick Cheney was inspired by this history when he invited Judge Anthony Scalia on a duck hunt eight decades later. Besides dinner, the upshot of that bonding experience was that Scalia refused to recuse himself in a lawsuit brought by the Sierra Club and Judicial Watch to publicize the records of Cheney's National Energy Policy Development Group.[30] More on this critical group later.) Needless to say, secrecy prevailed.

Ask the average person how Congress pays for projects and he or she will say "taxes." Ask the same person where the money comes from that banks use for loans and he or she will say, "From deposits," or, "From loans that have been paid back."

Implicit in these answers is the belief that money goes round and round the world in an infinite circle.

But it's not a circle; it's a spiral.

Say you borrow $100,000 from the bank to start a business. Where did it come from?

Thin air. The Federal Reserve created it on the spot and doled it out to the banks because, like the child in the song, "I'm five," they're allowed. That's the power Congress gave them over Christmas vacation, 1913 (the enemy never rests), ostensibly to prevent another panic like the one that had occurred in 1907. In the 97 years that have passed since the establishment of the Fed, the dollar has lost an average of 1% of its original value per year, or 97%.

Someone has to borrow every dollar we have in circulation, cash or credit. If the Banks create ample synthetic money we are prosperous; if not, we starve. We are absolutely without a permanent money system. When one gets a complete grasp of the picture, the tragic absurdity of our hopeless position is almost incredible, but there it is.

Robert H. Hemphill, Credit Manager of the Federal Reserve Bank of Atlanta, 1934

Now that you've borrowed $100,000, you owe the bank $105,000, say. Where does the extra $5,000 come from? The answer to that question reveals the necessity for infinite growth in our economic system. The bank hasn't created it yet; it doesn't exist. They are obliged to create it now, the same way they created the first $100,000. When you pay back the $105,000, they lend it out to someone else who also owes interest and so the process gathers momentum. It's like a game of musical chairs, with everyone scrambling for too few chairs. To keep the game going, we are compelled to foster an infinite spiral of growth. If an individual tried this, it would be called a Ponzi scheme.

Meanwhile, who's doing the work of starting the business—the bank? No. But they're guaranteed their interest or whatever collateral you put down for the loan. Heads they win; tails you lose.

If you borrowed the money to buy a house and you can't meet your payments, you get nothing but what does the bank get? (In the case of the "liars' loans" leading to the foreclosure crisis, the collateral may have been worth less than the value of the loan but the bankers didn't care since they passed the risk on to unsuspecting investors such as Norwegian pensioners who had no idea that their triple A-rated investments were a sham.)

In other words, the banks neither do the work nor undertake the risk, which is why all three major Western religions initially eschewed interest though of course, they all eventually reconciled themselves, even Islam. (Call it "a commission" instead and the problem disappears.)   Thus interest came to pass, funding the Renaissance as well as the Industrial Revolution by leaving farmers to farm while freeing the educated classes to specialize in everything from art to scientific inquiry and invention.

The situation is compounded, if you'll pardon the term, by the rule of fractional reserve banking which allows banks to keep on hand only a portion of their total deposits; a percentage which, via relaxing regulations, gets smaller all the time.   That's another reason we need infinite growth.   If the economy contracts, people will get nervous and withdraw money from the banks.   Once that process starts and makes its way into the media, it acquires critical mass so that we end up with a run on the banks—aka a stampede— at which point everyone learns the precise meaning of the term, "fractional reserves."

What gets lost in this process is the hard fact that in the end, it is not money that matters.   Not only can money not buy you love; it can't necessarily buy you food or water either, if there's a scarcity.

We've had a good, long run with this system.   But what is happening now is that we are at the end referred to in the expression, "In the end...;" as when John Maynard Keynes— addressing the assertion that in the long run, the free market would work out its own problems—famously said, "In the long run, we're all dead."   We are at the point at which it is not money that matters so much anymore as oil, the product of sun and plant matter distilled over millions of years into a goo with a cornucopia of uses on which we have come to depend.   As the population grinds upwards to fulfill the demands of economic growth, the grease for that growth is sliding downhill.   And as anyone who's taken Economics 101 knows, when the direction of supply deviates from that of demand, the price goes skyward.

The Man Behind the Curtain Revealed

February 17, 2009

(In the blog post above this one, Mike Ruppert has written a letter to President Obama which ends with the admonition: "The President we need now is not Abraham Lincoln. It is Thomas Jefferson.")

As we all lunge towards Wikipedia to figure out what it is about Jefferson that makes him such an apt mentor, I believe Mike's referring to two things:

1. Jefferson's emphasis on local rather than federal government. (This is going to play out anyway in the coming years as globalization splinters into localities.)
2. Jefferson's resistance to the establishment of a central bank that was not beholden to the people whose taxes maintained it. Hamilton won the argument by conceding that the bank would have to retain a gold reserve.

The rest, as they say, is history; as are we about to become, when the end which President Obama mentioned we're at the beginning of arrives in force.

But even as we players strut across the stage in the final act of whatever drama this has been, it's gratifying to learn its name at last.

Turns out, we are living The Wizard of Oz.

First revealed by school teacher Henry Littlefield in 1964 and explicated superbly by Ellen Hodgson Brown in Web of Debt, the fable was written in1900 to protest events which would culminate in the establishment of the Federal Reserve.[31] Author Frank Baum did not trust gold which is in notoriously short supply; hence the failure of the yellow brick road to get Dorothy where she wanted to go. In the original story, the magic slippers that finally did the trick were not ruby (used in the movie to capitalize on the new techno trick, color film) but silver.

The Scarecrow represented farmers who felt intimidated by the city slickers who would go on to set up the Fed. The Tin Man represented factory workers who lacked the "heart" to revolt. And the Cowardly Lion was William Jennings Bryan whom Baum was trying to enCourage [sic] to fight the good Populist fight. I do not recall that Brown identifies the Wizard but he has the aura of a contemporary Alan Greenspan (J.P. Morgan?), his final disappearance in a hot air balloon evoking what Mr. Greenspan was always so full of. I also wonder if the tornado that got the story—as well as Dorothy's house—off the ground was a vortex of inflation or the crash of 1873.

Perhaps the symbolism in the book was clear to audiences when it was first published. Or perhaps, in the spirit of Baum's contemporaries, Messrs. Freud and Jung, the story was simply intended to resonate with the archetypal conflict over the establishment of a Federal Reserve in the collective unconscious.

As for Oz, that stood for 'ounces.'

We Have Met the Enemy and It Is Us

I guess everyone is a Keynesian in a foxhole.

Robert Lucas[32]

September 19, 2008

Congress is getting it and they are "stunned." This is where our economic paradigm has brought us, to the brink of destruction. It cannot all be blamed on greed, unless we acknowledge that the greed of the few bastards at the top is only a concentrated version of our own greed. Those of us who thought we could live on borrowed money forever—because didn't real estate values only go up?—were in fact living on borrowed time.

We thought the nebulous, Godlike "they" who ran the world would figure out a solution. Some Bill Gates of economics would come along and get us out of this mess because that's what has always happened in the past and history repeats itself.

History is indeed repeating itself, but it is not our recent history of ups and downs always to be followed by another up; it is the history of an economic 9/11, a thus far unimagined and, to our novice eyes, unprecedented "Black Swan" event.

This phrase, from Nassim Taleb's book of the same name, refers to a phenomenon that is rare but nonetheless real. A one-in-a-million chance seems negligible, resulting in a mindset that dismisses it as equal to zero. Thus one engages in countless acts with one-in-a-million "Black Swan" consequences. But "negligible" is *not* the same as zero and over an extended period, the chances add up; so much, in fact, that the odds of encountering a Black Swan event grow exponentially, becoming not only possible, but probable; even, if one probes deeply enough, inevitable.

The term "Black Swan" is deceptively benign for in the contexts discussed in this book, economics and the environment, the Black Swan events are disastrous. For instance, the Black-Scholes model, which led to Myron Scholes' and Robert Merton's sharing the Nobel Prize for Economics in 1997, brought the world the too-good-to-be-true notions of options and derivatives.

Scholes and Merton were partners in Long Term Capital Management whose risk of losing all its capital in one year they calculated at one in ten to the 24th power, or one in a trillion trillion.[33] Who could ever count that high? How long would it take? The universe itself is a mere fourteen billion years old. The event must therefore be far beyond the horizon; nothing to worry about.

Buoyed by such reasoning, the bold thinkers of LTCM programmed their computers to go to work. But how many transactions were executed per second adding up to how many over the years?

Enough so that in 1998, LTCM lost 80% of its equity in less than a month.

Because of the fear that the firm's demise could rock the entire financial system, a bailout was orchestrated by the Federal Reserve Bank of New York.

Does this sound oddly familiar, a sort of rehearsal for the Great Unraveling of the global economy that hit the news in 2007 and which, as of this writing, we're still in the throes of?

Thus the protests that our current financial crisis is unprecedented are unsustainable. It was not only imaginable by those who had some insight into how the system works; it was imagined, it was warned of and it was described, sometimes in unbearable detail, which is why many readers who chanced upon the description preferred to ignore it: Maybe it would go away.

At the same time as we are witnessing our house of cards tumble while we're still inside, both presidential candidates speak of change, the need for an overhaul of Washington.

But in their next breath, both candidates speak of restoring growth.

They have not faced the depth of change needed, *away* from growth and towards what Herman Daly, former Senior Economist in the Environment Department at the World Bank, describes as a "steady state economy." We have to get out of the house of cards and build a new, more sustainable house, based on a cyclical rather than a growth model.

This would undo centuries of dependence on an economic spiral, which, like Woody Allen's description of relationships as sharks, must continue ad infinitum or die.

Even less radical thinkers than Daly, such as Bill Bonner, the wry wit over at the Daily Reckoning, acknowledge that true capitalism is Darwinesque. If we are to put our money where our mouth is, we should allow the banks that screw up to go belly-up. But our concept of Darwinism is specious. From an eco-system in equilibrium, we have tipped the balance so that a few corporations and banks gobble up the smaller fish and when there are none left, turn on each other. Eventually all that's left is a Leviathan gnawing on its own tail.

This is a travesty of a free-market system. It is, in fact, socialism, only it is not for the benefit of the poor; it's a heads-I-win-tails-you-lose socialism for the banks and other institutions that we deem "too big to fail." We have become junkies for the immediate fix, blind to the long-term consequences of our solutions.

The notion of *interest* was originally frowned on by all three major Western religions. Although the risks involved in the field of shipping necessitated high insurance rates, the sages of the day may have understood that nothing can grow forever except cancer.

Over time, all three religions came around to the extent necessary to conduct business. And who can blame them? Something for nothing! And no one to pay for centuries, by which time we'll surely have thought of a way out of the ensuing quagmire.

Thus interest came to pass, then paper currency based on gold; then paper currency and forget about the gold; then derivatives.

Derivatives are an order of magnitude more potent than interest. Now nobody's doing any work; the whole game is risk. And the risk is infinite because you can bet with money you don't have. To top off this recipe for disaster, the usual regulations don't apply.

Nice work when you can get it, especially if you're so big, you're underwritten by the United States government.

Thus there are now $600 trillion worth of derivatives in the ether, more money than there is in the world.[34] Congress must grab the bull by the horns, to use an ironic cliché. A detective who solves a case doesn't explain just one or two aspects of it; he or she reconstructs the whole ugly picture.

Those in charge do not make this easy. They operate on the principal of compartmentalization, with everyone specializing in his or her own piece of the global puzzle and having no clue as to its true raison d'être, how it works or its ultimate consequences. We think we know but we lack some key pieces of information. This puts us in the position of the cargo cults of Post-World War II years who, after the troops departed and with them, their magical airdrops of goodies, returned to the airstrips with palm fronds on their ears in the forlorn belief that these could function as headphones with which to summon the planes' return. We wave subpoenas vaguely in the right direction at some banker fall-guy but all that does is let the real perp continue whatever he is up to.

April 28, 2010: This week Congress is indulging in what the British writer, E.M. Forster, called the most satisfying of human emotions and what H.G. Wells called, "envy with a halo:" Moral indignation. The object is the richly-deserving Goldman Sachs and the audience is salivating—as with Ponzi schemer par excellence, Bernard Madoff—at the spectacle of high fliers getting their comeuppance. These are worthy objects of hate but they're not the original cancer, which is our economic system. Until Congress is willing to face the truth, to follow the clues in our present predicament back to the crime itself, its Original Sin, we will continue charging ever further off course with consequences growing exponentially.

Spinning Out of Control

November 21, 2008

In a bygone Age of Innocence, calamities used to get fixed; these days, they are simply superseded by even greater calamities. Nothing surprises us anymore, but it is still possible to be left breathless by quotes such as the following:

From the day of its founding in 1913 to September 24, 2008, the Fed's assets—the aforementioned cornerstone capital for the U.S. financial system—grew to $1 trillion. By November 14, 2008, the amount had grown to over $2 trillion. And in a speech in Texas, the head of the Dallas branch of the Fed said he expected the total to reach $3 trillion by year-end.[35]

We re-read the paragraph. Yes, in the seven weeks that ended last Friday, the fed's assets grew by the same amount which had previously taken 95 years. And even as we speak, the Fed is doing the same trick again.

It is as though you've just become aware of how fast the earth is spinning beneath your feet. You feel a little off balance, about to fall, which indeed you are. And when the United States dollar loses its reserve status which, along with our military arsenal, has been propping up our economy, we cross the event horizon.

Addendum 2011: The talk on the rialto is of "haircuts," a cute way of saying that it's time to pay our debts. But since the money isn't there, the question becomes: Whom shall we stiff—the pensioners or the bondholders? The tactics formerly employed to seize resources in Third World countries are encroaching on European shores: First Greece and the other PIIGS, but it is only a matter of time before the unthinkable becomes not only thought but reality.

What are those tactics? Sell people things they don't need (in Africa or South America, this might be a white elephant of an airport.) Kindly lend them the money to build it; money which then goes to an American corporation to do the building. Then when the country can't repay the loan, negotiate a favorable deal for an oil company; or, in the case of Greece, for example, suggest they use their gold as collateral.

In the U.S., analogous tactics were applied in the housing bubble. Using low-interest "teaser" rates, banks induced buyers to take on mortgages, knowing the rates would likely float to unsustainable levels in a few years. By the time the buyer lost the house, the bank was out of the picture, having passed the dodgy mortgage on to investors in a bundle of similar mortgages stamped Triple A on the grounds that they couldn't possibly *all* default. (Yes they could, if the bank didn't do due diligence but who needs to do that when you're too big to fail?)

When One Udder is Milked Dry, the Media Turn to the Next

More is thy due than more than all can pay.

Macbeth, Act I, Scene iv

December 10, 2008

Call it heroic patriotism. Or touching, if pathetic, idealism. Or call it the final fukking over of the public before the Hugest Pop of the World's Latest Greatest Biggest Baddest Really Humongulous Bubble. In an article marveling over the zero yields of U.S. treasuries, this morning's *New York Times* calls these investments, "the world's safest."[36]

The *Times* is not a-changing; on the contrary, it is living in a time warp as well as a geography warp. For true to its xenophobic, solipsistic tradition, it is dismissing the bonds of "lesser" countries, not to mention emerging markets.

Keep on running, people. Just don't look down or you might notice that the ground beneath your feet has disappeared. Only then will we all go Splat.

Like a doctor who, hearing that his medicine has done no good, doubles the dose, the Fed responds to every disaster which the Fed itself has caused through money-printing by cranking the presses even faster.

Ostensibly, this is because they are focused on the immediate problem, deflation. And since we live in a constant state of emergency, they are "of necessity" responding with short term fixes or at least what they're calling fixes. Maybe they mean that in the sense that a baseball game is fixed.

But the faster we run, the sooner we hit hyperinflation. Does the word evoke in you a hint of hyperventilation? No? Don't worry; it won't be long.

In the vortex that is approaching, everything, particularly metaphors, will get blended together like the kaleidoscopic images in a dream. The United States and Zimbabwe, previously at economically opposite poles, will find themselves rubbing elbows in Hell on wheels.

And yet, even as I never cease to marvel at the sleight of hand of today's media, I'm grateful for the mindless reassurance. It means we have another day.

Waiting for the Other Shoe

January 25, 2009

Another day, another collapse. The meticulously predicted plot of global disintegration—blackouts first on the vulnerable fringes of civilization, the "developing world;" food shortages; riots; the rise of militias and vigilantism; the helpless "stand down" of law enforcement in those communities where the Recession has brought about cutbacks in emergency services—seems to be unfolding in slow motion, like a watched pot. The action junkie in us wants it to pick up speed. But that's because it's all still happening somewhere else; on the news, not to us.

I'm reminded of a friend who once saw ominous strangers with flashlights outside her house.

There was a knock at the door.

Unable to bear the suspense, just wanting to get the murder over with, she flung the door open. The visitors turned out to be the police who were looking for a thief.

My friend's behavior suggests how a part of us feels about collapse. The anxiety of waiting for the other shoe to drop can become unbearable.

For those who don't know, that expression originates from the phenomenon of listening to the upstairs neighbor getting ready for bed. He takes off one shoe. Then you can't help listening for the inevitable.

Only in this case it won't only be the other shoe that will fall. It will be the ceiling.

Rock and Hard Place Closing In

May 22, 2009

To paraphrase Tolstoy: All happy families (or car outings or civilizations on the upswing) are alike, but each unhappy family (or car wreck or collapse of civilization) is unhappy in its own way. (Actually that's false about families, as many an unhappy family has noted. And civilizations tend to go under shortly after some version of an "economic stimulus package" otherwise known as "printing money.") However, just as there are only 36 basic plots in literature yet we keep reading books or at least, going to the movies, we'll continue to gawk until our own personal car wreck or collapse puts an end to our voyeurism.[37]

Pick Your Poison

April 29, 2009

Call me the scummiest hypocrite but right now with infinite relief (which feels a whole lot like gratitude,) I greet you from the heart of Corporate America—Burger King, which is my sole access to the Internet at the moment.

Before me is a photo of a workman sitting atop a steel girder which is attached to exactly nothing—like a forty-storey flagpole—having not yet met its horizontal mate in the construction of what is probably the Empire State Building; it's hard to recognize the New York of seventy years ago although given a minute, one could figure it out from the ever-mercurial orientation of Broadway.

The workman is waving triumphantly with his left hand while holding a half-smoked celebratory cigarette (as well as the top of the girder) in his right. His right leg is also wrapped around the back of the girder. Or perhaps he only has one leg; it's all a little dizzying.

Then again, that may be in the eye of the beholder. Life is a Rorschach, as a shrink friend of mine says. And we are feeling a little dizzy these days as the global economic crisis gets forgotten faster than a one night stand (I'm trying to write like a guy for one sentence) in favor of the supposed global bird flu pandemic.

Staying Sane

When last week's terror seems like history
as with an addict who seeks newer thrill,
the mutual destruction of Israel
and Arab world replacing Kim Jong Il,
when leaders who should model saving grace
are, rather, all-consumed with saving face,
and hopes of peace grow by the day more faint,
allusions to it brushed aside as quaint,
when hurricanes swirl metaphorically,
sooner, more intensely than before,
the dollar falls as the sea level climbs
so even Murdoch longs for boring times,
in refuge from outrageous Fortune's slings,
it helps merely to contemplate true things.

Farewell to Brooklyn

Spring, 2009

As part of my own personal preparation for collapse, I moved out of a living situation in which I'd been ensconced for ten years to an apartment in Manhattan; one which would be easier to pick up from in flight, should that need arise.

This feels like Step One in the process of disengaging from life-as-we-have-known-it. Had a farewell party a few nights ago with some of the heftier pieces of furniture, including the dining room table I'd bought at Mike's request from the Salvation Army as well as the walls which contained all the frantic research of the early days (which turned into years) following 9/11.

Physically, the move was less hellish than most. Knowing this day would come, for several years I've traveled light, shedding books as soon as they were read.

The new apartment offers a sliver of a park view–a few minutes of sunset once the clocks retreat an hour in November. But it evokes no memories and therefore no sentiment.

Yet through an ironic fluke, it is within shouting distance of where I was born. I don't like to think about what that might mean: Closing the circle, tying up loose ends before the absolute end and all that. Did I have unfinished business here? Or is it a case of the dog returning home to die?

Don't Frighten the Horses

November 15, 2008

I suggest that the peak oil community minimize its efforts to awaken the world to the near-term dangers of world oil supply. The motivation is simple: By minimizing our efforts in the near term, we may not add fuel to the economic fires that are already burning so fiercely.

Businesses and the markets are in what might be called a free fall. If the realization of peak oil along with its disastrous financial implications was added to the existing mix of troubles, the added trauma could be unthinkable.

Robert Hirsch[38]

Hirsch is right. It *is* unthinkable. We should know. We've been thinking it for the last several years.

Hirsch is a really nice guy. We've had occasional e-contact (as well as meeting at the ASPO Conference in Sacramento) since he answered a few questions after his first report in '05. (Such was the suppression of Peak Oil back then that the article[39] based on that e-interview used to show up in third place when you googled, "Robert Hirsch" and "Peak Oil.")

But the suggestion that we should tiptoe around the subject for fear of frightening the horses smacks of the same patronizing attitude we saw after 9/11 when the government lied about the record-breaking levels of toxics and carcinogens downtown for fear of creating panic. As a result, untold thousands are sick and some are dying; most of them, unnecessarily.

Thus History is repeating itself yet again with respect to the sacrifice of human lives on the altar of the economy.

What is this panic that everyone is so afraid of?

Fear is the underrated emotion, the nerd of human behavior that has its day of vindication in the end.

"We have nothing to fear but fear itself," ring out the statesmen as they lead us (deftly, without going themselves,) into war. Perhaps it is they who are afraid of our fear. Perhaps that is why they are depriving us of it at all costs.

If there's a fire, shall we keep mum for fear of creating panic? Or shall we point out the exits?

Unfortunately, in the case of Peak Oil, the exits are hard to find and without major compromises on all sides, there won't be enough of them.

Still, who are we to decide that The Public is not mature enough to handle the reality that we realized years ago?

Particularly if the bad news comes coupled with some solutions, however meager—the way a doctor would present a grim diagnosis—it will be more palatable.

Addendum 2011:   With the rise of the Tea Party, one can sympathize more with Hirsch's position. Despite its recognition of the roots of our malaise, the movement is rife with disinformation born of misplaced blame and vice versa.

CNN Lullabies

February 4, 2009

There we were placing bets on whether the U.S., Europe or China would be the first to cave to economic collapse when all the while it was Australia, dying of drought on the one hand and floods on the other even as Ireland succumbs to Peak Oil.[40]

Psychologists have observed that a baby, instinctively knowing that it can't survive without its mother, may, however paradoxically, die in order to allow its mother to live.

The innate biological response of the baby at least allows the mother to have other babies, thereby ensuring the survival of the species.

But as a social policy, it's a tad cart-before-the-horse or snake-eating-its-own-tail. Individually we are killing each other but in the aggregate, we're killing ourselves. Meanwhile, the mother of it all, our economic paradigm, remains intact. (When I ask my students if the environment should be sacrificed for the sake of jobs, they, who came here precisely because we are the land of opportunity, almost uniformly answer *Yes*. "Who knows what will be in twenty years?" they shrug.)

American optimism dies similarly hard. Along with the monetary system, it may be the last remnant of us to go, like the Cheshire cat's grin, after we ourselves have been lulled into oblivion by CNN anchors crooning, "When the economy recovers…"

If you think there's a snowball's chance in Hell of saving someone, you grab him by the lapels, treat him like an adult and tell him what he needs to do. If you don't think there's a chance, you treat him like a child and try to make the inevitable as painless as possible.

Which brings me to the final scene in the Barbara Stanwyck version of "The Titanic,"—A Night to Remember.

Everyone who hasn't gotten into a lifeboat is on deck, watching as the ocean rises all around. (The movie doesn't dwell on those who get locked into steerage.)

The only person who doesn't understand what's going on is a four-year-old boy who's looking for his mother.

An old man takes him by the hand asserting, "We'll find her." He repeats the soothing bromide while staring into the last horizon he'll ever see.

We who are older than four might not be so easily taken in by the old man with the haunted eyes. How much more effective, then, to use news anchors who are as clueless as we are.

Yet brimming on the other side of the porthole, the truth seeps in.

Now It *Is* Time to Frighten the Horses

Or: A Time to Reassure People and
a Time to Scare the Cr*p Out of Them

December 11, 2007

Might it sometimes be appropriate for the government to lie in order to reassure the public? Asked this question during a Court of Appeals hearing yesterday in Benzman vs. EPA, the case brought by residents, students and office workers exposed to and, in many cases, sickened by the environmental hazards following 9/11,* EPA lawyer Alisa Klein answered, "Yes."

Competing interests such as the economy or the "return to normalcy" [sic] might supercede that of public health, she argued. In other words, when it suits them, the government may legitimately opt to keep the people "fat, dumb and happy" as a teacher of mine used to call it.

There's no question that Ms. Klein accurately represented EPA's position. In addition to their compelling urge to <u>reopen Wall St</u>[41] ASAP after 9/11, the protocols they have developed to respond to a <u>dirty bomb</u>[42] also take into account the economic import of the area exposed, regardless of the fact that an area that's important to the economy will also be more <u>densely populated</u>.[43] (April, 2011 addendum: The response of the EPA to the Fukushima nuclear power plant disaster in Japan has been to raise the level of radiation considered permissible.[44])

Accepting, for the moment, the mind-bending reasoning that requires us to trust a government which has admitted that it will lie whenever it feels like it, let us turn now to some situations in which said government has seen fit not to assuage our fears but in fact, to scare the sh*t out of us.

The lead-up to the Iraq war, when Condoleezza Rice dropped a metaphorical bomb into the conversation with her allusion to a mushroom cloud comes to mind, as do the "Hoo-oo-oo—Be very afraaaaid" references at the time to chemical and biological weapons labs.

Ditto Iran, up until last week.

Then there are all those toxic toys and that contaminated toothpaste from China. I'm not saying they're safe. I'm just wondering why they've garnered such prompt headlines while the press on American products such as <u>Zonolite,</u> an asbestos-containing insulation material in millions of American homes, has traditionally been sluggish; never mind Agent Orange and depleted uranium. Some of the interests that have rightly decried lead-contaminated toys from China have, on the other hand, put up the strongest resistance to changing the lead laws in New York City housing, for example. Also compare the press on avian flu with that on the numerous offenses of the American food industry.

And remember the good old days of Homeland Security orange alerts and Osama's sneak previews? The ones that tended to come just before an election or some other politically sensitive event?

The government may not be consistent about wanting to reassure us but it certainly is consistently entertaining.

*I was one of the original plaintiffs in the case.

A Kinder, Gentler Holocaust: Peak Oil and
the Rebuilding (Or Not) of Ground Zero

July 12, 2008

Battles to publicize unpopular issues such as the lethal air quality following 9/11 or the arrival of Peak Oil c. 2006 have two phases. The first consists of sailing into the wind. The mainstream press ignores the issue or repeats the government's lies. This is unpleasant but after the arrival of Phase Two, one looks back at it with some nostalgia.   For the second phase occurs when the problem has grown so big and ugly, it can no longer be ignored.

Legend has it that Joseph Kennedy knew the stock market was about to crash in 1929 when his shoeshine boy gave him a tip on what to buy. Kennedy sold. The story is no doubt apocryphal (Kennedy was surely planning to sell anyway; the shoeshine boy, if there was one, was just the last straw,) but it makes the point: When everyone knows something, it's too late.

So it's with some ambivalence that we note the growing acceptance of earth-changing upheavals ahead. 9/11, Hurricane Katrina, the "Shock and Awe" campaign that morphed into a living example of "the war that will not end in our lifetimes..." One disaster after another has ended not in abatement but in simply being supplanted by a new disaster. Obama's catchword is "change" and many will vote for it, but how many really expect it? When AOL, not normally considered a tinfoil hat website, publishes an article on people preparing for Apocalypse in 2012, you know you're being psyched for something big even if the story, with its Nostradamus-like allusions to the Mayan calendar, has a New Age-y tinge, or should I say "aura?" (Since this article was first written, the History Channel has launched a widely publicized series on Nostradamus himself as well as one on UFOs. Even with all the dutiful caveats and airtime allotted to skeptics, the mere publicity given these issues by the channel which calls itself "History" constitutes an implicit nod of respect.)

The fact that oil plays into our bleak zeitgeist is also accepted even as people sputter in protest, "But what about wind/geothermal/solar/Brazil/hybrids/algae/electricity/Angola/bikes /fusion/some-genius-coming-along-with-something?" Pick your "solution," which may be a wonderful thing in itself but will not replace oil in our autophagous economy that depends on infinite growth in a finite world.

Clearly, the worst is yet to come. Despite Congress' scolding of "speculators" for the current financial crisis, those speculators are not the main source of the concurrent oil dilemma. (This is not to exonerate them; only to point out that the math would indicate they're but a fraction of the problem, though it's fun to have someone on whom to fix your hate.) Unlike the Hunt brothers who cornered the silver market in the seventies, oil speculators do not take delivery of, much less horde, oil. Few speculators have tankers of the stuff in the back yard. But when did reality ever trump a populist, vote-gleaning stand? How much easier to go after a profiteer (however justifiably) than question the entire system from which we all profit.

The country's fast heading into what we'll euphemistically call a "recession," interrupted only by speed bumps like the "economic stimulus package" of a few hundred dollars that many of us received several months ago. On the financial front, we have the collapse of stalwart institutions like Bear Stearns Bank, sold off at a fire sale price to J.P. Morgan/Chase via a "non-recourse loan," a.k.a. "gift," of $30 billion courtesy of the American public. And that was just for starters. Now Merrill Lynch, Citigroup, Fannie Mae and Freddie Mac are following suit.

Yet everyone's still going about their business, if they can afford the gas to get there. And here in New York City, the rebuilding of Ground Zero has been moving right along, or so we are supposed to believe.

Up until a couple of weeks ago, that is, when the Port Authority's Christopher Ward took a deep breath, quoted the philosopher George Santayana (the thinking man's equivalent of saying a prayer) and announced that regarding the goal of a grand opening by the tenth anniversary of the attacks... fuggedaboudit.

Maybe all the squabbling parties downtown should just learn to play better together. Or maybe someone with his/her ear to the ground is getting, if we may mix metaphors, cold feet.

For ignore it or not, Peak Oil is here. Writing for the European Tribune, Jerome a Paris informs us[45] that the relentlessly upbeat International Energy Agency has sobering data it's anxious to release. But they have been told by the Bush administration to withhold the truth until after the election. And the Bush administration's own Energy Advisor Matthew Simmons <u>maintains that oil could easily hit $500 p.b.</u>[46]

The titans of Ground Zero may not know these precise facts. But they probably have a canny sense of where things are heading. And while it's in their interest to keep up the front as long as possible, they must surely recognize that it's not in their interest to invest in a project whose future is iffy.

The match has been struck for the burning of "Rome," but this time Nero isn't playing the fiddle; he's talking about A-Rod and Madonna. Fascism is on its way only this time with more polish, at least so far; instead of goose-stepping in jackboots, it walks softly and wears a nicely cut suit. The gas chambers are subtler too: The fires that burned the toxic debris at Ground Zero for over three months; the formaldehyde-contaminated trailers provided to the victims of Hurricane Katrina, are doing the same job, only over a more extended time. And we "Jews" are swallowing the sweet pablum that the nice man on T.V. is offering (up tick in the stock market today!) because this new kind of Holocaust "could never happen."

Heart of Darkness: The Egg Comes First

It is interesting to contemplate an entangled bank, clothed with many plants of many kinds, with birds singing on the bushes, with various insects flitting about, and with worms crawling through the damp earth, and to reflect that these elaborately constructed forms, so different from each other, and dependent on each other in so complex a manner, have all been produced by laws acting around us.

Charles Darwin
On the Origin of Species by Means of Natural Selection

When you're a kid, you wake up, have breakfast, go to school, come home, do your homework, have dinner, go to bed, wake up…

So it goes day after day and you imagine it will continue forever, an infinite cycle.

But no.

When I was ten, my family moved to England. The infinite cycle broke. Uprooted and transplanted, I'd acquired the third dimension of a past.

One day about a year later, a triumphant classmate confronted the rest of us with the chicken and egg conundrum, that staple of infinite cycle thinking.

After some pondering, I realized that it lacked a key element. If you factored in evolution, the egg came first. What had laid the egg was not a chicken but something that preceded chickens in the evolutionary scheme of things.

What looks like an infinite cycle in the two dimensions of life while you're living it, changes when you add the third dimension of hindsight. Stepping back to take in the whole picture, you see that the cycle was in fact a spiral, with a direction, an agenda.

That's on the individual, micro level. How does that lesson apply on the global level?

The market goes up; the market goes down. What goes down must come up again. Not because of any law of physics, God knows, but because in our narrow experience, that is what it has always done. Therefore it will continue to do it, for whatever reason, known only to itself and those nebulous Experts in these matters who sound as though they know what they're talking about on CNN. Who cares why?

Again, no.

What looks like a cycle of history is also not an actual cycle. It, too, has a direction, an agenda.

We are the turkey, living a life of abundance, never questioning our good fortune. Then the day before Thanksgiving, we find out what the point of it all was.

One thing we *can* see now: Whoever is pulling the strings, they use us humans with diabolical ingenuity. And we let them.

First they unleash the furies of the Islamist world, ready and willing accomplices in the destruction of the Wicked Witch of the West, which is us.

Then they do the opposite, unleashing a backlash stateside.

Hard to know whom to point the finger at more. There's no shortage of candidates. Simon Bolivar's admonition springs to mind again: An ignorant people is the instrument of its own destruction. Everyone becomes a pawn on the Grand Chessboard. The best way to destroy your enemies is to let them destroy each other. It's a great energy saver, at least of your own energy. And they don't seem to mind. As E.M. Forster said, "There is nothing so satisfying as moral indignation;" particularly among young men with energy to burn, scores to settle and selves to prove.

Like Nature, we humans abhor a vacuum. We rush in to fill it with mischief. The point is not, as some commentators on the recent Madoff debacle have eagerly pointed out, that Madoff's victims were sold out "by one of their own." (So far, no one outside of the most bottom-feeding websites has spelled out what that phrase means.) The point is, **deregulation allowed it to happen**. Whistleblower Harry Markopoulos said of the SEC's role in the case, "Then you had Christopher Cox, because he wasn't going to do his job. That's why he got the job."[47] Given that wink-

and-a-nod environment, some Madoff somewhere was inevitable and indeed, several others have sprouted up since, though for relatively piddling amounts—a billion here or there. Is that because they were more moral than Madoff himself? Possessed of greater self-control? Or because they lacked his opportunity or savvy?

What might have prevented all these Ponzi schemes was a rigorous legal framework. That's why society as a whole constructs laws, if it does: to control the appetites, the runaway mayhem of individual sociopaths.

But the attenuation of regulation was no accident. It had been methodically expanded since Reagan, not only in the field of finance, but also in the Environmental Protection Agency and the Food and Drug Administration; in agriculture and in communications. The farce of allowing industries to police themselves removed the sorts of checks and balances for which the Framers had strived in the Constitution, leaving the field open for monopolies to feast and grow ever larger. It's a fitting metaphor for our age that one of its foremost distractions has been athletes who have evolved with time-lapse alacrity courtesy of a generous dose of steroids.

As always, precedents abound: Vacuums which permitted events to take place that changed the course of history. For just as our bodies are constantly being assaulted by bacteria, so is society constantly under threat from potential attackers. Security agencies are society's equivalent of the immune system. For a potential attack to come off, the normal protocol must let down its guard; this passivity will allow the aggression to take its course. And if there isn't enough natural aggression handy, we have cures for that too.

Acts of war which were allowed to happen, or even provoked, are mentioned in greater detail elsewhere. For now, we'll focus on assassinations:

1. The security lapse that allowed the assassination of Abraham Lincoln.

Lincoln, of course, had innumerable enemies; among them the promoters of a Central Bank, as his government had issued greenbacks to finance the Civil War. In such a case and at such distance, it's almost impossible to tease apart who was responsible for what and what their motivations were. But the modus operandi, for all its apparent simplicity, bears a resemblance to that of future assassinations.

Lincoln's customary messenger, Charles Forbes, had been at the theatre box early on the evening of April 14, 1865, but had left on an errand. Forbes' replacement, according to historian Theodore Roscoe, author of *The Lincoln Assassination, April 14, 1865: Investigation of a President's Murder Uncovers a Web of Conspiracy*, had to be Constable John Parker.[48] The lapse allowed John Wilkes Booth, a matinee idol who knew *My American Cousin*, the comedy being performed that night, to wait for the line that invariably drew uproarious laughter, and upon that cue, open the door to the box.

2. The egregious security lapses that allowed the assassination of President John F. Kennedy. Among them: Open windows, absence of adequate personnel and slowing down the motorcade while making the turn at Dealey Plaza.

None of these would have been allowed had Chief of Special Operations for the Joint Chiefs of Staff Colonel Fletcher Prouty been performing his accustomed function. But just before Kennedy's fateful trip, Prouty had been dispatched to a point at a safe distance from Dallas: The South Pole.[49]

Prouty writes:

"I recall, when we walked down Avenida Reforma in Mexico City before Eisenhower's trip, being told that if we found a place where Eisenhower could not be properly protected, the Secret Service "manual" stated that the "President's car must maintain

not less than 44 mph until clear of any danger zones." I joked with the Secret Service officer about the "44 mph." Why not "45 mph" or "50 mph." He answered that tests had determined that a car traveling 44 mph was going fast enough to guarantee all but 100 percent assurance that the President would be safe. It was Secret Service men working under the provisions of the same manual who let the President's car creep around that corner at Dealey Plaza at 8-9 mph. Why?...

I happened to be far away in New Zealand at the time of JFK's murder. I was on my way to breakfast (the crime occurred at 6:30A.M. on the 23rd of November there) with a member of Congress from Ohio. As soon as possible, we purchased the first newspaper available -- the Christchurch Star. It is amazing to re-read the front page of that paper today and find all of the detail, the remarkable detail, about Lee Harvey Oswald, about his service in the Marine Corps, about his living in Russia, about his Russian wife, and then the full scenario of the crime.

Then one begins to wonder -- understanding full well the capability of modern-day communications and reporting -- who it was that was able in so short a time to come up with such a life history of so obscure a twenty-four-year-old "loner." Even the Dallas police had not charged him with any crime by the time that paper had hit the streets. In the crime scenario it states that two Dallas cops, J.D. Tippit and M.N. McDonald, had chased Oswald into a theater and that Tippit was shot dead "as he ran into the cinema." Who fabricated all of that news? Who was at the right place at that moment to flood the whole world with all of this news about Lee Harvey Oswald, when even the Dallas police weren't too sure of their man, they said, because he carried two identities (Oswald and Alek Hidell) in his pocket." [50]

Prouty later wrote a memoir entitled *The Secret Team*, which disappeared as soon as it was published, all record of it expunged from the Library of Congress:

[O]ne day a business associate in Seattle called to tell me that the bookstore next to his office building had had a window full of books the day before, and none the day of his call. They claimed they had never had the book. I called other associates around the country. I got the same story from all over the country. The paperback had vanished. At the same time I learned that Mr. Ballantine had sold his company. I travelled to New York to visit the new "Ballantine Books" president. He professed to know nothing about me, and my book. That was the end of that surge of publication. For some unknown reason Prentice-Hall was out of my book also. It became an extinct species.

Coincidental to that, I received a letter from a Member of Parliament in Canberra, Australia, who wrote that he had been in England recently visiting in the home of a friend who was a Member of the British Parliament. While there, he discovered The Secret Team on a coffee table and during odd hours had begun to read it.

Upon return to Canberra he sent his clerk to get him a copy of the book. Not finding it in the stores, the clerk had gone to the Customs Office where he learned that 3,500 copies of The Secret Team had arrived, and on that same date had been purchased by a Colonel from the Royal Australian Army. The book was dead everywhere.

The campaign to kill the book was nationwide and world-wide. It was removed from the Library of Congress and from College libraries as letters I received attested all too frequently.[51]

However, some of Prouty's work is now available at www.prouty.org where he has provided innumerable vital details that had been withheld from the Warren Commission, thus allowing Arlen Specter to fill in the empty space with virtuoso imagination.

"How could it have happened that the Secret Service, contrary to all good sense and all professional 'Protection' practice, permitted the President and the Vice-President to be in close proximity in the same city, in the same procession? This is unheard of. The Secret Service dates back more than a century and they had never permitted that to take place before. Why this time?"[52]

Like Lincoln, Kennedy had made the mistake of thinking he could combat the forces of the military-industrial complex. Not only did he flout the CIA in the Bay of Pigs incident, he also fired three of the agency's top officials including Director Allen Dulles; he disregarded the wishes of his own generals by conducting a secret correspondence with the purported "enemy," Nikita Khrushchev, using his brother Robert as intermediary while Khrushchev used Ambassador Anatoly Dobrynin.[53] And he even entertained the notion of a joint mission to the moon.

Researcher John Judge has written about information he acquired from his mother who, at the time of Kennedy's administration, was the highest paid woman at the Pentagon, working in manpower analysis. In April of 1963, orders had come from the White House to reduce manpower in Vietnam to zero. These orders were reversed Monday, November 25, the first working day following the assassination which had taken place the previous Friday. The new memo "project[ed] instead a 10-year war with 57,000 dead."[54]

But the coup de grace was Kennedy's decision to sell wheat to the Russians, rather than let them starve.

In a speech to the Coalition on Political Assassinations in 2009, James Douglas, author *JFK and the Unspeakable,* said:

> *The violent reaction to his decision was represented on Friday morning, November 22, 1963, by a threatening, full-page advertisement addressed to him in the Dallas Morning News. The ad was bordered in black, like a funeral notice.*
>
> *Among the charges of disloyalty to the nation that the ad made against the president was the question: "Why have you approved the sale of wheat and corn to our enemies when you know the Communist soldiers 'travel on their stomach' just as ours do?" JFK read the ad before the flight from Fort Worth to Dallas, pointed it out to*

Jacqueline Kennedy, and talked about the possibility of his being assassinated that day.

"But, Jackie," he said, "If somebody wants to shoot me from a window with a rifle, nobody can stop it, so why worry about it?"[55]

According to John Judge, the complex details of Kennedy's assassination are available in the Warren Commission investigation though the report that summarizes it is a cover-up:

> *I mean, when you go into the evidence of the John F. Kennedy assassination, you'll find that Oswald didn't own a rifle; he didn't own a pistol. He didn't fire a gun that day. There were no nitrate samples on the cheeks or on his palms. He didn't shoot a gun. He didn't kill anybody...*
>
> *The person that actually wrote the report is a fellow named Otto Winnacker. He was on TDY, transfer from the Pentagon to the Warren Commission, to do that job. He was also, historically, one of 26 official historians of the Reich who worked directly under the Reichschancellor, Adolph Hitler, and was brought here into the United States...*
>
> *The current world cover for the training of these assassins, I believe, is an evangelical right-wing organization known as World Vision. Among its employees at the Fort Chaffee Refugee Camp it was running for Laotian, Thai, and Vietnamese refugees was a young man named Mark David Chapman—responsible for the death of a very political musician who could have brought a million people out in response to Reagan's war efforts in a single day, named John Lennon.*
>
> *Mark David Chapman had military training. He was in Beirut, interestingly enough, when military training was going on there by Wilson and Terpil. And he moved to Hawaii, worked for the large military firms. You'll remember he took a military stance at the time. The*

chairman of the board in those days of World Vision was none other than John Hinckley, Sr.   [A discussion of Hinckley's son, John Hinckley, Jr., who attempted to assassinate President Ronald Reagan, follows.] The funding for World Vision was, primarily, during the Vietnam period, CIA directly funding it.   They now still admit 5% coming through USAID, which was the cover.[56]

Like Lincoln, Kennedy also foiled the Central Bank's agenda of debasing the quality of the money. As a minor example, quarters produced prior to Kennedy's death retain real silver; after 1963, that system ended, for we were living beyond our means.

The United States had promised, on its honor, not to inflate beyond its gold holdings when, at the Bretton-Woods agreement of 1945, the dollar was given the enviable status of becoming the world's reserve currency. In 1971, sensing that we'd broken our promise, France demanded the value of their dollar holdings in gold. Rather than declare the United States bankrupt, Nixon, at the behest of Paul Volcker and others, simply took us off what remained of the gold standard.[57]   The vacuum was filled by "Petrodollars" (the requirement of OPEC that oil be traded in dollars) until 2000 when one member of OPEC decided to break out of that bind. That member was Saddam Hussein.[58]

3. Sara Jane Moore, the would-be assassin of President Gerald Ford, had been questioned by the Secret Service the night before the shooting. They had confiscated a .44-caliber weapon but did not detain her because the San Francisco Police Department told them she had worked as an informer for them as well as "for what they called two federal agencies." Moore herself told police she was an informer for the FBI.[59]

4. Security lapses in the assassination attempt of President Ronald Reagan:

Reagan was told not to wear his vest that day -- his protective vest. I'll bet he wore it after that. They did not call the procedure with the limousine. He should have come out the door and gone directly into the limousine. That's how he arrived.

He came, the Secret Service formed two rows on either side of the back door, they opened the back door and he goes in. When you hire a limousine, they don't go to the house down the street, they come to your door. When you're the president, they'll move it six inches to make sure that it's in the right place. It was in the right place when he arrived. He got out and went in through the phalanx of the two rows of agents. He's safe into the VIP entrance.

He comes out the same exit and where's the car?' It is nowhere near the door. It's 40-50 feet down the pavement. So, he's got to walk out into the open. What's supposed to happen? The Secret Service is supposed to surround him like a diamond and protect him. One guy goes forward, McCarthy, to open the door for him. The rest don't surround him. They all file out like a line of ducks off to the right and they leave Reagan walking in the open with Brady and these other guys. Then, the shooting happens...

This I believe was a coup. The black box disappeared for several hours. . . There was that kind of transition-of-power going on -- who was actually going to control things and there were switch-overs about the Strategic Air Command bomber pilots, again, not having code books aboard on March 31, 81 like they didn't on November 22, 63. This was a classic transition-of-power situation.[60]

5. Security lapses surrounding the assassination of President Anwar al-Sadat of Egypt:

"I was just getting ready," Robinson said, "to ask our expert on assassination conspiracies how four to eight men

*were able to insinuate themselves into a military parade,
leap from a truck at precisely the moment that the Egyptian
Air Force was staging a spectacular flyover, and with no
opposition from the security guard, advance to the
reviewing stand and shoot President Anwar el-Sadat to
death at point-blank range? ...."*

*"The Times even referred to what it called a striking
breakdown in security around Sadat. That's a curious fact
when you consider that Sadat's bodyguards were trained by
our Secret Service and were required to spend a year in the
United States in on-the-job training. Nixon started that in
1974 and later the CIA gave Sadat a lot of advanced
communications gear to increase his security. It didn't
seem to help."*[61]

6.   In an interview with Sir David Frost on November 2,
2007,[62] Pakistan Prime Minister Benazir Bhutto mentions,
"Omar Sheikh, the man who murdered Osama Bin Laden."
Frost does not interrupt or ask about this slip-of-the-tongue
bombshell: Was it a matter of mistaken identity or did the
world quietly lose its Most Wanted villain years before his
much-trumpeted, if peculiar, assassination? There's no record
that anyone followed up after the interview either because seven
weeks later, Bhutto herself was assassinated, the UN blaming
inadequate security precautions.[63]

7.   The most recent lapses of historic significance are the at
least six war games taking place on the morning of 9/11, which
diverted military planes to Northern Canada and Alaska, leaving
a vacuum in air defenses on the Eastern seaboard. One of the
war games introduced twenty-two pieces of "chaff" or
superfluous debris onto radar screens, which stymied pilots who
wished to pursue the hijackers.[64]

Prior to the attacks, innumerable lapses had been documented by FBI agents Colleen Rowley and Robert Wright. And highly out-of-whack put options on United and American Airlines ostensibly went "unnoticed" although the CIA monitors the stock market in real time.

Things are happening fast now. As in nuclear fission, each change will precipitate others at an exponential rate. When the growing spiral changes direction, it will become a vortex until it implodes.

Meanwhile, threats of further terror attacks fuel the public's fear and rage. In the West, we are told to blame Islamists, while carefully observing the fine distinction between them and your average, garden-variety Muslim.

The Muslims, who have first-hand experience of the dirty tricks of the Americans and know the story isn't that simple, are similarly put off the scent by propaganda instructing them to blame the Jews. Then, like Christians who've been placated to shut up about their poverty with the line that their reward awaits them in the Afterlife, a select cadre of Muslims, so far mostly young men, are indoctrinated to believe that if they sacrifice their lives, they'll be considered heroes and get seventy-two virgins forever after (although seventy-two virgins doesn't seem like enough for Eternity. Virginity is quintessentially transient, but young men are not known for thinking ahead.)

Meanwhile, their white bread American counterparts are indoctrinated to believe that they must bring democracy to Iraq whose people will throw flowers at their feet. If that line doesn't work, how about some free tuition?

Thus the ancient foes go at each other while those in power make off with the loot.

The Shell Game of Evading Responsibility

(Based on Thom Hartmann's Unequal Protection: How Corporations Became "People"—And How You Can Fight Back)

The poor don't work because they have too much income; the rich don't work because they don't have enough income.

John Kenneth Galbraith[65]

It all comes down to the eternal battle between the individual and society, particularly where the individual is a monopoly. This is the conflict that sparked the American Revolution, for it was the licensing advantages bestowed on the East India Company that did away with small businesses (sometimes referred to as "pirates"), which in turn led to the Boston Tea Party.

Corporations soon sprouted again, however, for unlike humans whose rights they pursued for over a century, they transcend individual mortality.

Originally created for the purpose of sharing risk, European corporations soon figured out how to evade responsibility by shielding personal assets behind the corporate veil. Then in the U.S., via the Federalists, they manipulated the wording of the Constitution to refer simply to "persons" rather than "natural persons," which achievement allowed them eventually to win the same rights as *human* persons covered by that seminal document. "[T]he Federalists [also] fought hard to keep 'freedom from monopolies' out of the Constitution. And they won."

Over the course of the ensuing century, the corporate takeover of the world unfolded. Being immortal, not to mention wealthier than most human persons, corporations had time and resources on their side. Thus after the Civil War, 289 of the 308 Equal Rights Protection cases heard by the Supreme Court were brought not by individuals but by corporations.[66]

The pursuit of corporate personhood persisted despite the fact that the very raison d'etre of corporations is antithetical to human interests: Their primary allegiance is to their shareholders. Corporations are not only permitted, they are *mandated* to sacrifice interests that might conflict with that priority. If the law allows them to pollute a certain amount, for instance, it may be a violation of their fiduciary duty not to, if taking precautions would hurt the bottom line.

Not only are the personal assets of corporate officers protected; the officers themselves are protected from guilt the way the members of a firing squad escape sleepless nights by the placement of a blank among their collective bullets. This way, each can tell himself that his was the blank; the fatal bullet came from someone else's gun: "Lots of people were involved in making this decision;" says the CEO. Or: "Everyone does it; if I hadn't done it, someone else would have." By such reasoning did an Italian court recently rule that participants in gang rape should not be sentenced to jail.[67]

I sometimes ask my students if they would be capable of killing someone if they were ordered to.

Yes, many of them say, because the decision wasn't theirs.

Would they be capable of giving the order?

Yes, they go on, unfazed by the contradiction, because they weren't the one to pull the trigger.

Guilt loves company. The word "morals" derives from the Latin "mores" which means, simply, "customs." The word "ethics" derives from "ether." Either way, what is good or acceptable is determined simply by looking around and seeing what everyone else is doing.

And we wonder how so many millions could have gone along with Nazism.

(The famed studies by psychologist Stanley Milgrim at Yale indirectly corroborate this thesis. Participants were told that the study focused on how pain affected people's ability to learn. Actors were hired to stay in a different room and respond to questions which purported to test their scholastic abilities. If they got a wrong answer, the participant was to press a button which would [supposedly] administer electric shocks of increasing strength in response to which the actor would scream with corresponding intensity before eventually lapsing into ominous silence.

In reality, of course, the subject of the study was the people administering the "shocks." If they had doubts about continuing, the psychologist in charge would calmly tell them it was OK; they should just carry on. A few subjects eventually refused but the results were unsettling for everyone, particularly the people who had engaged in what they believed, however erroneously, was electrocution. The study was carried out in the aftermath of World War II, Milgrim wanting to see how concentration camp guards could have so mindlessly carried out orders to torture.)

The corporate agenda gained particular momentum with the deregulation ushered in by Reagan so that today, over half of the hundred largest economies in the world today are corporations rather than countries. In 1999, sales of General Motors were greater than the GDP of 182 nations. And most of the business of the country's 11,000 magazines is controlled by only three corporations.[68]

Of Monopolies and Monotheism

While the road to our current collapse was paved with the removal of checks and balances to restrain all-consuming greed, there's another force at work as well.

The licensing of monopolies takes place at the upper echelons of the social structure, among those eminences grises whose presence in the media is low-key. It's a dry, cumbersome process, nothing you fun-loving folk need worry your heads over. Leave it to the wonks who will tell you what they've done after they've done it and you can't undo it.

Meanwhile for your reading pleasure, here are the antics of Brangelina and their ilk. With their ever-entertaining entanglements, they serve the function of the gods of yesteryear. Appearing in close-up on screens twenty feet high, they are literally larger than life. The public are nurtured to believe that this cluster of Superstars came into being not through the machinations of some Hollywood studio marketing department but according to Divine Law: The unknown actor may have had the same talent on Tuesday as he has on Wednesday, but the public will not give him a second glance until he has been anointed by the press. At that point, a spotlight is cast on him whose glare blinds us to the human beings around; for our mindset seems to allow for no more than one such hero at any given moment, some form of Dad.

Perhaps the ancients, in particular, Moses, underwent the same thought process: The pantheon of gods who populated pagan belief was messy in the way democracy so often is; the gods were wont to squabble. Why not dispense with this inconvenience by paring the number down to one? A survival-of-the-fittest, Unified Field Theory, one-stop shopping God who did it All, being omnipotent. And lest anyone argue about His intentions, He puts them in writing which is literally set in stone. The earlier acceptance of duality goes by the boards. In her book, The Dark Side of Christian History, Helen Ellerbe points out that the original Trinity consisted of a man and a woman, creating a synergy that is greater than the sum of its parts. This was replaced with a Trinity that exalted sameness.[69] (She also points out that the word "heresy" comes from the Greek "hairesis," or "choice.")

But as soon as you introduce one Supreme Being, you create a hierarchy into which everyone else must scramble to find a place, and one which is, of necessity, inferior. Thus reality is forever imperfect when compared to an ideal somewhere off in Never-Neverland. The hitherto revered Earthmother, ever-changing Nature, the source of empirical knowledge, is now to be supplanted by the immutable Sky God representing abstract thought which was considered to be the province of men. There are insiders and outsiders and those in power get to define who's what. Some centuries later, the passage of time having brought about little change in attitude, women who show a streak of independence by living alone are declared to be witches, particularly if they own property which is then seized to pay for the trial which ends in their death. Also they may possess knowledge of herbal medicine, particularly in relation to childbirth, which is a repulsive business. (Death, leading to one's ascension to a pristine Heaven, is in some ways more respectable.) Henceforth, the only people who can practice medicine shall be graduates of "accredited" medical schools, which, by the way, only men can attend.

And so, finally, Dad trumps Mom, forever and ever, Amen.

One Giant Step Backwards for Womankind

August 30, 2008

Whether to cry or vomit, that is the question that so frequently pops into mind these days. Any woman, possibly disgruntled at the defeat of Hillary, who cheers the choice of Sarah Palin as a running mate for a presidential candidate needs to stop and think ahead a step or two: Say McCain, who, whatever theoretical good qualities he may have, has rarely been accused of youth, becomes indisposed or dies. We now have our first female president. Inexperienced and, in a party not short on machismo, anxious to prove herself one of the boys, Palin is a tad overzealous in an era that calls for depth of thought and understanding.

As the world is on the brink of disaster anyway, her mistakes are magnified and the results, calamitous.

The country, or whatever is left of it, says, "You see? We had a woman president and what happened?"

It will be the end of female power for aeons; again, if there are any.

If Obama wins, he too, will be biting off more than he can chew (since it's more than anybody can chew) and will be destined to fail. But he does not face the same fate as far as history goes. He will be blamed for what happens, but more as an individual; less because of his race (except among racists who were against him anyway.)

For, while racism is alive and well, it is not so pervasive as anti-feminism. It's not politically correct to be a racist and there has been a sea change in progress over the last fifty years.

Feminism has seen progress in tangible areas such as admission to medical school and token CEOs, but less in the more nebulous realms of attitudes and assumptions. The supposed differences between men and women are still the stuff of arguments and sitcoms. Nobody would ever write a book saying that one race is from Mars and another, from Venus.

So if the moment the wrecking ball strikes, McCain steps out of the way (possibly via a heart attack) and Palin is left standing in his place, then like Eve, she will earn her honorary male status as the fall guy.

Palin, Perfect Patsy

September 06, 2008

In an era when what counts above all is selling toothpaste, Sarah Palin has it all: Looks (the Barracuda even has toothpaste-selling teeth), the Reaganesque savvy to disarm her critics with self-effacing humor ("What's the difference between a hockey mom and a pit-bull?   Lipstick."), and to top it all off, Wonder Woman prowess at hunting and skinning a moose. We know-it-all East Coast city slickers are impressed in spite of ourselves. Even the Peak Oilists have to admit that, however perversely, she has some of what it takes to survive the hard times, at least on a personal level.

What makes the package even better for the Repubs is that her handlers, operating, as always, on a need-to-know basis, will keep her pumped with disinformation so that she'll continue to preach the party line: Drill, Baby, Drill! Nukes! "Clean" Coal! Then, as an afterthought, wind/solar/geothermal and whatever other renewables you want to throw in.

Americans, who every day become more incapable of analysis any deeper than sound bite level, respond to her poignant yet sitcom family dilemmas, her spunky ability to bounce back and what's more, to project her own problems onto a national scale, promising, for instance, that other families with special needs children will have a voice in the White House.

In sum, what a great package! Her ignorance of the true facts behind our energy crisis only makes her a more effective proponent for economic growth, which is the original cancer of our mortally ill civilization. If you want to convey the impression that your solutions to various impending crises are innocent of environmental or social havoc, there's nothing like sending out a messenger who genuinely doesn't know any better.

Like W and Obama, she's being bought with power. After all, look where her zealous promotion of the party platform has gotten her so far. And like W and Obama, she's being set up to take the eventual and fatal fall.

A Final Fling with Optimism

Oscar Wilde said that second marriages represent the triumph of hope over experience. So it is with elections.

In January 2009, the world was in a heady mood and inclined to give Obama the benefit of the doubt. The honeymoon lasted about two weeks before the couple (Obama and the United States) returned to their roach-infested apartment.

January 2009

Asian cellist, Jewish guy on violin, disabled, to boot! Venezuelan woman on piano; African-American on clarinet. The signal came through loud and clear: This is going to be an ecumenical administration, dedicated to the proposition that all men are created equal, even women. Which is to say, we're all going down together.

It has been breathtaking, the swift, sure dismantling of Executive Orders whose only purpose was to serve not the people of the country but the people who had issued the Executive Orders in the first place.

The secrecy that for eight years, in the interest of "national security," has been invoked across the board—even to the EPA, where Policy Analyst Hugh Kaufman, railed, "We're the country's janitors, for God's sake!"—is going into reverse.

Guantanamo is being closed and the United States is forgoing policies of "enhanced interrogation" otherwise known as torture.

Scientists are sighing with relief that once again their disciplines will be considered objectively rather than twisted to serve industry's needs.

And the one-hand-washing-the other, inbred "military industrial *congressional* complex'—as Eisenhower called it before some antsy speechwriter intervened—is not going to have such a smooth ride.[70]

No question: This guy's showing what he's made of. He's got good intentions.

Ah, but the road to Hell....

Will this inspiring start turn out to be no more than a wistful salute to idealism before reality returns from its heady few weeks of euphoria?

So far, Obama's got the wind at his back, universal approval for his reforms. But that won't be the case when it comes to the economy. The inevitable correction that must follow the parade we've witnessed of ever larger bubbles is not going to be popular. The biggest bubble, in Treasuries, is going to make the biggest pop. Were Obama to tell the truth, much less do what needs to be done which is to say, allow nature to take its course, he would be booed, Congress would vote down his initiatives and the people would run him out of office ASAP.

For contrary to popular belief, we are not a capitalist society. Our biggest failures are not permitted to die, on the grounds that they are "too big to fail." Instead, we feed the dinosaurs taxpayer trillions.

The True Color of a Chameleon

January, 2009

A trillion here, two trillion there... In between you go to the store, pay for your coffee and walk out, just the way you did three orders of magnitude ago.

"Freefall," reads another headline.

Between conception and realization falls the shadow. And that's a good thing. We are at the legs-spinning-above-the-abyss phase, oblivious to said freefall until we land.

Americans, being the most spoiled people in the history of mankind, not only want the good life back; they want it now. Man-on-the-street interviews reveal that some, woozy with the advent of Change Incarnate, expect the President to be able to turn things around in a matter of months. The more circumspect allow him a second term. But unless there's some major editing going on, no one dreams that perhaps it is the President, not to mention we the people, who will be turned around.

What we have lost in the period of ease since World War II is a sense of time, investment and history. Having never known hunger, we believe it's obsolete, like, oh, getting places on horseback (which some Peak Oilists envision making a comeback in the not-so-distant future). Why should it return, now that we have so much cool stuff like cell-phones and computers? Not only do we lack imagination, we're unaware of our shortcoming.

But the basic laws of physics stubbornly remain: What goes up must come down, especially if the "up" part was artificial. Everything returns to equilibrium, reverts to the mean. Taking in the big picture, the balance of our consumption with the depletion of resources somewhere outside of frame and therefore of consciousness, this abundant garden is turning out to be mortal. It could have nourished us forever but not without some stewardship on our part.

We are learning this, but not fast enough.

And Obama, being the people's hero, is not far enough ahead of us. Rather than offering us what we need, he is offering us what we crave. Now that the birthday boys have gotten their supersized bailout, it's time for party favors for everyone else.

There's something goofily fitting about the stimulus package, like balancing the loss of a leg by cutting off the other one. But the tragedy of it is that it is throwing—I want to say, "good money after bad" but by now, it's worse money. (I'm also tempted to call the stimulus package a knee-jerk response but for the two amputated legs of the previous metaphor.)

When are we going to get our "blood, sweat and tears" speech? Churchill didn't give his until the Battle of France was underway; the people had to be confronted with brutal realities before they were willing to entertain his offer.

Obama has the potential to be a great president. The question is: Will we let him?

The Mightiest Fall Guy

2009

Pity Obama. He will be viewed as the knight ("Obamalot") who rode in with such promise, yet whose advent in fact ushered in disaster such as the world has never known. My East European students speak earnestly of Vanga, a Bulgarian seer who, blinded at the age of twelve, has supposedly provided uncannily accurate predictions, to whit: The United States will elect a "chocolate-colored" President under whose guidance we'll go to the dogs.

Have you ever seen a piece of chocolate the color of Obama? I respond.

My students then protest that Vanga predicted that "Kursk" (which, so far as anyone knew at the time, was nothing more than the name of a landlocked city in Russia) would be underwater, leading to the shedding of many tears. No one could figure out what to make of this. Ah, but then look what happened to the Kursk *submarine*! An explosion led to the death of its entire crew; hence, the tears.

However, what my students did not know, because they had never bothered to investigate, is that Vanga made her prediction before the submarine was constructed. Is it not possible that some wag among the thousands involved decided that "Kursk" would be a fitting name for a submarine whose very raison d'etre is to go underwater and participate in dangerous activity, possibly to include destruction, thereby causing the shedding of tears?

Does Obama know he's been set up? Have they minced words in telling him what's in store? He seems awfully serious these days. And his speech started off on a grim note of warning.

But soon enough we were back on the familiar track of hope triumphant.

Perhaps eventually, depending on one's definition of "triumph." But to quote T.S. Eliot, "Between the conception and the realization falls the shadow." Between now and then, an awful lot of s*** is going to hit the fan.

Update: January 22, 2010. The cover of this week's New Yorker depicts the career of Obama in successive panels. In the first several, he walks on water, then on thin ice. In the last panel, he drowns.

GOVERNMENT RESPONSE TO PEAK OIL/RESOURCES

Knowledge is power; thus, anyone who wants to stay in power needs accurate information. Unlike the People who, as a group at least, allow themselves to be manipulated because it's easier than educating themselves, those in power can't afford to be beguiled by wishful thinking; at least, not in the long term.

So for a number of decades, governments have been asking themselves and by extension, their hired experts, how long they could depend on oil to maintain their power.

M. King Hubbert told the U.S. in the fifties: Your peak is around 1971. And for the world, it's in a few decades. And Dick Cheney acknowledged Peak Oil in a 1999 speech at the London Institute of Petroleum.[71]

The major powers have responded to this in different ways, depending not on their relative degree of righteousness but on the means they had available, always bearing in mind the Prisoner's Dilemma and the Tragedy of the Commons discussed below.

We begin in China and India because their approach to Peak Oil, while subtle and behind the scenes, has nonetheless thus far been more straightforward than that of the U.S.

Strange Bedfellows: Making Friends in a Post-Peak World

Speech for the Petrocollapse Conference in Washington, DC

May 2006

One of the hallmarks of addiction is that you use escalating amounts of the substance you're addicted to.[72]

Our economy, which is based on interest, guarantees addiction. Not only is growth inevitable; it's essential. The substance which feeds that growth—energy—must by definition become addictive.

Because our economy depends on growth and therefore on the oil on which that growth in turn depends, we have become oil addicts. So what should we do now that it's heading down its post-peak production slope?

One option is, we can change drugs. We can build nuclear power plants, thereby switching our addiction from oil to uranium supplemented by ethanol, coal and renewables because suddenly, now that Mother Nature is striking back with a vengeance in the form of earthquakes and hurricanes, we care about the environment. Switching drugs means we don't have to wean ourselves from addiction at all.

Or we could go into Rehab. That would take a real effort and seriously cramp our style. But we might be willing to do it as long as no one else was having any fun either.

Trouble is, everyone else is an actual or aspiring addict, too. What if we go into Rehab but the other crazed addicts remain at large? They'll get all the good stuff, which will fuel them with a manic energy to grab even more.

That is the Prisoner's Dilemma that we're faced with.

The original Prisoner's Dilemma is this:

Two suspects get arrested. The police don't have enough evidence to convict either of them and need testimony. If one prisoner testifies against the other and the other remains silent, the betrayer goes free and the silent accomplice receives the full 10-year sentence. If both stay silent, the police can sentence both to only six months in jail for a minor charge. If each betrays the other, each will receive a two-year sentence.

Each prisoner must choose whether to betray the other or to remain silent. However, neither prisoner knows what choice the other prisoner will make. For the best total outcome, a sentence of six months for both prisoners, each prisoner has to rely on the honor and shrewdness of the other prisoner.[73]

A variant of this problem is the Tragedy of the Commons: A group of farmers share common grassland for their respective flocks of sheep. If one farmer wants to "grow" his flock, it will have to eat more than its share of grass. This will benefit the farmer, at least in the short term, but at the expense of everyone else. In the long term, since the commons will not be sustained, everyone loses.

Those are the dilemmas we face if we go into Rehab with respect to our energy addiction. If everyone else also goes into Rehab, fine. But if one country reneges on the deal, they get all the good stuff, i.e., resources.

Can we trust other countries to stick to the deal?

Only if it's in their own best interest.

Will they perceive it to be in their own best interest?

Only if they feel they need us.

Do countries need each other?

Not if they're at the top of the heap.

So that is what everyone has decided to do: To scramble to the top of the heap because they think that with a little help from their friends, they have a chance of making it.

Thus there's a lot of saber-rattling going on. Recently Iran conducted Holy Prophet naval exercises complete with flying boats to show their neighbors their "peaceful intentions."[74]

By way of response, the United States conducted naval exercises in the Bahamas in order to show our peaceful intentions towards Venezuela, which has sought closer ties to Iran as well as to our erstwhile Pinko enemies, Russia and Cuba.[75] And India sent a ship to the Maldives to patrol the Exclusive Economic Zone, a phrase that refers to fishing and seabed mining.[76]

Certainly no one's putting brakes on their economy. Those U.S. wannabes, China and India, are obsessed with feeding theirs, like the doting parents of monster children who refuse to see that when those children grow up, they'll eat their parents, too. And since neither country is endowed with the natural resources on which said growth depends, they're doing what anyone does who needs something: They're making friends.

China is jumping into the Free Trade Agreement fray with New Zealand and Australia and has pledged $374 million in loans to Pacific allies to boost economic cooperation.[77] Chinese Premier Wen Jiabao said, "[T]he loans would target various industries including mining, agriculture, forestry, fisheries and aviation...

"China has funding and technical expertise," [Wen] said. 'The island countries are rich in natural resources. Herein lay huge potential for bilateral cooperation.'"[78]

Translation: *We'll provide the money to help you help us ravage your country.*

Wen maintained that the agreement came with no political strings attached. But it included only those South Pacific countries whose governments have diplomatic relations with China—the Cook Islands, Fiji, Micronesia, Niue, Papua New Guinea, Samoa, Tonga and Vanuatu and excluded six countries that have relations with Taiwan—Kiribati, the Marshall Islands, Nauru, Palau, the Solomon Islands and Tuvalu.

Other friends are being cultivated for the purposes of securing energy, ports and alternative routes for oil delivery as well as strategic partners in the event of war. China is making agreements on gas from Turkmenistan, a power plant with Kazakhstan, electricity from Russia, energy from Nigeria, Kenya[79] and Saudi Arabia and alternative energy via a bus service to Pakistan. Agreements on ports with Cambodia[80] and in the Mekong River will allow China to become more independent of the Malacca Straits.[81] And rail links are being established to the Republic of Korea and Tibet in spite of the risk posed by the latter of spreading plague.[82]

This may seem odd since China has suffered more than one headache from its association with a dread disease. As the putative source of Severe Acute Respiratory Syndrome (SARS) and the infamous bird flu, which, despite best efforts on the part of researchers, could not be found to have spread from a single migrating bird, China is the international version of the kid with cooties.[83] To show the sincerity of its stand against cooties, China recently hosted a meeting of Asian Pacific Economic Cooperation against emerging infectious diseases.[84]

On the military front, it is providing advisors to Equatorial Guinea and making defense agreements with Saudi Arabia, Vietnam and Singapore. Not picky about going where angels like the U.S. Department of Energy fear to tread, China readily deals with regimes to which the DOE has given "pariah status" such as Myanmar and the Sudan.[85] (Perhaps their coziness with China is the very reason they have earned such status. The recent "concern" of the United States with Sudanese human rights abuses, for example, is ironic because, according to a Human Rights Watch Report of 2003, many of those abuses are the work of foreign oil companies.[86])

Meanwhile India has been cultivating friends across the political spectrum like the new kid in school who wants to be head of the class, but also doesn't want to get beat up by bullies.

It has signed a comprehensive economic pact with the six-nation Gulf Cooperation Council, as well as similar agreements with ASEAN, Singapore, Taiwan, China, Russia, South Africa and

Brazil and cultural agreements with Iceland.[87] In addition, Deutsche Bank, Barclay's and J.P. Morgan are all expanding their Indian operations.

To lock in the energy supplies on which its optimistic trade agreements depend, it has Memoranda of Understanding or similar agreements with Afghanistan, Japan, Saudi Arabia, Myanmar, the Sudan, Qatar, Finland, West Africa, the European Union and the United Kingdom, and defense agreements with Mozambique, France, the Philippines, Saudi Arabia, Oman, Mauritius, the Andaman Islands, Tajikistan and the Maldives. Playing it safe, India also has defense agreements with Iran as well as the United States;[88] and, in the East China Seas, with China as well as Japan.

This headlong pursuit of growth on the part of both China and India persists despite the fact that both countries have already experienced an alarming share of growth's Picture of Dorian Gray effects.

In India, drought caused in part by climate change and a rising population has resulted in crop failures which have driven hundreds of farmers to suicide.[89]

Drought also plagues the Northwest Chinese province of Ningxia where, unable to survive as a farmer, 23-year-old Wang Zhanguo has been forced to work instead as a coal miner, a building site manager and a long-distance truck driver, which uneco-friendly professions, of course, only exacerbate the problem. Wang's case is not unique, however: 67% of China's farming is in the north whereas 80% of its water is in the south.[90]

Acid rain falls on 30% of China's land area[91] and desertification has been so vast as to necessitate a logging ban to protect China's own forests.[92] However, Chinese companies remain undeterred in their zeal to satisfy the world's appetite for cheap furniture; they have simply turned to slashing through the forests of Burma, Russia, Malaysia, Indonesia, Gabon and Borneo. (One such company is Shanghai Anxin Flooring in which the Carlyle Group invested $30 million.[93] 9/11 researchers will recall the Carlyle Group for its directorship which included former President George

H.W. Bush as well as members of the Bin Laden family.[94]) As a result, soil erosion, landslides and floods are being globalized.

To combat these effects, the Chinese government has taken the heroic step of imposing a 5% tax on chopsticks.[95] The measure is having disappointing results although it does serve as another weapon in China's arsenal against Japan, which gets 97% of its chopsticks from China.[96]

China's other solution to industry-induced water shortages is sure to delight the gods of irony who rule the universe: It is using artificial rain.[97]

At the opposite end of the weather spectrum, China has also created an artificial sun, this time to address its energy crisis. By extracting deuterium from the sea and combining it with tritium via nuclear fusion, the pseudo-sun can produce energy from just one liter of seawater that is equivalent to 300 liters of gasoline. What a relief to know that nature will no longer be necessary, since there will be so little of it left. The only thing standing in the way of this brave new invention is a device that can withstand 100 million degrees Celsius.[98]

In high school French class we once read a fable about an oak tree and a reed. A storm came in which the reed bent with the wind and survived. The oak tree stood firm and was felled.

The twist in the story was the oak tree's dying words: "I am still an oak."

While India and China are making friends to help them bend with the oncoming storm over finite resources, the United States has stated its position: "The American way of life is non-negotiable." (*We are still an oak.*) We suck up to no country and when we keel over, those will undoubtedly be our last words.

Water in Central Asia

September 29, 2006

At a dinner party, it's the empty chair that garners curiosity. In this case, the chair belongs to Turkmenistan, which did not participate in the recent Astana summit, culminating in the pact to preserve the Aral Sea.

Yet they're hardly immune to the problems afflicting their neighbors. 80-90% desert, Turkmenistan has the lowest "operational resources of groundwater" of all the Central Asian states.

The other piece missing from the Astana pact is Russia. The Central Asian states agreed, as they have in the past, that the way to resolve their water problems is to divert waters from the rivers of Siberia.

How does Russia feel about this? It has "yet to come up with any official reaction to the Siberian river diversion scheme. However, some officials have indicated that Russia, or at least some regions, may eventually face shortages of quality drinking water. In the meantime, competition for water is increasing in Central Asia at an alarming rate, adding tension to what is already a volatile region."[99]

U.S.

The United States' recent response to Peak Oil represents a desperate power grab. Since we have gone beyond assertively acquiring friends (if only for their resources) into the realm of naked aggression, we have followed in the tradition of what any self-respecting government does in such a position—we have disguised our efforts as self-defense.

There is a grand history of false flag attacks from the Spanish-American War to the Reichstag fire which, executed by the Nazis—with help from a young, embittered stonemason who'd become permanently disabled on the job—was blamed on the Communists, thus catapulting Hitler to the position of Führer. (Does, "Consolidating power in the Executive branch" sound familiar?) War is a cure-all for certain economic woes but it requires a cover story, which is to say, an enemy. Now that Communists no longer fit the bill (the Soviet Union having collapsed,) conveniently, terrorists (who were once armed and trained by the CIA to drive out those same Communists) have rushed in to fill the vacuum.

Conflict of Interest, a 9/11 Windfall and
the White House Council on Environmental Quality

www.fromthewilderness.com, www.oilempire.us, Michael C. Ruppert's Crossing the Rubicon and Paul Thomson's 9/11 timeline (*www.historycommons.org*) chronicle the myriad evidence, both circumstantial and otherwise, of Bush administration involvement in the attacks of September 11. A brief synopsis includes:

1. Multiple warnings from foreign intelligence agencies from Italy, Indonesia, Germany, Israel, etc.[100] *which were uniformly ignored.*

2. The assertion in a document written prior to 9/11 by a consortium known as the Project for a New American Century—"Further, the process of [military] transformation, even if it brings revolutionary change, is likely to be a long one, absent some catastrophic and catalyzing event—like a new Pearl Harbor." Though tangential to the current discussion, it is interesting that the passage continues, "advanced forms of biological warfare that can 'target' specific genotypes may transform biological warfare from the realm of terror to a politically useful tool."[101]

3. Multiple requests from FBI agents such as Coleen Rowley and Robert Wright for authorization to investigate Zacarias Moussaoui's laptop. These were methodically denied or, like the warnings of an attack during the week of September 9, ignored.[102]

4. Highly anomalous put options on United and American Airlines. "A jump in UAL put options 90 times (not 90%) above normal between September 6 and September 10, and 285 times higher than average on the Thursday before the attack."[103]

One might argue that the placement of these options is evidence only of terrorists' affiliates who wanted to profit from the attack. That argument misses the point, which concerns not illicit gains but foreknowledge: If only for the honorable purpose of uncovering insider trading, the CIA monitors put options in real time.[104]

5.   The at least six war games taking place on the morning of 9/11.

In addition to diverting planes from the East Coast to Northern Canada and Alaska, the war games introduced false blips onto the radar screen, stymieing any pilots who might have tried to intercept the hijacked planes.   One exercise taking place at the same time as the actual attacks, though not a war game, involved a plane going off course and hitting a building, the National Reconnaissance Office.[105]

(Numerous other plane-into-building-or-national-icon threats had occurred in the course of the previous decade, including a plane flying into the Eiffel Tower.[106]   *These should be borne in mind when weighing the testimony of Condoleezza Rice to the 9/11 Commission that the administration never expected a plane would fly into a building.*[107])

Such planes as did remain on the East Coast, both at Otis Air Force Base in Massachusetts and Langley AFB in Virginia, went off in the wrong direction, towards Russia,[108] *on the supposition that the attack was a carryover from the Cold War which had ended ten years before.*

But the environmental disaster that followed in the wake of the attacks affords the opportunity to investigate a previously overlooked piece of evidence of foreknowledge at the very least—the White House Task Force on Energy Project Streamlining.[109]   *This group, which sprang into existence with the advent of the Bush Administration, was led by James Connaughton, Chairman of the White House Council on Environmental Quality, the entity that was largely responsible for the lies told to New Yorkers about their air quality following 9/11.*

James Connaughton, Cheney's Boy Wonder

June 27th, 2007—James Connaughton, the Chairman of the White House Council on Environmental Quality, which coordinated with the National Security Council to edit EPA's press releases following 9/11, faced the music last Wednesday with a nimble tap-dance. Padded with cliché allusions to the "unprecedented" attacks and a homespun vignette about his son's fear that dad was dead, Connaughton's testimony at the Senate Hearing Into Federal Government Failures on [the] Environmental Impact Of [the] 9/11 World Trade Center Attacks deftly passed the buck, pointing out that there was a flurry of press releases; they were the work-product of many people and that anyway, the public doesn't read them.[110]

But in the course of this fancy footwork (first the blame is over here, now it's over there), the Chairman slipped on the banana peel of a detail.

In response to a question about the EPA Inspector General's Report of 2003, which showed how the White House CEQ "tweaked" EPA's press releases—for instance by changing cautionary statements about asbestos to reassurances and by omitting advice to obtain professional cleaning—as well as why (in order to reopen Wall Street), Connaughton asserted that the 9/11 Commission later did a thorough investigation of the same issue, coming to very different conclusions.

During a recess, I asked Connaughton if, by "thorough investigation," he was referring to the footnote on page 555 of the 9/11 Commission Report, the only mention the report makes of the environmental aftermath of the attacks.[111]

"I am," he replied gamely. (His demeanor throughout the hearing was chipper, as of one who has nothing to hide; who is, in fact, eager for the chance to tell his side of the story.)

During the Commission hearings, Commissioner Richard Ben-Veniste had regretfully told me that the Commission would *not* investigate the environmental issue.

I relayed that information to Connaughton.

"They changed their minds after the Inspector General's Report came out," he asserted. "They did a thorough investigation, interviewing lots of people."

The footnote in the Commission Report containing the fruits of said "thorough investigation" is four paragraphs long. One paragraph reads in its entirety:

"We do not have the expertise to examine the accuracy of the pronouncements in the press releases. The issue is the subject of pending litigation."

(I was one of twelve original plaintiffs in one of the pending lawsuits.)

As for coming to very different conclusions from the Inspector General's Report, while it is true that the Commission Report's footnote offers EPA Administrator Christie Todd Whitman some support, it also says:

The EPA did not have the health-based benchmarks needed to assess the extraordinary air quality conditions in Lower Manhattan after 9/11. The EPA and the White House therefore improvised and applied standards developed for other circumstances... Whether those improvisations were appropriate is still a subject for medical and scientific debate.[112]

I then asked Connaughton about his less well-known but potentially even more explosive role as Chairman of the White House Task Force on Energy Project Streamlining, which was established on the recommendation of Vice President Dick Cheney's infamously secretive National Energy Policy Development Group. (Two years later, its mandates were amended to include the security of pipelines.)

The Task Force included representatives from 21 Federal agencies: the Departments of State, the Treasury, Defense,

Agriculture, Housing and Urban Development, Justice, Commerce, Transportation, the Interior, Labor, Education, Health and Human Services, Energy, Veterans Affairs, the Environmental Protection Agency, the Central Intelligence Agency, the General Service Administration, the Office of Management and Budget, the Council of Economic Advisers, the Domestic Policy Council and the National Economic Council.[113]

Connaughton frowned in concentration.

"Ah yes!" he said triumphantly, as though retrieving a bauble from the depths of memory.

"How does this position expand the normal powers of the CEQ?" I asked.

"It doesn't!" he asserted. "I inherited it."

The Task Force was created, and Connaughton appointed its Chairman, by Executive Order 13212[114] on May 18, 2001, two weeks after Connaughton was appointed to the Council on Environmental Quality, so it is difficult to understand from whom he "inherited" it.

Concerning why so many disparate agencies had to be involved, Connaughton said, "The Defense Department because often the energy is located in other countries. The CIA? I don't know; I don't think they came to any meetings."

Serving at the pleasure of Cheney's Energy Task Force, Connaughton and the CEQ faithfully carried out the Vice President's environmental agenda of relaxing regulations (that is how "streamlining" takes place), the better to serve business interests.

In fact, so lax did regulations become, they managed to offend Administrator Christine Todd Whitman, whom Cheney had brought into the EPA, a feat that is comparable to shocking Larry Flynt.*

"It was Cheney's insistence on easing air pollution controls," says the Washington Post, "not the personal reasons she cited at the time, that led Christine Todd Whitman to resign as administrator of the Environmental Protection Agency."[115]

In response to the Inspector General's allegation that a major reason the CEQ downplayed dangers in EPA's press releases was the need to re-open Wall Street, much has been made of the fact that one smoking gun press release was issued *after* Wall Street re-opened; ergo re-opening the markets couldn't have been a motive.

This reasoning is simplistic; bosses don't necessarily spell out their wishes. In an article entitled "Leaving No Tracks," the *Washington Post* quotes Paul Hoffman, a former Cheney Congressional aide, who says, "Cheney never told [Hoffman] what to do... He didn't have to...

'His genius is that he builds networks and puts the right people in the right places, and then trusts them to make well-informed decisions that comport with his overall vision."[116]

Through the CEQ, Cheney turns up again in the furor over climate change. When NASA scientists complained of the Bush Administration's censorship of the issue (once again by editing press releases), the spotlight fell on one Philip Cooney, who reported to Connaughton.

...And the Horse He Rode In On

Before becoming the eager hatchet man of the White House's environmental policies, James Connaughton was a partner in Sidley Austin (now Sidley, Austin, Brown and Wood), which has been ranked among the top five law firms representing the 250 largest companies in the U.S. for business litigation and as the top provider of legal services to the hedge fund industry.[117]

Clients have included J.P. Morgan Securities,[118] Deutsche Bank, Chinese National Offshore Oil Corporation, Monsanto and GlaxoSmithKline. Sidley Austin represented Searle when it was cleared of price fixing;[119] and Marathon Oil when the federal government was ordered to provide it with a refund of $156 million.[120]

The ties between Sidley Austin and the Bush Administration are extensive. Besides Connaughton, partner Patrick Morrisey has served as the Deputy Staff Director and Chief Health Counsel to the House Energy & Commerce Committee and Sidley's Senior Government Affairs Advisor Dean Clancy is the former Program Associate Director of the Office of Management and Budget. According to the Washington Post, Clancy is a " 'proclaimer' for the Separation of School and State Alliance, which favors home schooling over compulsory public education in order to 'integrate God and education.' "[121]

In addition to public schools, Clancy also opposes stem-cell research and federal taxes for which reasons Esquire magazine has called him a fanatic.[122]

In 2007, President Bush appointed Sidley Austin partner Daniel M. Price, who had served in The Hague as the U.S. Deputy Agent to the Iran-U.S. Claims Tribunal, as Deputy National Security Advisor for International Economic Affairs.

Then there is Bradford Berenson who returned to Sidley, Austin, Brown & Wood after two years as Associate Counsel to the President.

According to his biography on Sidley's website, his responsibilities to the President *"included work on judicial selection, executive privilege, and responses to congressional oversight efforts. In the aftermath of the September 11 attacks, he played a significant role in the executive branch's counterterrorism response. He worked on the USA Patriot Act, the military order authorizing the use of military commissions, detainee policy and anti-terrorism litigation, presidential action against terrorist financing, and the restructuring of the federal government to create a new Department of Homeland Security.*

'He previously worked on the defense of complex white-collar criminal matters...

'Mr. Berenson has defended criminal cases at every stage of development, from corporate internal investigations and grand jury proceedings through trials, sentencings, and appeals, in areas as diverse as government contracts, environmental crime, health care, and public corruption."[123]

Conflict of Interest Alive and Well

At the White House, Berenson worked closely with Cheney's Chief of Staff, David Addington, and fended off critics who demanded the recusal of Judge Antonin Scalia, after he went duck hunting with Cheney, in the Sierra Club case which sought access to Energy Task Force records.

Conflict of interest objections were apparently waived in this case because the Government Accounting Office also hired Sidley Austin[124] to sue Cheney to obtain a list of officials from Enron and other companies who met with the energy task force.

The ubiquitous Mr. Berenson also served as the attorney for former Rove assistant Susan Ralston during the investigation of White House ties to Jack Abramoff as well as for Kyle Sampson, Alberto Gonzalez' Chief of Staff. Berenson defended the habeas corpus stripping provisions of the military commissions bill and has stated: "[T]he Geneva Conventions do not apply to Al Qaeda terrorists."[125] He has even maintained that the "process that's now in place in Guantanamo is, in many ways, superior to an Article V process.... [The prisoners] all get annual administrative review board hearings, and this is far in excess of the international law obligations and the law of war obligations."[126]

Like Connaughton, Berenson is a zealous executant of the Cheney philosophy, stating, "[W]hen we are at war, we weigh the risks to innocents entirely differently than we do when we are not at war. Grievous damage to the lives and liberties and property of innocents are a regrettable, but daily function of a state of armed conflict, of warfare the kinds of injuries that are totally unredressable in war time, but which we would never tolerate in peace time, if we were not at war."[127]

And concerning executive privilege, he stated: "It's the President in time of war, the executive branch, that's responsible for our security."[128]

Cleverly, he suggests that a little fascism acts as inoculation against the ham-fisted variety: "Were there to be more attacks on the scale of 9/11 or God forbid worse, there would inevitably be a far more draconian response than we've seen thus far. And so in the name of preventing that kind of response, which the public would demand, and in the name of ensuring our ultimate victory over an Islamo-fascist ideology, a religiously inspired fascist ideology, that is as illiberal as any the world has ever seen, we all need to keep first and foremost in our minds the need to wage this war effectively and ensure that the forces of right and the forces of liberalism and democracy prevail in the end."[129]

Sidley Austin, then, may be justifiably described as an eminence grise of the executive branch. But lest it be viewed as biased towards the right, it is also the law firm where, as a summer associate, Barack Obama met his future wife, Michelle.

How Sidley Survived 9/11 Not Only "Intact...."

On 9/11 Sidley Austin, which had merged with Brown and Wood in May 2001 (the same month that Connaughton left for the White House), had its offices in the World Trade Center. In an article written in 2003, Sidley describes how it accomplished the feat of "surviv[ing] 9/11 with vital records and employees intact."[130]

Some of these vital records, which included client, personnel, vendor and services lists, backup tapes, floor plans with personnel locations identified, inventory lists of equipment, furniture, and supplies, procedures manuals, docket calendars, and blank checks, "were available because they were part of a planned dispersal in which they had been copied and sent offsite for safe keeping."[131] Weekly computer backup tapes were also being stored in New Jersey.

The article is written in a breathless style, pausing to pay lip service to the dreadfulness of the day before going on to the myriad resourceful steps Sidley had taken to the benefit of their cherished clients.

Then comes the punch line.   As far as Sidley Austin is concerned, September 11 had a silver lining made of real silver.

...But Also with a Windfall

In addition to all its other prudent measures, on September 1, 2001, Sidley had taken the extraordinarily felicitous step of not only renewing but also of doubling its insurance.

"When it was announced that the firm's insurance policies had just been renewed and doubled on September 1, 2001, applause filled the room.   The insurance policies not only covered reconstruction costs for the files but for the organization's valuable art collection and personal effects as well."[132]

This move joins a distinguished line of coincidences leading up to the attacks, such as highly anomalous put options on United and American Airlines; numerous war games including "practice Armageddons" which diverted planes away from the East Coast and introduced chaff onto the radar screens to paralyze pilots who wanted to respond; as well as dozens of warnings to agencies which are normally overlooked by the mainstream press.

Sidley confesses that "some individuals listed as having supervisory roles in the disaster recovery plan ended up not having job assignments, which was frustrating to those sitting around on 9/11.   Part of the problem stemmed from a lack of testing of the plan the year before."   But despite the frustration, over the entire firm, to use a Grishamesque phrase, dubbed its recovery effort a success.

One Minor Glitch

And so the reader comes away believing, even after encountering this sentence:

"By September 13, only one individual had not been located."

Written this way, the account relays the information concerning "only one individual," as an example of yet another triumph.   What the article neglects to say, however, though it was published nearly two years after the disaster, is that the reason the individual had "not [been] located" is that she was dead.[133]

A telephone operator who dreamed of opening a candy business, Rosemary Smith was the only member of the firm not to make it out of the building alive. And while Sidley mentions her elsewhere on its website and has apparently put up a memorial to her somewhere in its offices, it is difficult to understand what the writer of the article means by the phrase, "employees intact."

The "good news" about the firm's assets, however, seems to be abundantly accurate.

Jenna Orkin was one of twelve original plaintiffs in a class action lawsuit against Christine Todd Whitman and the EPA.

King George and the Knights of the Oval Office
or 9/11 for Dummies

(In the triple meter of, 'T Was the Night Before Christmas)

Sir Richard, surveying his fiefdom, the earth,
said to staffers, "I wonder what it'll be worth
in ten years. For you know, 'neath that rich-looking soil
lie ever diminishing volumes of oil.
Wonderfully handy for large SUVs,
Halliburton and Co., and for killing off trees,
essential in anything made out of plastic,
the loss of all which calls for actions quite drastic.
And China's cars multiply, though ours are bigger
and fortunately, we are quick on the trigger."
He scanned the horizon. "What I'm looking for
is justification for unending war.
As sure as my annual trip to the barber,
what I could use now is a modern Pearl Harbor."

That night as Sir Donald lay sleepless in bed
staring up at the ceiling, he feelingly said,
"Oh Sir, if you're there, then you know why I'm here.
My wife lies beside me; I guess I'm not queer.
But let's face it, I'm getting quite long in the tooth
and am not so strong as I once was in my youth.
Such a vigorous flow I had then like Niagara,
while now I need doses galore of Viagra.
A stallion I was who humped all like a pup,
whereas now, as you well know, I can't get it up.
And I feel with each tick of mortality's clock
ebbing from me the power to Awe and to Shock.
So, Sir please, if it isn't much trouble, gosh dang,
Let me exit not whimpering but with a bang.
I know we've had this conversation before
and your mind is made up so I won't be a bore.
I'm changing my tactic, my tune, my request;
Will obligingly settle for third or fourth best.

Let my glory be for all just once more unfurled
If not here in the bedroom, at least in the world."
On this heartrending note and without further word,
Sir Donald slept, not knowing if he'd been heard
and little suspecting that in a few days,
his Lord would respond in mysterious ways.

For who would have thought, upon hearing Sir Don,
such a hard-bitten realist and Neo-con
as he prayed to his personal saint, Mussolini,
that what he'd called up would look more like a genie.
Soft-spoken in turban and robes he was clad,
while also a touch of the Wise Man he had
as he made his way shepherd-like over paths steep
yet his relatives claimed he was, more, a black sheep.
A family outcast, though with a few wives
and surrounded by men keen on losing their lives,
the deus ex machina star of our drama
's a not-so-poor shepherd who goes by "Osama."
Hearing the good knights' lamenting and prayer
(for he had the most up-to-date kind of software)*
he summoned four airplanes on nine eleven
by telling recruits they'd go straight up to Heaven.
For all his unlikelihood, this noble hero
obligingly leveled the towers at Ground Zero.

First the North Tower's hit; then the South Tower too,
then the Pentagon by a plane out of the blue.
Then Flight 93, with the packed words, "Let's roll,"
Added forty-four victims more to the death toll.

Sir Donald knew nothing for hours, not tracking
the planes though (ironic) he spoke of hijacking;
conjecture of course, since no one could foresee
a plane hitting a skyscraper, especially
since the FBI, acting both dumbly and foully,
suppressed all the warnings of Williams and Rowley
and Robert Wright and all the other intelligence,

saying, "To hell with intelligence, schmelligence."
And about those put options that smell kind of funny?
It's one of those things; just don't follow the money.
As for George to whom all eyes turned, on television,
at that crucial time, he embodied decision:
The prize of Supreme Court's majority vote
stayed the course by continuing with The Pet Goat.

Both NEADS and NORAD stood poised at the ready
well armed with America's true blue and steady,
all waiting to intercept planes that were errant
at moments like this. Oh wait, Oops! No they weren't.
At this moment of truth they were being upstaged
in an exercise up 'round Alaska engaged.
What a lousy coincidence. Darn it, but wait!
Andrews base! Alas, help came a little too late.

Sir Donald, Sir Dick and the other good knights
lost no time before rallying for the good fight.
Or rather, since others could hardly ignore them,
they sent in those others to fight the fight for them.

Such a brilliant maneuver came next, with such wit!
A war that in our lifetime will not quit!
What a grand opportunity for Awe and Shocks!
Talk about thinking outside of the box!
With a logic that lesser minds found a bit cloudy,
considering that the hijackers were Saudi
and while in America learned to hijack,
King George's knights upped and invaded Iraq.

And so our legend of exploits so royal
ends with our heroes securing their oil.
The war, an excuse for more government spending,
provides us with this, our most happy ending.

For a discussion of Promis software, the basis for Total Information Awareness, see Michael C. Ruppert's Crossing the Rubicon.

From the Bread and Circuses Department:
Muddying the Waters

As a piece of PR, 9/11 was a work of art, complete with a swarthy villain straight out of Central Casting who kept the entertainment going by continually eluding the bumbling sheriff (a role which is continually being recast among various security agencies.) Will they get him this time? Stay tuned! Then, "We'll smoke him out," metamorphosed into, "He's not important anymore" and the public turned their attention elsewhere. (Addendum May, 2011: Then we got him, flags flew high once again and the U.S. will be able to withdraw troops from Afghanistan with honor intact.)

In supporting roles, a steady stream of bearded ruffians kept the press busy with their plots to destroy the West because "they hate our freedoms."

Whether they are Jungian archetypes or Hollywood stereotypes, the storyline has worked. Anyone questioning it gets eggs of ridicule thrown at him.

Whereas in the areas of science and finance, the weapon of the government and its mouthpiece, the media, was the soporific potion of boredom—hiding the smoking-gun data in a deluge of bureaucratic documents—here, it is entertainment. 9/11 research is a rabbit-hole of Byzantine complexity, full of snares and delusions and peopled with false friends, lunatics, earnest lost souls and a few heroes.

The problem is distinguishing them all. Those in charge have taken pains to muddy the waters of legitimate inquiry with murky claims and downright howlers.

As in the case of the Kennedy assassination, where the fling of the head upon the impact of the bullet is conclusive evidence of where that bullet came from, physical evidence is hopeless. According to www.oilempire.us: "For every Ph.D., there is an equal and opposite Ph.D." And when it comes to the lone researcher vs. the United States government, guess who has more resources to spare on sussing out the hired guns and granting them contracts.

9/11, [. . . Phrase Removed]
and Twelve Foot Reptiles in the Royal Family

2005 At the request of a person described in the original version of this article, two thirds of it has been removed with apologies for offense caused.

...In preparation for a 9/11 conference at which I was invited to speak, the PR agent for the event has arranged for a dozen radio interviews around the country about the enviro-disaster that ensued in the aftermath of the attacks. This is a bonanza, although my colleagues in the environmental movement caution that we must have nothing to do with the 9/11 conspiracy theories [a policy I modify, though only on my own behalf. However, my insistence on distancing myself from certain members of the conference has, predictably, resulted in my dismissal. Nonetheless, the schedule of radio interviews proceeds.]

No problem, say the first eleven programs and they stick to the agreed on topic.

Then comes interview number twelve. The interviewer, John,* [some identifying details have been changed] calls the day before to confirm what we're covering.

No conspiracy theories, I say. OK he says. "But I hear you're no longer [involved in the conference.] Can we talk about that?" Better not, I say.

The show is forty-five minutes. We address the enviro-disaster of 9/11 in the first twenty. Also Peak Oil, which I've mentioned to the show's producer with the thought of suggesting possible guests for a future program.

John is not a great believer in Peak Oil. He fears that scientists who warn of a potential war over it with China are saying that we need to get rid of the Chinese people, our rivals for the precious, diminishing resource. I point out that warning of war is not the same as advocating it; quite the contrary.

I'm wondering how we're going to spend the remaining 25 minutes of the show—call ins?—when John says, "I have a surprise in store."

I have a strong sense of what the surprise is and contemplate hanging up but I don't want to look like a coward.

"My next guest writes for the American Free Press."

Of course it's all a set up. The writer from AFP (not to be confused with Agence France Presse) knew I'd be on the show. I didn't know he would be. The "surprise" is an ambush.

The American Free Press was founded by Willis Carto, one of the leading American Neo-Nazis of the twentieth century. Its website shares office space with and links to Barnes Review, a Holocaust denial site which advocates that a posthumous Nobel Peace Prize should be awarded to Hitler.[134] It is the presence of the writer from AFP at the 9/11 conference that was a major reason for my reluctance to take part. I stipulated as a condition of participation that I be allowed to preface my speech with a disclaimer stating that I departed radically from some of the other views being espoused. After an exchange of emails in which I was described as "not a team player" (Yes, that was the point), I was politely, and not surprisingly, disinvited.

The interviewer, John, asks what I think of the 9/11 conspiracy theories. Remember, this is after he agreed we wouldn't talk about them. I say there are valid questions about the official story of 9/11 and there are wacky theories; it's important to distinguish between them.

John then asks both of us about the conference and me about the lawsuit I'm involved in against EPA, two more questions he'd agreed not to ask.

I tell him about the link between the American Free Press and Barnes Review with its suggestion about Hitler and the Nobel Peace prize.

John accuses me of calling his other guest anti-Semitic; like I invited him on the show and raised the subject in public?

"Don't you owe him an apology?" John asks.

No, I say, because my disclaimer as a condition of speaking at the conference wasn't personal. It was to avoid linking the issue of the 9/11 enviro-disaster to the American Free Press.

John asks if I'm funded by the Jewish Anti-Defamation League and B'nai B'rith.

Lawyers know that you shouldn't ask a question in court unless you know what answer you're going to get. Journalists should take a leaf from their book.

I say that to my knowledge, I've never met anyone from ADL or B'nai B'rith and I certainly don't get funding from them. I don't get funding from anybody; wish I did.

The AFP writer says that no one blames the whole New York Times for Judith Miller. (I won't bother to analyze the irrelevance of that analogy.) Barnes Review is a "historical publication," he says (like the Smithsonian?), a "revisionist historical publication." (Not a great venue to be linked to when you're supposedly on a quest for truth.) He doesn't know about the Hitler/Nobel Prize suggestion; he's lived in Israel; that's why he knows it so well; he was married to a Jewish woman and he speaks Hebrew.

I respond about the founding of the American Free Press by Willis Carto. (A call from American Free Press a few weeks later informs me that Carto was one of several founders. Carto's own website says: "In 1994 he founded The Barnes Review, a bimonthly magazine of authentic history, of which he is the publisher. In 2001, he began publication of the American Free Press, a weekly newspaper."[135])

John interrupts to end the first hour of the show. The next segment belongs to the other guest alone.

After the show, I Google John. His guests have included a reknowned comedienne as well as Oliver North. And on the bottom of his home page is a banner advertising Barnes Review.

৯   ৫

"You may call me a conspiracy theorist," says Kennedy assassination expert and 9/11 investigator John Judge, "if you're also willing to call yourself a coincidence theorist."

The official story of 9/11 in which we were attacked by forces from outside (forces which, however, we'd recently supplied with weapons to fend off the Soviets) is a conspiracy theory. But it's widely held so people don't speak of it in the scornful tones with which they write off the less popular "conspiracy theories."

Those theories, which tend to get lumped together, the legitimate with the insane, are hard for Americans to swallow, though not so hard for the rest of the world. They involve the participation of our government in orchestrating 9/11 in order to psych the country for war, as well as for the increasingly heavy hand of the government itself via the Patriot Act. (Recent articles indicate that another root of the invasion of Iraq was that country's decision to upend the OPEC practice of accepting only dollars for oil.)

Examples of false flag attacks serving as excuses for initiating or escalating combat are too plentiful to enumerate. Some recent examples are the knowledge of the Roosevelt administration that the attack on Pearl Harbor was coming, since the U.S. had broken the necessary Japanese codes.[136] The attack was allowed to proceed in order to goad the otherwise unwilling American people to enter World War II, thereby ending the Depression.

Putting aside the diametrically opposed reasons for wanting to enter their respective wars (somewhat noble versus wildly rapacious), the parallels between Roosevelt's modus operandi and the Bush administration's are obvious. And in his book, Body of Evidence, James Bamford discloses Operation Northwoods, a plan during the Kennedy administration (which Kennedy nixed) to attack an American plane—either a drone or an actual flight filled with real passengers—and blame Cuba.[137]

In Germany, they had the Reichstag fire. As with the Kennedy assassination, the official story focuses on a solo operator, which is what Lee Harvey Oswald was referring to when he protested, "I'm the patsy."

Marinus van der Lubbe was a Dutch bricklayer, unemployed after a work-related accident. Angry and disaffected, he joined the Communist Party and has traditionally been accepted as the only arsonist. (Four possible accomplices were acquitted.) However, a tunnel connected the Reichstag to the presidential palace where Hitler, Goebbels and Goering were dining the night of the fire. In the course of the evening, Karl Ernst, a former bellhop who'd become the Berlin SA leader, led a contingent to the parliamentary building where they scattered gasoline and self-igniting chemicals to "grease the way" for Van der Lubbe.[138]

Like Oswald, Van der Lubbe was never tried. Although arson was not punishable by death when he committed it (with or without assistance,) a law passed the next day changed that and was made retroactive so as to include him.

In addition to these circumstances, analogously to 9/11, the fire was oddly felicitous for the Nazis, allowing them to blame the Communists and make a case for consolidating power in the executive branch of government, to wit: To promote Hitler from Chancellor to Führer.[139]

The "lone gunman" executes the operation; he is the muscle rather than the brains. Van der Lubbe was supposedly willing to shoulder full responsibility just as the 9/11 hijackers were apparently proud to become suicide bombers and young Americans are proud to "serve their country" in Iraq. The allure of heroism entices young men with machismo to prove; their handlers are happy to afford them the opportunity.

But according to some 9/11 researchers, setting the stage for the Afghanistan and the Iraq wars was only part of a grander scheme. The ultimate purpose of the attack was to justify invading a host of Middle Eastern and other countries on the grounds of terrorism and seize such oil resources as remain. In the meantime, the terrorized American people would also be more receptive to giving up ever increasing quantities of their civil liberties.

The truth of 9/11 may well be odder than the official story. And some of the people who get the most attention for doubting the official story are themselves, odd. Activism tends to attract people who are looking for a cause through which to vent their anger. And because it's anti-establishment, it also attracts, among others, social misfits with a grudge against the in-crowd.

Complicating matters further is the fact that even the full-fledged nutcases can be entertaining.

Having been fired as a member of the 9/11 conference that featured the Neo-Nazi publication, with my new-found leisure, I journey down the rabbit hole and spend the evening with one of the "Truth" movement's more charismatic, if way-out-there figures, to whit: I click on David Icke's website.

According to his bio, the British Icke is a former football goalie turned sports commentator. Then in 1991 he donned turquoise because it channeled energy (and brought out his eyes?) and found his true calling as a unique brand of New Age guru. People called him a lunatic. But several years later, scientists at Johns Hopkins discovered that turquoise was the color of the young universe, or the average of all the colors in the universe, depending on whom you read. (Has turquoise also become more fashionable at Johns Hopkins since this discovery?)[140]

All this is stuff you'd normally pay attention to only if it was pasted at eye level on the corner streetlamp where you happened to be waiting for the light to change. But Icke's five-hour long lectures command standing ovations (as well as protests outside). And his message isn't even about freeing yourself of inhibitions.

According to Icke's website, Hitler was a Rothschild. His grandmother was a servant in the Baron de Rothschild household and the master got up to some hanky panky.[141]

Forty-two presidents were also Rothschilds. Clinton seems to be an exception as he's a Rockefeller.

How do the Rothschilds know where all the future Presidents are going to be born so they can make sure to mate with the Presidents' ancestors of the opposite sex?

Icke covers that base by explaining that some of the Presidents weren't literally Rothschilds; they were "clones" or under the influence. The Rothschilds achieve their vice-like hold over the U.S. presidency by betting on both sides in all elections so whoever wins owes them. (They are far from alone in doing this; Goldman Sachs was one of the top funders of both the McCain and the Obama campaigns.)

Is this view anti-Semitic?

No, answers Icke, it's the Rothschilds who are the anti-Semites; they abuse Jews as much as they abuse everyone else. And anyway, the Rothschilds aren't Jews.... they're reptiles. They "shape shift." The Queen is a reptile, too; Princess Di said so. So is Kris Kristofferson (whom Icke resembles.)[142]

"The reptiles are anti-Semites?" asks my son when I explain Icke's worldview.

"The reptiles are Jewish?" asks my friend Lita, who knows it's not so easy to wriggle out of Jewish ancestry.

The reptiles are twelve feet long (or is it tall?) There are 15-25 "reptilian races" including the Crinklies who are pink and cuddly with old-looking faces, and the Tall Blondes.[143]

Wouldn't shape shifting into a reptile be grounds for divorce? All right, so the law didn't anticipate this particular problem but doesn't it constitute fraud? Icke doesn't address this point.

The reptile metaphor is intriguing. I can see saying that someone you hate shape shifts into a reptile. It's not clear, however, the extent to which Icke thinks he's dealing in a metaphor. And what's with the twelve feet?

Courtesy of a computer program to delight the heart of any eight-year-old boy, an Icke lecture opens with a portrait of the Queen and a photo of George Bush Sr. transmogrifying into snakelike creatures.

An effective rabble-rouser, Icke (who is not wearing turquoise for this lecture, but maroon) compares people to sheep and tells a story about some pigs who, sensing what's in store, bolt from the slaughterhouse.

"They made it to the news, these pigs," he says in incredulous North country tones.   (*He's* no scion of the inbred reptilian "bloodlines.")

Icke is also preoccupied with the Illuminati—a secret society along the lines of the Freemasons and Skull and Bones—which, according to some links in this netherworld, was founded by a Rothschild and four other men including the Marquis de Sade. (Women are nowhere to be found among these blood oaths and traditions that go back to the knights of the Holy Grail.) And to muddy the waters further, since his concern is shared by many esteemed researchers, Icke also rails about the Trilateral Commission and the Council on Foreign Relations.   (2009 addendum: A comment to www.mikeruppert.blogspot.com points out that if you type into your browser the word "illuminati" spelled backwards followed by .org, you arrive at the website of the National Security Agency.   No doubt some wag at the NSA ascertained that itanimulli.org was up for grabs, grabbed it, then sat back to enjoy the spectacle of "troothers," drunk with conspiracy, thinking they'd stumbled on a find.)

I'm reminded of Bruno Bettelheim's observation that lunatics did surprisingly well in concentration camps; the outside world mirrored their inner one. Maybe we, too, are living in a distorted world, which is why, in reference to 9/11, my friend Lita said, "I think in this case, the crazies may turn out to be right."

I'm also reminded of a line from a professor I once had: "The reason the devil gets as far as he does in this world is that there's a little bit of truth to what he says."

So where, finally, is the devil in this mosaic of Bush-bashers, Neo-Nazis, snakes, pigs, sheep and a purported Chicago grandmother/researcher who goes by the name of "Web Fairy?" As always, he's in the details.

Homage to the Cannon Fodder

Written before I understood the bigger forces behind 9/11, this doggerel on the plans to rebuild Ground Zero focuses on the motivation of the troops.

On one side, you have Muslims such as the "muscle hijackers" who overtly carried out the attacks of September 11; legions of Angry Young Men who hurl themselves to death for the sake of eternal glory among 72 virgins who may, in fact, turn out to be white grapes. (The translation is apparently unclear.[144] But the Christian bible also has a history of misleading interpretations of the word that has come to be accepted as "virgin." According to some scholars, it merely meant a young girl.) On earth, they would be forever praised by their proud and grateful families who perhaps received a hefty reward for the martyrdom of their child.

On the other side are the opposing legions of Angry Young Men who hurl themselves to death for the sake of heroism in the eyes of whomever they want to impress with the corresponding, though perhaps even more pathetic, rewards offered by the American government. Mutatis mutandis, the whole thing brings to mind the words of Tom Lehrer:

> *Oh, the Protestants hate the Catholics,*
> *And the Catholics hate the Protestants,*
> *And the Hindus hate the Muslims,*
> *And everybody hates the Jews.*

Machismo in Real Estate

The latest plans have been unveiled
each looking rather like the next,
laid out with the latest virtual magic,
accompanied by awestruck text.
A tower pointy like a spire,
towers shaped like DNA,
towers just a little higher
than before as though to say,
"So there! We've risen from the ashes.
See the triumph of our will.
Here are trees 'cause people want 'em
and culture so they can have their fill.
Here's the hollow, hallowed ground,
reminder of that dreadful hole,
with space for the Memorial;
wouldn't touch it with a ten foot pole."

But doesn't all this miss the point?
This tit for tat, bigger and better
tribute to both God and Mammon,
for poor as well as the go-getter?
After all, what were Al Qaeda
really interested in?
Not Jews or Palestine for sure
nor our blithe disregard of sin.
It wasn't money that they wanted.
Who has more than Mr. Bin Laden?
The underlying deep object
of their jihad is self-respect.
The attack was not about the wheeling
and dealing in those palaces.
The towers stood for something else:
Hundred storey phalluses.
I feel obliged then, to point out,
and more, to bitterly bemoan
the carte blanche, the free-wheeling ride

that this world gives testosterone.
We cannot afford to let
this struggle go on any longer.
It will surely do us in
as each side proves itself the stronger.
For the mess this world is in
there surely are no simple cures
but it would help if we would stop
needing to prove, "Mine's bigger than yours."

The Norwegian Massacre Was Not Simply an Act of Madness; It Was an Act of Hate Fueled by Insecurity

July 24, 2011

The main stream media's summary judgment of Anders Behring Breivik, the Norwegian gunman whose victims number at least 85 so far, is that he's a crazed loner with a beef against Muslims. Where the latter information derives from was originally left unmentioned but few people ask such questions anyway; terrorists are assumed to be Muslims first and foremost but when that avenue abruptly shuts due to the Nordic features of the assailant, we're used to making a right turn towards some breed of neo-Nazism and getting somewhere soon enough.

However, one ignores the origins of "madness" at one's peril.

On his business, Breivik Geofarm, Facebook says only: "No information has been provided... yet." (Who's going to add it at this point? But it does seem that this farm served as the cover for Breivik's ordering amounts of fertilizer which he could not have otherwise legally obtained.)

The website of another company listed on his CV, Brentwood Solutions (assuming it's the same one), is under construction. Other companies he founded were "Front[s]—milking cow[s] with the purpose of financing resistance/liberation related military operations."[145]

The anti-Muslim angle, however, derives from a 1518-page document, sent around to journalists prior to the attacks, known as *A European Declaration of Independence* by one "Andrew Berwick," (whose identicality with Mr. Breivik is revealed on page 1398) although many of the articles contained in it appear to be by other people. One of these, who goes by the single name, Fjordman, was thought by some of Berwick's associates to be a pseudonym but Berwick claims he is simply a like-minded thinker. Wikipedia describes Fjordman as an anonymous blogger. His blog contains articles in a sardonic style similar to Berwick's and on similar themes. One, with the intriguing title of *A Brief History of Pasta*, opens:

"In recent weeks I've been on two major travels, one to Beijing, China, and another to northern Italy. I couldn't really afford to go, but then I got some money from the CIA and the Mossad for my Islamophobic essays. I also remembered that I had not cashed in on my annual white privilege bonus for a few years. Once I had done that, I could go for a holiday, anyway."

A cursory perusal of *A European Declaration of Independence* yields the impression that for the most part, it's in excellent English; that it is, with some exceptions which, under normal circumstances, would be considered laughable, well-researched or at least well-footnoted; but most significantly, that it is not, in any "normal" way, crazy.

Much of the document consists of an idiosyncratic account and history of various forms of Islam. I'm in no position to assess how accurate or twisted these are. Berwick is more knowledgeable than most Westerners but in situations like this, a little knowledge can be an especially dangerous thing.

He then tackles the assault on Western culture of feminism, hitting the usual milestones—Chesler, Steinem (again, better than the average Joe or even Jane.) But while any woman, regardless of literacy, could knock over some of his arguments with a feather boa, he does get in some decent lines:

"For all the talk about "girl power" and "women kicking ass" which you see on movies these days, if the men of your "tribe" are too weak or demoralised to protect you, you will be enslaved and crushed by the men from other "tribes" before you can say 'Vagina Monologues.' "

Berwick is concerned about the feminization of Western man while the "alpha-males" of Islam are encouraged to wage war. Also, "many ethnic Norwegian girls, especially in Muslim dominated areas, despise ethnic Norwegian boys because they consider them as weak and inferior with lack of pride, seeing as they are systematically 'subdued' by the 'superior Muslim boys.' "

In an autobiographical "interview," he says that his father refused to speak to him and his siblings for several years; in Berwick's case, this was partly due to his involvement in graffiti and hip-hop which he engaged in to gain the respect of girls. On the subject of his past he continues, "I do not approve of the super-liberal, matriarchal upbringing though as it completely lacked discipline and has contributed to feminise me to a certain degree."

One might be forgiven for speculating that one of the unconscious purposes of his mass murder could well have been to overcome that "feminisation" and assuage his need for alpha male-hood, for he drops this insight: "Sex is probably the most powerful and under analyzed motivator for man on earth."

And it's on the subject of sex where, unsurprisingly, Berwick most flagrantly reveals his dorkiness. He purports to "analyze" the breakdown in sexual ethics in eighteen countries, based on "young women's susceptibility to have one night stands, pre-marital sex and the average amount of sexual partners for women during a lifetime." No attempt is made to explain why it is the behavior of young women, rather than men, which provides the criterion.

This "scientific" study draws its conclusions from "the experiences of my network of male friends (my own included). We have visited all these countries and our combined experiences and findings thoroughly document a relatively precise picture of the current sexual moral in the various European countries." (Oh, did they ever "thoroughly" do their homework to obtain that "relatively precise picture.")

He goes on to name members of his family and the number (sometimes in the hundreds) of sexual partners they've supposedly had. However, we are not to think that he does so out of envy: "I could easily have chosen the same path if I wanted to, due to my looks, status, resourcefulness and charm." (But maybe not so easily if you've been overly "feminized," Andrew.) He then details their purported bouts of STD. But it's the behavior of his mother and half-sister that disturbs him most.

We also learn that Berwick is no garden variety neo-Nazi; he professes to hate Hitler because the latter destroyed Europe while also sullying the reputation of eugenics. And he doesn't object to Jews, especially conservative ones, because there aren't enough of them to cause a problem. The wishy-washy multicultural ones, however, earn the same opprobrium as his fellow Europeans whose liberalism is destroying their cultural identity.

He also manifests a concern for the "carrying capacity" of the earth, professing that it is approximately 2.5 billion and discusses a return to the gold standard. The circa two billion figure for a sustainable population is in line with some mainstream calculations.[146]

The document contains a narrative about a fictitious Holy War some time in the future and argues that Muslims should be given the option of assimilating into Europe only by abandoning their religion, their native tongues, even their Muslim names and by bearing no more than two children per couple.

Then, in a chapter entitled "Planning the Operation," Mr. Berwick lays out, in meticulous detail, how to execute attacks. Under the chapter heading reads a quotation: "Violence is the mother of change."

He suggests telling family members, "that you have started to play World of Warcraft or any other online MMO game and that you wish to focus on this for the next months/year. This 'new project' can justify isolation and people will understand somewhat why you are not answering your phone over long periods."

This may explain his reputation for being a loner—despite an apparently active social life—not to mention his purported interest in World of Warcraft which, however, also seems to be genuine.

On page 1472 of the text portion of the document, Berwick signs off in a way which will quicken the hearts of moviegoers familiar with the Da Vinci code:

I believe this will be my last entry. It is now Fri July 22nd, 12.51.

Sincere regards,
Andrew Berwick
Justiciar Knight Commander
Knights Templar Europe
Knights Templar Norway

The Truth Movement Dies Hard

September 11, 2006 8:35 A.M.
Ground Zero

Silent crowd standing eight deep. On the top floor of a building to the left, a sign reads, "Dissent is Patriotic." Next to it, a peace symbol. In the tradition of sneakers flung over telephone wires, high in the fence surrounding what used to be called "the pit," someone has placed a rosary.

A solemn drum beat as a distant, unseen Scottish brigade from the Fire Department begins a funeral march. The crowd-silence deepens. From the other side of the pit, the Star-Spangled Banner rises. A woman to the left cries as does another woman to the right. What is it about music that brings out the deepest emotions? Freud said it was the words with which the music was associated. Say the words of the Star-Spangled Banner (if you know them) without the music; see what happens.

Nasal tones. An oboe? No, it's Mayor Bloomberg. The list of names. After several, I move on.

In front of the Path Station, two men in 9/11 Truth T-shirts hold a banner proclaiming the Bush regime was responsible. A woman with a poster of a lost loved one shouts, "Traitors!" Then, to passers-by, "These people want to destroy the Constitution and have Shariah law. Islamic fascists were responsible for 9/11. America is good."

The banner-bearers get into a shouting match with her. Winning converts one at a time? In Alice in Wonderland, the Red Queen asks, "What's one and one and one and one and one and one and one and one and one?"

But most activists operate on a principle not of arithmetic but of exponential progression: "If I email ten people and each of those people emails ten people..." A reasonable principle that somehow never works.

Someone walks around with a sign that reads, "9/11/2006: Five years of the Clinton legacy."

Someone else is wearing a T-shirt that says, "Bush was responsible. Bed bugs bite in Brooklyn." Asked what that's about he explains, "They found bedbugs in a police precinct in Brooklyn. I wanted to lighten the message a little."

A well-known activist's T-shirt reads, "Planehuggers did 9/11." By that he means, he says, "The people who think real planes hit the towers." Apparently, there is an alternate theory that the plane everyone in the world saw hit the second tower was, in fact, a hologram. Flagrant lunacies like this make easy straw men for the media to use as distractions from the legitimate questions that swirl around that day.

Every camera in the area has come to check out the shouting match which other members of 9/11 Truth have now joined. All this energy going to argue with one strident, desperate woman.

A young 9/11 Truth member says to a fellow activist, "Get all the people in 9/11 T-shirts. We shouldn't be part of this."

A man in a black Harley Davidson T-shirt complains to the people in 9/11 Truth T-shirts, "It's a moment of silence." Then, to his friend, "I gotta slap somebody."

A Japanese woman points to her sign that says, "Peace" in Japanese and English.

More drums, this time held not horizontally according to Scottish tradition but in vertical, Japanese style. Four Buddhist monks and a gaunt Western woman of about sixty stake out space for a concert.

A woman asks a 9/11 Truth member, "Do you have another DVD?" She shows him the one she'd been given which has been crushed by a hostile passer-by.

The shouting match is over; the crowd disperses. Nobody won.

George Bush, the Joint Chiefs, and Me

When I was in third grade, the Cuban Missile Crisis leapt to the forefront of the national consciousness. All of us kids were scared that our middle-aged fathers would be called to war. Even the teachers were nervous.

So on Parents' Day, they asked us how we would solve the crisis.

I suggested, "Why not paint the Cuban missiles with the American flag? Then the Cubans will destroy them themselves."

Miss T. smiled indulgently. "How would you get to them?" she asked.

I didn't have an answer and sat down feeling defeated.

Forty plus years later, I have been vindicated by a kindred spirit of my devious third grade mind:

"President Bush said, 'The U.S. was thinking of flying U2 reconnaissance aircraft with fighter cover over Iraq, painted in UN colors. If Saddam fired on them, he would be in breach.' "[147]

Apparently, it is not just great minds that think alike, but also immature ones.

This wasn't the first time the vibes I sent out into the universe in third grade got legs. During the Bay of Pigs itself, the Joint Chiefs hatched a scheme known as Project Northwoods, which involved attacking Americans and saying the Cubans did it. But wouldn't you know, Kennedy vetoed the plan.

While most people might think that these two plots, launched at the highest level of government, were hare-brained, as the former third grader who came up with them I have to say, "No, they're *not*! *You're* hare-brained!"

From 9/11 down the road of nonexistent yellowcake to Iraq:

Dubya's Lament*

(To the tune of, "If I Only Had a Brain")

Oh, I'd seem intelligenter
an authentic presidenter
in ways I can't explain.
I could answer probing questions
and make sensible suggestions
if I only had a brain.

So let's bomb the evil axis
and do away with taxes
though it might seem quite insane.
Here's another great idea,
we can just ignore Korea
since I haven't got a brain.

What the hey, let's drop a bomb
on—What's his name?—Saddam!
though it goes against the grain.
'Cause while there's a war on
No one dares to call me "moron"
I don't even need a brain.

In Cynic Magazine's Best of 2005

Notes from the Brooklyn Front

March 20, 2003

Iraq has struck back at the U.S. for jamming radar screens with chaff at 4 AM this morning: With the ruthlessness for which the U.S. was compelled to invade them in the first place, they have released a video of a man with a mustache.

As the video is critical in determining whether Saddam is alive, experts have been summoned in force to determine whether the man in the video is, in fact, Saddam. Comparison with archival photographs has yielded discrepancies both in jowl size and number of chins. The mustaches have been determined to be identical which, however, is inconclusive since they are also identical to the mustaches of 20 other members of Saddam's cabinet and 158 members of his family as well as the entire Republican Guard and the Arab League.

"That's what makes the East so goshdang inscrutable," said one expert who wouldn't give his name.

Eyebrows could be a significant indicator but unfortunately, the man in the video is wearing glasses. Saddam experts say they don't look like his usual glasses but then, he might have gotten a new prescription. Hairline could also be a dead give away but the video Saddam is wearing a beret.

Analysis continued until this afternoon when it was halted by the release of another video. Experts are currently trying to figure out whether the man in this video (who has a mustache) is the same as the one in the first video.

Further confusion emerged at a press briefing today when someone asked Defense Secretary Donald Rumsfeld whether or not the war had begun.

"Sir, we've all seen the bombs and mortar and we've heard the explosions," said a reporter later identified as a rookie. "But we were told we'd be filled with shock and wonder. Did you mean we'd be wondering what the hell we're doing in Iraq?"

"Not 'wonder,' you moron," Rumsfeld replied evenly. "Shock and *awe*."

"Oh. Well yes, I guess I'm awed that we're in Iraq but frankly, Sir, shock? Are you kidding? Anyway, Sir, my question is, are we having fun yet?"

"You'll know it when you see it," Rumsfeld replied with the half smile that accompanies his more sadistic responses.

March 21, 2003

Operation Shock and Awe got underway today when U.S. and British forces liberated the shit out of Baghdad. Meanwhile at the port of Umm Qasr on the Kuwaiti border, in a moment of inappropriate exuberance, U.S. Marines hoisted the American flag.

"Take that down, you dumb fucks," their commander ordered.

"Why, sir?" asked one of the Marines. "You mean we're not American?"

"No, faggot," the commander responded. "This isn't a conquest, it's a liberation."

"Shall I hoist the Iraqi flag, then, Sir?"

"Do whatever you want."

"But the Iraqis are dead, Sir."

In the North, hostilities between the Turks and the Kurds prompted one viewer to wonder who would be the first reporter to Spoonerize the pair into "Kurks and Turds." The prize went to Wolf Blitzer.

Today's press briefing was dominated by reporters pestering Ari Fleischer about whether President Bush was watching the war on television. They were disappointed to learn that no, he wasn't; the President was no fan of the tube. Some reporters voiced skepticism about this since they had noted the President's increasing resemblance to the recently deceased Mr. Rogers, as though he had donned the departed soul's gentle mantle. For instance, the President had taken to speaking in a folksy manner of Iraq's "neighborhood."

"Look, the President goes to bed at ten o'clock," an exasperated Fleischer told CNN's John King. "He doesn't have time to watch the news and if he did, it wouldn't be CNN."

The protestation served only to fuel reporters' suspicion that the President gets up at seven in order to watch Mr. Rogers reruns.

Work continued on determining the identity of the man with the mustache in the video released by Iraqi officials yesterday. The CIA concluded that the voice was indeed Saddam's and that therefore the rest of the man may also have been Saddam. But sources within the intelligence agency told news reporters that they had been in touch with a former mistress of Saddam, now in exile, who maintained the man was neither Saddam nor even any of his forty body doubles. The sources did not reveal how she knew. She did not, for instance, have access to the sort of data that would enable Monica Lewinsky (and now, thanks to her, anyone in the world) to identify President Clinton under particular circumstances.

"That's why you shouldn't take a mistress," concluded CNN's Aaron Brown at the end of the report, to the titillated delight of the control room.

"Or if you do, don't exile her," grumbled a producer who'd been around the block a few times.

The CIA vigorously denied having used the consulting services of Saddam's ex-mistress.

"Maybe it was the Pentagon," they suggested, an indication that their longstanding rivalry with the FBI may have been supplanted.

For What It's Worth: Report on Peak Oil "Lobbying" or Whatever It's Called When You Don't Get Paid

July 2005

(The date will become obvious to anyone who's been keeping tabs on the National Debt which currently stands at $14 trillion and is growing exponentially. I was in D.C. anyway, to speak at a 9/11 conference and decided to give "lobbying" a shot [in the dark.])

Have seen about seventy House and Senate staff members on Energy. I know this because of the number of Xeroxes remaining of the packet left in each office: Roscoe Bartlett's first Special Order Speech and the home page (which prints out at nine pages) of www.lifeaftertheoilcrash.net.

After lobbying for four years, I've gotten used to the perky blond ponytails swinging down the halls of Congress, the upbeat, Stepford-wives-in-training greetings (one receptionist hummed, "When the Caissons Go Rolling Along,") but it's always disconcerting to be reminded that this country is run by twelve-year-olds, particularly on this trip when what I'm peddling comes down to a warning of the potential death of a good chunk of the population.

It's hard to tell what reaction the message is getting. Mostly, the staffers just nod politely. Some get a deer-in-headlights expression, then set out to show that they've done their homework on the issue: "I read the Dreyfus book," says one of them eagerly, probably meaning Deffeyes. Others plug their bosses' energy initiatives.

Phase 2 of the conversation concerns the need to reform the economy since it's not going to keep on growing forever.

This elicits bemused smiles. Nobody pretends to know anything about the idea. Neither do I so I refer the staffers to Herman Daly, former Senior Economist in the Environment

Department of the World Bank and advocate of a Steady State economy. Though he's still the gold standard, these days I'd add the Daily Reckoning, Ellen Hodgson Brown, Max Keiser and Chris Martenson.

Only a couple of aides are overtly hostile. One is from the office of a Congressman from Virginia. "I suggest you check your sources, Ma'am," he says. "We need to drill off the coast."

I cite the Lundberg Letter—the "Bible of the oil industry"—and Matt Simmons of the Bush administration. "Drilling off the coast" can mean drilling in deep water through several miles of rock. [2011 Note: This article was written five years before the BP disaster in the Gulf.]

"Thank you for stopping by," says the aide and strides off.

McCain's office has a whole wall devoted to family photos. After initially claiming he'd "love to see" Roscoe Bartlett's material on Peak Oil, the aide, a straight shooter, says the Senator doesn't approve of this sort of approach since it would involve subsidizing wind farms. (So?)

Ed Towns' office says they'll contact Bartlett's and endorse whatever bill he's proposing.

Outside the offices of several Senators stands a placard that reads, "National Debt: $7,854,000,000,000. Your share: $26,000." Outside Lautenberg's office is an exhibit entitled, "Let Us Never Forget: Faces of the Fallen," which consists of ID photos of dead American soldiers in Iraq.

In a Georgia Congressman's office, the receptionist's desk bears a wooden paperweight with the legend carved into it, "Pray." It's a forbidding imperative and sizing up this office as a lost cause for the Peak Oil message, I walk out again.

Warner's is the only office that says you can't see any staff person without an appointment.

Specter's is the most Senatorcentric office as it is dominated by dozens of photos of the boss with world leaders: Mrs. Thatcher, Nixon, the Queen, the Pope.

Waiting in one reception area, I gaze at the map of the Congressional district it represents: It looks like a sick octopus. There should be a caption that reads, "Gerrymandering in Action."

The receptionist is on the phone: "I'm sorry; he's in Labor at the moment."

Where else in the world could you hear someone say that?

Kathryn Harris' office features a picture of trapeze artists hanging upside down stiffly, like chrysalises or inverted mummies. However, the centerpiece painting is of—I kid you not—a herd of charging elephants.

At lunch I'm reminded that our legislators, or at least their staff, are a captive audience for sub-mediocre food as well as Coca Cola.

As I wait for a receipt the cashier says, "You don't have to sign; we know what you did." She seems oblivious to the ominous sound of her words.

༄ ༺

Last Thursday I turned a corner in the Cannon building and came face to face with an entire corridor of ID photos of dead American soldiers, one poster in front of each office.

A man comes out of the first office. From the directness of his eyes, I suspect he is the boss. Also, he's over twelve.

"I'm Congressman Jones of North Carolina," he says. "You can probably tell from my accent."

There follows banter about Southern accents.

"I saw you looking at our exhibit."

"I wanted to see if they were all from North Carolina," I say and peer at the captions.

"No," he says. "This one's from California. I went to his funeral."

He describes the funeral and I start to cry. (Hormones play a role, dissolving barriers.)

"I have a nineteen-year-old son," I say.

"Who died in Iraq?"

"No, he's OK.... I've seen this exhibit before but never a whole corridor of them."

Here the account goes off the record since I'm not wearing a press pass.

"Well X suggested we all do it and everyone agreed, Democrats and Republicans." (Can you imagine a Congressperson hearing the suggestion and daring to say, "Thanks, I'll pass?")

He asks where I'm from so I go into lobbying mode and talk about how Peak Oil is recognized by a Congressman with impeccable Conservative credentials (which should appeal to Jones:) Roscoe Bartlett.

I also mention the other exhibit in the halls of Congress, about the debt. His response will remain off the record but it reveals a level of understanding not often publicized in the media.

This is the guy who introduced a resolution changing the name of French fries to freedom fries. But the impression he leaves is of a decent man with integrity who is open to reason.

Change is afoot but far from enough to overwhelm the forces against it.

Meanwhile, Back at the Ranch: How the U.S. Treated Its Own People in the Aftermath of the Attacks

How Can We F*ck Thee? Let Us Count the Ways

Any teacher (or parent) learns that her effectiveness depends not just on what she teaches—the content of her message—but on when. Writing is teaching on a wider scale and a writer on a particular topic may find herself spinning Variations on a Theme: Pointing out the innumerable places and ways in which an idea appears, particularly when the "idea" is a strategy of the enemy that is all the more effective for not being recognized.

The present strategy is: The Devil's in the Details. Anyone who's ever gotten an unpleasant surprise from a contract they signed has learned the necessity of reading the fine print. It is here, rather than in the main text, which most people never get past, that the other fucks you over.

Following are articles and testimony illustrating just a few examples of this phenomenon in the enviro-disaster of 9/11, so that they may serve as a word to the wise in the event of future disasters. Already, the same tactics have been echoed both eerily and drearily in the BP disaster: Relying on sensory perception (smell for BP, visual for 9/11;) allegations that the offending substance (oil in the case of BP, a plethora of contaminants in the case of 9/11), could have come from somewhere else so it should therefore be dismissed; arranging the equipment so it won't detect a problem;[148] the use by politicians of their own children to make a point. After 9/11, Senator Charles Schumer kept his daughter at Stuyvesant High School, located four blocks from Ground Zero. After the BP disaster, President Obama was photographed swimming in the Gulf with his younger daughter, Sasha. This repetition of history has even led to the comeback of some of the same whistleblowers, such as EPA Senior Analyst Hugh Kaufman.

And now those tactics are playing out yet again in Japan, with respect to the Fukushima nuclear reactor.

But even more important is to expand one's understanding of governmental Modus Operandi to other areas as far ranging as safety and the financial meltdown. Here again, the same tactics of esoteric terms, designed both to intimidate and to make the eyes glaze over with tedium as the poison takes effect, are being applied in the arena of mortgage financing and speculative financial instruments. (Think, "Alan Greenspan.")

For, while history repeats itself, it is never verbatim. Just as the French writer, George Polti, maintained that there are only thirty-six basic plots in all of literature, it is the underlying theme that is the same. If nothing else, the following fragment of a record stands as a warning regarding the danger of relying on headlines and soundbites.

How Science Was Abused to Perpetrate Lies after 9/11:
A Cautionary Tale for the Approaching Peak Oil Disaster[149]

November, 2005

September 11 was, among other things, a Big Bang that signaled the birth of a new universe. As this universe unfolds, we're learning that it operates under laws that are antithetical to the ideals we grew up with. Human life is no longer sacred. Democratic ideals are no longer upheld. Nor are any other ideals, certainly not those of health or compassion. The new universe upholds pragmatism above all else, even to the point of cynicism. For what is at stake now, given the arrival of Peak Oil and the depletion of water and other resources, is survival. Towards that end, The Powers That Be will tolerate all means necessary.

Whose survival? Not America's, much less the world's, but their own.

This new attitude of blatant indifference to human health, suffering and life itself first manifested itself in the environmental disaster of 9/11, which began when the twin towers and the other five buildings at Ground Zero collapsed and the fires ignited by the two planes burned and smoldered for over three months releasing record levels of some of the most toxic and carcinogenic substances that flesh is heir to.[150]

The World Trade Center was a city with its own zip code. When it fell, hundreds of tons of asbestos were pulverized to particles of an unusually small size—which some scientists believe to be especially dangerous to human health—and carried to Brooklyn and beyond. The towers also contained 50,000 computers, each made with approximately four pounds of lead and that doesn't include the five other buildings that were destroyed that day. Tens of thousands of fluorescent light bulbs each contained 41mg. mercury per four foot bulb.[151] The smoke detectors contained radioactive americium 241.[152] According to my calculations, which were presented at three scientific conferences where they were not challenged, dioxin reached 150 times its previous records and PCBs in the water, 75,000 times their previous record. ["PCBs were detected at high concentrations. The Toxic Equivalency (TEQ)... is 151pg/L. In previous harbor work...the highest observed PCB TEQ was 0.002pg.L."[153]] The alkalinity of the dust attained the level of drain cleaner.[154] And a month after the disaster, Dr. Thomas Cahill of U.C. Davis found very- and ultrafine particles that were the highest he'd recorded of 7,000 samples taken around the world, including at the burning Kuwaiti oil fields.[155]

These are just a few of the over 2,000 contaminants that were released. (This figure comes from the Sierra Club report of 2004. But over 80,000 chemicals are manufactured in the United States,[156] many of them behind the veil of privacy or "trade secrets" invoked by corporations. So it is likely that the number of chemicals released on 9/11 is in fact higher.)

Yet a week after the attacks, EPA Administrator Christie Todd Whitman told the people of New York, "Good news. The air is safe to breathe."[157] I should disclose that I was one of twelve original plaintiffs in a class action lawsuit against Governor Whitman and EPA.

Whitman's announcement, she has maintained ever since, was based on the best science available at the time. Also ever since, science has been used in the service of lies and the economy at the expense of human life.

How is this possible? Science is objective. Instruments and facts don't lie.

It depends on who's using the instruments and what ax they're grinding. It depends on what facts are told and more pointedly, what facts are left out.

This is not the conference in which to discuss the fact that when Whitman told the people of New York the air was safe to breathe, not only did EPA lack the data to support that statement, but EPA actually had data which contradicted it.[158] Nor is this the conference to go into Whitman's potentially felonious conflict of interest in speaking about the World Trade Center at all when her husband owned shares of Port Authority stock and she had sworn in her oath of office to recuse herself from cases in which she had a personal stake.[159]   This is a conference about science so we will look at how science was used to promote the lies perpetrated by the EPA and the White House Council on Environmental Quality, which edited at least one of EPA's press releases, replacing cautionary statements about asbestos with reassurances.

The technique was simple: Make a mockery of science. Perform scientific tests but use the wrong equipment in the wrong places the wrong way.

The tactic was put into effect immediately, when EPA conducted its initial tests for asbestos. First of all, query why they focused so exclusively on that contaminant. There were over two thousand released in the disaster, some of which had never before existed.

But even if this autistic focus on asbestos had been plausible, how could EPA's tests have come up with the wrong results?

Dr. Cate Jenkins, an EPA whistleblower, told the *St. Louis Post-Dispatch* that EPA had used 20-year-old instruments to conduct their tests. For every fiber of asbestos that EPA found, independent contractors found nine. The risk of cancer from the asbestos alone could be one person in ten.[160]   EPA's Region 8 out West offered Region 2 in New York up-to-date equipment, which they could conveniently summon from New Jersey. Region 2's William Muczynski said, "We don't want you fucking cowboys here."[161]

Also, EPA used a 1% standard for asbestos in the dust. But this standard was established for intact materials such as water pipes. If a minute piece of the pipe broke off that contained more than 1% asbestos, that was considered dangerous because it might be inhaled. EPA applied this 1% standard to Lower Manhattan where none of the material was intact. All of it had been pulverized. All of it could be inhaled. Furthermore, there was tons of dust.

Oh, what a tangled web we weave/When first we practice to deceive

My father used to say, "Mistakes are made in the beginning." Since 9/11, EPA has been nothing if not consistent. Having uttered the initial big lie, EPA could not turn back. So they forged ahead down the road of cover-up and further lies with local agencies such as the New York City Department of Health close behind, urging residents to clean their apartments themselves using a wet rag and where the dust was particularly bad, to wear long pants. Pregnant women, they said, did not need to take any special precautions. When it came to their own lobby, however, EPA used professional asbestos abatement contractors.[162]

In their treatment of the public, also, no one can say EPA wasn't consistent. In addition to using out-of-date equipment, they have routinely deployed the wrong tests. For instance they advocated a wipe test for polycyclic aromatic hydrocarbons on soft surfaces whereas the test was intended only for hard surfaces. They resisted testing on horizontal surfaces where dust falls or in corners where dust was likely to be found, favoring vertical surfaces and countertops which had been frequently cleaned. They fought the use of ultrasonication, a sensitive test for asbestos which they themselves had developed. They based their determination of whether an area was contaminated on a "visual inspection" which means one of their reps would eyeball a given site and say, "Looks good to me." In some cases, this visual inspection was performed—I kid you not—from an airplane.[163]

This medieval attitude that what you can't see won't hurt you persisted despite evidence that the smaller the particle, the more dangerous it may be to human health; both because it eludes the protective mechanisms that cough it out and because its relatively large surface area to volume ratio allows volatile organic compounds to adhere to its surface.

(In the Madoff scandal, the Securities and Exchange Commission employed a strategy similar to EPA's Keystone Cops approach: Send in the Clowns. Advised to investigate the astoundingly lucky investor, they dispatched neophytes who, in addition to lacking the experience to see their way through the labyrinth of booby-traps, were told that Madoff was on track to be the head of the SEC himself, i.e. their future boss. One young lawyer did, however, warn of Madoff's dubious dealings. She was told to stop pursuing the case by her superior who later married Madoff's niece.[164])

And how did EPA determine whether the dust they found was from the World Trade Center? In one building, they asserted, "That's not WTC dust; WTC dust is grey and gritty;" in another, "That's not WTC dust; WTC dust is brown and fluffy."

Other abuses of science included EPA's writing off of deposits of magnesium because it's a nutrient. If only we'd known we were supposed to eat WTC dust instead of breathing it, perhaps everything would have turned out all right, although I doubt it. Ground Zero workers who ingested WTC dust now suffer gastro-intestinal as well as respiratory and other illnesses.

Then there was the issue of spikes.

When my son was twelve, he wanted to be a magician. As he underwent his sorcerer's apprenticeship, I picked up some tricks of the trade. Rule number one is, when you're doing your sleight of hand, say, "Look over there!" EPA and other authorities knew this trick, too, and dismissed high levels as spikes or "outliers," thereby shoving unpleasant data under the carpet.

A corollary of this practice was "averaging" in which the "spikes" were averaged out over a lifetime or a large area and thus made to disappear. The human body, however, doesn't average. When the lungs are exposed to too much water, you drown. When someone overdoses on drugs, the human body doesn't say, "I'll average this out over a lifetime;" you die of an overdose.

Dr. Cate Jenkins has written several memos detailing other EPA lies. The latest (October, 2006) is subtitled: *Cover-up, corrosive alkalinity of WTC dust by EPA, OSHA and NYC.*

> *Falsification of the health implications of the alkaline pH data.*

Fraudulent reporting of pH levels for smallest WTC dust particles.

She shows how the Agency for Toxic Substances and Disease Registry and New York City relied on outdated texts that tolerated lead levels sixty times as high as those now considered safe. And she provides evidence of their lying and criminal malpractice.

EPA's execution of tests and cleanup was as shoddy as their research. In their so-called cleanup of 2002, residents found them performing air tests with the required fan turned off or facing the wrong direction.

The additive effects of the contaminants were also not taken into account, much less their explosive synergistic effects, about which little is known. However, work performed at Mt. Sinai has shown that if someone is an asbestos worker and a smoker, for instance, the risk of cancer is not simply twice as bad as being one or the other; it's eighty or ninety times as bad.

Since 9/11, there have been several blue ribbon scientific panels which have convened to consult with EPA on next steps. At the first one, EPA neglected to tell the panel that the document on which they were supposedly conducting peer review was already being implemented downtown. The panel learned this from community members who were allowed to speak for two to three frantic minutes each in public sessions.

The final panel, which lasted almost two years, spent much of that time on a quixotic quest for a World Trade Center fingerprint or signature as though it were the fountain of youth or the alchemical formula for gold. For once the fingerprint was found, that would be it. If you had it, you had WTC dust and EPA would give you a cleanup, however shoddy. If you didn't have it, you didn't get said cleanup and you could get on with your life.

However, a couple of us activists and scientists have always maintained that either metaphor was misleading. The World Trade Center was not a person; therefore it didn't have a fingerprint or a signature. Its contents were not stirred into a homogeneous blend in that great mixing bowl in the sky along with two eggs. The thousands of contaminants released were spread unevenly according to their various weights and chemical and aerodynamic properties as well as the wind conditions of the moment. But the quest for the ever elusive fingerprint went on. First it was asbestos, then gypsum with a soupcon of, if I remember correctly, manmade vitreous fibers and a specific PH, then slag wool because in the dozen or so samples that one study had collected close to the site, slag wool, which is a component of glass, had been uniformly present.

One must ask, and one did: If a fingerprint or signature is unique and irrefutable, why did the WTC fingerprint or signature keep changing? One must also ask, and many did, if the signature is, in fact found and determined to be a particular assortment of contaminants, what do we do about all the rest?

That question was never answered because EPA closed the panel process when an independent panel, commenting on their latest plan, in effect accused them of fraud: [The independent panel raised questions as to whether] "... EPA's evaluation and interpretation of the study data were performed fairly. Peer reviewers pointed to several non-standard steps taken to enhance the study's ability to distinguish WTC dust from background dust. These steps could be interpreted as attempts to prove the method's success rather than to objectively evaluate its real-world potential for fingerprinting WTC dust."[165]

Let's go back to the assertion at the beginning of this talk that 9/11 was a watershed moment when the laws and precedents we previously relied on all got turned on their heads.

In the case of environmental disasters, what that means is this: Prior to 9/11, in the event of a release of toxic substances, EPA followed scientific protocol and conducted representative testing in concentric circles to determine the path of contamination.

But in the World Trade Center case, they did no such testing. Instead, 9/11 set a new precedent for testing and cleanup: the quick and dirty method, a lick and a promise in order to get back to work ASAP. **The cleanup standard they used in Lower Manhattan— a 1/10,000 cancer risk—exposed residents to a hundred times the cancer risk of previous standards.**

At a City Council hearing in March, 2003, EPA's Dr. Paul Gilman (who would resign from the agency in November, 2004) was asked under what circumstances EPA had previously used the standard that put a hundred times as many people at risk of cancer. He responded: Where the area was sparsely populated or few contaminants were released. Clearly, neither description applied to Lower Manhattan.

Another reason EPA officials gave for using the more lax standard in Lower Manhattan was that the more protective standard was impossible to achieve because their instruments clogged. To anyone who challenged this excuse—(Isn't the clogging of the instruments an indication that there's a significant amount of potentially toxic dust?)—they responded, "This disaster was unprecedented." In other words, "What do you expect us to do?" On the other hand, they also continued to maintain that there was no problem.

The result is of potentially far-reaching concern. For **this new standard, exposing citizens to a hundred times the contamination levels previously accepted, is serving as a precedent for the new standards which they plan to implement in the event of a dirty bomb.**

Antinuclear activists have complained, "The exposure allowed under the contemplated advice would create almost 100 times as much cancer risk as those usually allowed from other kinds of contaminants, like chemicals, or from radiation in other settings."[166]

Why would the feds do this?

The answer appears in an earlier article and sounds all too familiar:

"...an attack using conventional explosives to spread radioactive materials—a dirty bomb—would probably occur in a far more prominent location than a toxic-waste site or a power plant, and the need to resume using the site would be higher, said [radiation specialist for DHS] Mr. Buddemeier, in his presentation to a National Academy of Sciences group.

'When balancing the risk of radiation exposure against the benefit of returning to normal activity, the government safety recommendations will weigh the importance of the contaminated location to economic or political life, said a radiation scientist who works for one of seven federal agencies drafting the document.

'Thus a major train station, cargo port or building in Lower Manhattan might be reoccupied sooner than a suburban shopping mall, said the scientist, who asked not to be identified because the document had not yet been published."[167]

Just as the Inspector General's Report of 2003 found that the White House CEQ edited EPA's press release out of the "need" to reopen Wall Street, EPA has matter-of-factly stated that if the area affected by a dirty bomb is important to the economy, human health will be sacrificed.[168]

In other words, **EPA's standards prior to 9/11 have now been officially turned upside down: The *more* people who are likely to be exposed (since economically important areas tend to be highly populated) the greater the likelihood that standards designed to protect human health will be overlooked.** If you live in the suburbs, the federal government will give your health high priority. But as soon as economic interests enter the picture, the bottom line trumps health and science.

What Lessons Can We Learn From The Environmental Disaster of 9/11?

The answer to this is the reason I felt it important to speak at this conference. What we can learn from the environmental disaster of 9/11 is that it is up to us to educate ourselves. We cannot trust those in charge, the suits. We cannot bow to their supposed greater authority. To do that, knowing what we know, is to put our collective head in the sand and abdicate responsibility.

This lesson is of enormous importance as Peak Oil takes over the world. For the same scenario is playing out in this new arena. First, those in charge tell us there is no problem. Then, when the elephant in the living room grows too large, they acknowledge the problem but say, "Look over there!" and point to the tar sands in Alberta or to ethanol.

But will these solutions really work?

Just as after 9/11 it was necessary for the community—non-scientists—to teach themselves enough science to recognize rampant lying, in order to understand what's really happening with Peak Oil, it is necessary to do the math. It's not hard math; about sixth grade level, if that's when you study ratios.

So what does doing the math tell us?

The light, sweet crude oil we've been relying on to run the economy gave thirty barrels of oil for every one used to produce it. Around last December, the world's supply of that so-called easy oil went into permanent decline. Tar sands and heavy crude are not the same stuff. It takes steam, water injection or chemicals to extract them which in turn requires energy (to heat the water to make the steam, for example.) And the discoveries off the coast of Brazil and Angola which have been announced with such fanfare may require drilling through several miles of underwater rock. In fact, all the alternatives and renewables added up together don't come close to the Energy Returned on Energy Invested ratio for easy oil. The EROEI for ethanol, for instance, is 1.3; it barely gives back more energy than is required to make it in the first place.

You might think, "This is a blessing in disguise, just in time to save us from climate change." But oil is not only used for cars. It's a key ingredient of pesticides and fertilizers, which, however much you might turn up your nose at their toxicity, are necessary to feed our current population of six and a half billion people.

Answers to the problems we're facing do not lie in British Petroleum's changing its name to Beyond Petroleum, or in politicians' soundbites. They require crunching the numbers: How much oil is necessary to keep the economy going? What will it take to sustain life as we know it?

The answers to these questions are not happy. The current economic paradigm is a Ponzi scheme that requires infinite growth. The earth is finite. There is no reconciling these two facts, not with all the renewables and nifty techno-fixes in the world, however useful those may be on a limited scale. But between the two, we have more control over the economy than over the finite resources of the earth, so it is this that we must reform. **It must become localized rather than global.** Peak Oilists are fond of pointing out that the era of the fifteen-hundred-mile Caesar salad is over. We'll have to rely on food sources located within approximately a hundred miles. And it would be better to transition to that lifestyle now than have it thrust upon us the hard way. (Some of this relocalization is already being implemented, both voluntarily and in-.)

Why are people resistant to looking at these facts? Why do they persist in writing off the Peak Oil movement even as it is being corroborated by headlines and world events?

Though more and more people have lost faith in George Bush and lies have been uncovered that make Watergate seem halcyon, the American people have not extrapolated.

"Yes," they say, "there was the Downing Street memo, and the WMD never existed, and we invaded Iraq based on lies, and the government lied about the air quality following 9/11 and betrayed the heroes of Ground Zero who are sick and dying as a result, but the U.S. government caused the attacks? That's crazy. As for this

Peak Oil business, if it's true, why aren't they talking about it on CNN?"

They're not talking about it on CNN because the people running the show at CNN don't want them to. They're keeping up the façade as long as they can while they clean out the cupboards. By the time you figure out the cupboards are bare, it'll be a fait accompli. As ABC's Reuven Frank once said, "News is something someone doesn't want you to know. Everything else is advertising."

Everyone knows the old saw: "Those who do not know history are condemned to repeat it." What's happening now is that those who *do* know history are repeating it anyway.

They're not repeating it verbatim. Peak Oil isn't going to poison people; no one's going to get a deadly disease from it, at least, not directly. It's the *structure* of the drama that's being repeated. Again, those in control are withholding the truth or actively lying. Again, they are doing so in order not to panic the public. Again, the media are complicit or clueless. And again, the public trusts them anyway because that's what they've always done and doing the legwork themselves is just too hard.

After 9/11, the people of Lower Manhattan were enticed by the government, like children by the Pied Piper, to return to an area which every instinct told them was poisonous. They did this even as a few voices, some of them belonging to independent scientists, cried out, "This will kill you."

Some went back because they believed the government or they had nowhere else to go. But others went back because they were blinded: By wishful thinking because they wanted to go home; by ambition, because Lower Manhattan was where their jobs were; or by arrogance, smugly writing off the naysayers because it is comforting to feel superior.

Some of these people who allowed themselves to be misled boasted impressive achievements, advanced degrees, high IQs. But these credentials got in the way of their ability to perceive the truth.

They were not open to the opinions of those who didn't represent an agency or hallowed corporation. Who did we think we were?

What we can learn from the environmental disaster of 9/11 is that contrary to the adage, "Eight million Frenchmen can't be wrong," Yes, they can. Think of the tens of millions of Germans who answered Hitler's call to arms.

The people who recognized early on how bad the air was and how egregiously the government was lying were a small minority. We lacked critical mass while the masses themselves were anything but critical. We were the kids whom the cool crowd looked down on. But we would rather have been wrong. This particular battle leads to Pyrrhic victory.

If any good is to come out of the environmental disaster of 9/11, it is as an inoculation against even greater disasters in the future. Those disasters will be both unique and universal. They will repeat history not in their superficial details—Fascism does not always march in a black shirt—but in their fundamental structure. Not to recognize this is to repeat the mistake of the French who, in 1939, were exquisitely prepared to fight World War 1.

Those who lived through the lies and the terrible consequences of the environmental disaster of 9/11 must learn:

Truth doesn't always come dressed with the trappings of authority.

The smarter and more educated we are, the more we must be on guard against arrogance. We must keep an open mind and listen even to those from out in left field. Our lives depend on it.

In addition to the scientific arena, countless federal, state and city legislatures and agencies held hearings on the environmental disaster of 9/11, ostensibly to get to the heart of the problem but in reality to stall for time.

The tragedy is that one cannot prove that this is their purpose until after the fact when it's too late. Until then, one has no evidence of intent and is, as per Gandhi's maxim, ignored, ridiculed and greeted with rage. (The last phase of Gandhi's dictum is less likely to come to pass: "Then you win.") And the longer that action is delayed, the more people have been exposed, the more evidence has dissipated and the easier it becomes to argue that whatever toxic dust is found inside buildings comes from sources other than the World Trade Center.

The following excerpts document more of the government's infinite ingenuity when it comes to ways to screw the public. Mutatis mutandis, the reader may extrapolate to situations which may arise in his or her own life.

Testimony to the New York City Council

January 11, 2007

I got involved in the environmental disaster of 9/11 as a Stuyvesant High School parent. In the process of working with other activists to get Stuyvesant properly cleaned, I learned of ultrasonication, a highly sensitive asbestos test developed by no less an authority than EPA themselves. Using that method, a cadre known as Concerned Stuyvesant Community found an astronomical 2.4 million structures per square centimeter of asbestos in a carpet segment from the Stuyvesant auditorium.

Following that success, if you can call it that, I had ultrasonication performed on the carpet in my apartment in downtown Brooklyn, an act that led to my becoming one of twelve original plaintiffs in the class action lawsuit, Benzman vs. EPA. The result came back 79,000 structures per sq. cm. a gray area, according to the experts I consulted. (There are no established health-based benchmarks for ultrasonication.) I had the one bedroom apartment abated, which took four burly men 22 hours. The apartment passed its subsequent air tests. But **one of the tests showed a level of asbestos that was almost ten times higher than EPA claimed it was achieving in Lower Manhattan.** Bearing in mind EPA's history of using the wrong equipment in the wrong places the wrong way, you may draw from this anomaly whatever conclusions you wish.

Council members, this hearing has the air of a reunion. For over five years, EPA has shown up at hearings at all levels of government. Each time, experts and citizens who've been forced into de facto expertise have chastised the agency for innumerable flaws in innumerable plans. Each time, EPA has been sent back to the drawing board. And each time, after months of dragging their heels, they have emerged with a new plan that has outdone the last in scientific shoddiness. Then the process has started all over again.

The tail is wagging the dog. We should not be spending time on EPA's latest outrage. The appropriate response to environmental disasters is well-established: testing in concentric circles emanating from the center with cleanup to follow as warranted. In this case, the testing should be for a broad spectrum of contaminants since that's what was released.

Testimony: WTC EPA Panel

April 12, 2004 (during Passover, a widely observed holiday in New York City, at which the question is asked: "Why is this night different from all other nights?")

Why is this environmental disaster different from all other environmental disasters? The word "unprecedented" is used ad nauseam to describe it. But in crucial ways, the environmental consequences of 9/11 *do* have precedent and EPA has long-established protocols to clean up the contaminants that were released. Why are they not following them here? Why are they reinventing the wheel in the shape of a triangle? If this disaster was greater than its predecessors, all the more reason why state-of-the-art testing and cleanup should have been and still should be instituted ASAP...

On the Draft Generic Environmental Impact Statement for Ground Zero

February 18, 2004

This is a rush job. Although the rebuilding of Ground Zero will be one of the largest construction projects in the world, the usual three-year Environmental Impact Statement process has been condensed to one for reasons that have nothing to do with the environment or public health. Once again, the reasons have to do with image and politics. In this respect as in others, the rebuilding process shows signs of repeating the reckless behavior of the cleanup operation.

The DGEIS consists in large part of sanguine projections into the future and assurances that where there are problems they'll be handled appropriately "when practical."

Who determines what's practical?   Who defines it and according to what criteria? During the cleanup, it was often found to be *im*practical to wet down dust—a measure mandated by science—during the winter for fear the water would freeze. Is that going to happen again? Will other actions protective of human health be considered impractical because they require too much time or money? Will it be considered impractical to enforce the rules against truck and bus idling? And *how* will those rules be enforced—simply through fines? Bus and truck companies are known to consider fines a necessary part of doing business and to write the expense into their contracts. The fines, therefore, don't deter anybody.

The DGEIS also asserts that P.M. 2.5 was not much of a problem outside Ground Zero. This, too, is false. **For half the days until February, P.M. 2.5 was higher at Stuyvesant High School than at Ground Zero...**[169]

Testimony to the World Trade Center
Expert Technical Review Panel

February 23, 2005

1. The Draft Generic Environmental Impact Statement (February 18, 2004 testimony) assert[s] that **the dioxin levels until January 2002—some of which were the highest ever recorded, attaining to 170 times the previous record**—are "not expected to cause serious long-term health problems."

2. Not expected by whom?   There are many venerable scientists who *do* expect serious long-term health consequences. In this assertion, the DGEIS is engaging in **"averaging:"   When levels are uncomfortably high, dilute them over a larger time or space and they'll go away.**

3. OSHA action levels for lead have been exceeded at 130 Liberty St. yet so far as we know, no action has been taken. The levels simply get posted to the website.

4. At the City Council hearing, Kevin Rampe (Chairman of the Lower Manhattan Development Corporation) spoke of applying for variances. This is troubling because a variance is what you seek when you want to avoid a regulation.

5. We've made some progress on Deutsche Bank but even as we speak, 4 Albany Street is being demolished. This has a private owner who is not subject to the same kind of public process requirements as a state agency. Nevertheless the public has a right to know how the demolition is proceeding. We have reason to fear it may fall short of what's necessary to protect the public health.

6. Regarding the eternal issue of EPA taking the lead on the demolitions: EPA has taken to using the phrase but that's far from doing the deed. "Taking the lead" means taking responsibility; being the [ultimately responsible party]. What EPA means by it is that they're busy on the phone fobbing off responsibility onto other agencies.   They've adopted an ever-so-polite stance of,

"Department Of Labor, you're such great experts in asbestos and you, Department Of Health, are the authorities on lead; you must, of course, take the lead." Then when it's time for the lawsuits, we'll have a room full of agencies pointing fingers at each other. That's what EPA is counting on. Their pseudo-solicitous attitude of, "After you, Alphonse," in which they defer to every other agency on matters that fall squarely within their jurisdiction, is exactly *not* taking the lead. Politeness is fine in a business-as-usual situation but this is not business as usual. It's a potential public health emergency and you need to rise to the occasion.

Testimony to the WTC Expert Technical Review Panel

September 13 2004

Two points:

1. Deutschebank: Heavy metals coat the structural steel. During demolition, the bending of the steel will cause these metals to flake and powder, which will pose a danger to residents (in addition to the astronomical levels of contaminants in the building). The building should be encased in Tyvek as was done after a release of asbestos in Gramercy Park. Similar protocols were used on the George Washington Bridge. Please recommend this to the Lower Manhattan Development Corporation.

2. This is a helpful EPA brochure called Protect Your Family from Lead in Your Home; it reads:

> a. "Lead dust, which you can't always see can be a serious hazard." One wonders, then, why in its initial cleanup, EPA recommended visual inspection.
> b. The brochure talks about the dangers of lead to children, which include not only cognitive damage but also hearing loss. And it says that lead is also harmful to adults. "Adults can suffer from: difficulties during pregnancy; other reproductive problems in both men and women; high blood pressure; digestive problems; nerve disorders; memory and concentration problems;"[170] etc.

The WTC contained approximately 50,000 computers each made with between four and twelve pounds of lead. And none of these calculations ever take into account WTC 7 [let alone 3, 4, 5 and 6.] We know from previous testing (never mind common sense) that some of the lead landed in people's apartments. So two things are indisputable:

1. WTC lead is in people's homes.
2. It's dangerous.

How, then, can we justify ignoring it? That it lacks some ineffable, "Je ne sais quoi" marking it as uniquely WTC in origin? This is why the fingerprint [or today, the "signature"] metaphor is misleading and dangerous. The WTC was a building like any other. The only unique thing about it is that it was really big. Apart from that, its lead was indistinguishable from any other lead. So it is disingenuous of EPA to ignore lead excesses in Lower Manhattan because the particles failed to arrive individually stamped, "WTC."

I also take issue with the statement that you already have the fingerprint for WTC dust. You only have it, possibly, for the immediate vicinity of the site since that's where the few samples being used to determine the fingerprint were collected. It's impossible to establish a universal fingerprint, if such a thing exists, *before* you've done representative testing.

2,000 years ago, Cato the Elder ended each Senate meeting with the words, "Et Carthago delenda est." (And Carthage must be destroyed.) By the end of the year, the Senate took the hint and voted to destroy Carthage. Likewise at each panel meeting we say to you, "Having been destroyed, Carthage must be representatively tested."

Damage Control After a Few Members of the Public
Figure Out They've Been Screwed:
Grant Face Time with Those in Charge and
Keep Activists Busy Addressing Ever Escalating Outrages

I let them say what they want and they let me do what I want.

> *Frederick the Great of Prussia*
> *(possibly apocryphal)*

Over the course of several years following 9/11, three scientific panels were convened to figure out what to do about the contamination that remained in homes, offices, workplaces and schools. In addition, a number of buildings that contained stratospheric levels of contaminants from the World Trade Center were scheduled for demolition as part of the ambitious "rebuilding" plans. The process by which this took place threatened to turn into 9/11, the Sequel, subjecting the citizens of Lower Manhattan, already debilitated by their exposure to the original contamination, to a fresh onslaught.

The first two scientific panels lasted for a few days. The final one, the blue-ribbon panel to end all blue-ribbon panels, was the hybrid brainchild of Hillary Clinton for the good guys and James Connaughton, progenitor of the government's original lies. It met approximately once a month for nearly two years.

The scientists, culled from a variety of disciplines and around the country in an effort to achieve "independence," were largely ignorant of what had been going on. Thus, much of the conference consisted of the public's bringing them up to speed.

The upshot of all this, which was studiously covered in the press, was... nothing: A slapdash testing program of which most people opted out because it was even worse than the first one in 2002.

It was for a meeting of this final panel that the following doggerel was written to summarize the process and urge the panel to prevent further environmental disaster, courtesy of the remaining demolitions.

Homage to the WTC Expert Technical Review Panel

(In the triple meter of, 'T Was the Night Before Christmas)

'T was two days after history changed its direction
as radically as a plane veering off course,
when mindful of Nasdaq and Dow's bottom line,
the White House, through Whitman, declared the air "fine."
Returning to offices, schools and apartments,
the residents, with baited breath having waited,
let out that breath in relief, not understanding
that they'd have done better to have kept it baited.
For who would have thought, under such circumstances,
the White House would lie, and to such a degree?
Americans couldn't begin to believe
that their leaders might poison them; call them naive.
They ignored the foul odor as harmless if gross
like their symptoms the experts said would go away
and armed with the buckets doled out by Red Cross,
they cleaned up their apartments that looked like Pompeii.
A year later, confronting rage and litigation
from people who said, "We should not have returned,"
EPA, in a moment of faux introspection,
came out with a document called, "Lessons Learned."
However, the residents weren't appeased.
EPA and the White House kept feeling the heat
so they set up a panel of experts to keep
the community busy and off of the street.
Five more buildings now face demolition and history

seems bent on repeating mistakes of the past.
Intervene, so years after this panel's adjourned,
your memoirs need not also be called, "Lessons Learned."

Saving Private Capital

2004

Narrator: September 11 was a unique tragedy in the history of our country. But while the victims' families and the rest of the world mourned, no one was harder hit than the nation's billionaires. For what was at stake for them was neither their lives nor their health from the record levels of contamination downtown; nor even the lives of their loved ones. The billionaires had been attacked where it hurt most:

Billionaires: (*covering their crotches*) My portfolio!

Narrator: But the billionaires remembered what was truly important in life. And so, after a lengthy thirty seconds of soul-searching, ever valiant in the face of the hardship of others, they rallied to restore that one truly important thing.

Billionaires: (*to the tune of "Daisy, Daisy, Give Me Your Answer, Do"*)

Wall Street, Wall Street, our love pure and true,
We can hardly wait to reopen you
We don't care for public health
But only for our wealth
So we lie and cheat
Upon this street
Full of people that we can screw.

Narrator: Meanwhile, back at the ranch, aka the White House…

Chairman of the Council on Environmental Quality is in his office, looking over some papers and frowning.

Enter Enviros 1 and 2. Enviro 1 holds a large sign. Enviro 2 holds papers.

Chairman: (*chipper*) Well, everything's looking fine to reopen Wall Street.

Enviro 1: But Sir, there are dangerous levels of asbestos—See this press release?

Enviro 1: (*shows Chairman sign that reads, "DANGEROUS LEVELS OF ASBESTOS"*)

Chairman: Give me that. I'm just going to do a little editing.
(He puts "NOT" in front of "DANGEROUS.")

Chairman: There we go.

Enviro 1: (*thrilled*) Oh, thank you, Sir!

Enviro 2: But Sir, there's also antimony, lead, dioxin and some stuff I can't pronounce.

Chairman: Hmm.... Let me see that.

Enviro 2: (*hands him paper which he looks at, frowning again*)

Chairman: (*reading to himself*) Antimony... no; arsenic, uh uh... Here's calcium, good. Dioxin, no, lead, no good. Here's Zinc, great!... And Copper, good... Well it's very clear. The environmentally responsible thing to with WTC dust is to recycle it.....as cereal. Sprinkle it, bake it, do whatever you want but just (*to tune of Michael Jackson's "Beat it:"*) Eat it, eat it.

Enviro 2: (*prostrate with admiration*) Oh Sir, now I understand why this administration is so reknowned for its brains!

Chairman and Enviro 2: (*To the tune of "Mares eat oats and does eat oats."*)

PCBs and VOCs, beryllium, asbestos
A kid'll eat gypsum too, wouldn't you?
Antimony, TCE, vanadium and benzene
A kid'll eat chlorine too, wouldn't you?

Narrator: So it was that in the face of danger to the nation and the people who had been attacked, the White House heeded a higher calling. They sacrificed more of the country's sons and daughters so that they could reopen that spiritual beacon to the world, Wall Street.

All: (*to the tune of Petula Clarke's Downtown*)

When the air's fine and you think it should be thicker
you can always go—downtown.
When you are healthy and you want to get sicker
take the number six—downtown.
Just listen to the White House with its bald misinformation
Breathe deeply of the lead and other foul contamination
The air is more toxic there
You can forget all your troubles, forget all your cares
'Cause you're Downtown.
Things are much worse when you're Downtown.
Get me a nurse for you Downtown.
Out in a hearse for you there.

Postscript: *In a Life Copies Satire moment, a recent documentary contained the nugget—no doubt, like the rest of the documentary, a toxic admixture of truth and disinformation—that during Operation Paperclip, whose purpose was to cleanse the war records of former Nazis in order to bring them to the U.S. and take advantage of their scientific insights, Werner Von Braun's biography was "edited" to change the phrase "an ardent Nazi" into "not an ardent Nazi." I saw this documentary several years after writing the above skit. I don't know when it was made.*

MEDIA

Introduction

[I]n the big lie there is always a certain force of credibility; because the broad masses of a nation are always more easily corrupted in the deeper strata of their emotional nature than consciously or voluntarily; and thus in the primitive simplicity of their minds they more readily fall victims to the big lie than the small lie, since they themselves often tell small lies in little matters but would be ashamed to resort to large-scale falsehoods.

Adolf Hitler

(*After World War Two, a number of former Nazi scientists, propagandists and other war criminals escaped prosecution by emigrating to South America or the United States to assist the government in its fight against Communism.*[171] *These "rat lines" were facilitated by the Red Cross and the Vatican.*[172])

Just as the checks and balance system enshrined in the Constitution has been hijacked, so, too, has the fourth estate. Even more than Congress who have been seduced or blackmailed by corporations, the independent press is openly owned by Viacom, GE and other energy and defense firms. (The ownership may be open but it is not often discussed since the ones who would do the discussing are the very subject of the discussion. Therefore it is not widely known, nor its implications understood.) The muckraking journalists of yesteryear have been replaced by "left-wing gatekeepers" who allow just enough real facts through for people to think that we have a functional free press while the smoking guns remain concealed. The previously detached observers have morphed not simply into players but into handmaidens to the stars.

The New York Times is a particularly smooth operator. The Op-Ed page continues to feature liberals like Bob Herbert and

Maureen Dowd, clever, angry opponents of the status quo. But theirs are opinions, not reports. The news pages follow the party line, particularly in what they *don't* say or in whole stories they don't cover. The paper might commission research which shows that most people don't get beyond paragraph fourteen of most articles, and then use that information to bury the pivotal information in paragraph twenty-three. Or they pay lip service to the truth, but couch it in such boring techno-speak, we skip the passage. Or, as in the case of the EPA Inspector General's Report of 2003 concerning the environmental disaster of 9/11, they may publish it late on a Friday in the heart of August.

In the case of alternative interpretations to the U.S. government's concerning 9/11 (referred to dismissively as "conspiracy theories" whereas the accepted narrative, involving "medieval-minded" Muslims guided from a cave by a dialysis patient, is no less conspiratorial), they take an opposite approach to death-by-injection-of-lethal-dose-of-boredom, gleefully high-lighting the more preposterous hypotheses: (*There were in fact no planes; what we all saw were holograms; the passengers were spirited away to Ohio.*).

Corporations have learned to play the game as well, for they are on the front line when it comes to exposing the public to the release of toxic substances. A speaker on Communications Strategy—How to Win the Media War at a conference of the American Chemistry Council recommended:

"Find a 'credible and comforting' person to drive the message of the chemical industry in times of disaster or in response to environmental/health issues. This person may not be your company CEO, it may be the fire chief, or the mayor..."[173]

They might have added, "Or a woman," preferably blond and blue-eyed.

The tactics are endless and those brandishing them, because of their agenda, have more energy than their unwitting customers.

*"I think this is the appropriate moment," Jonathan said quietly, "to put an end, once and for all, to the notion that Jonathan Blakely is nutty when it comes to his warning that the American news media have been deeply penetrated by our intelligence community. Confirmation of everything I have been saying on that score came less than two weeks ago, and I've been waiting for just the right moment to pass it on. It comes from no less a source than the New York Times. I would like to say that it was the lead story on page one but, alas, as usual it was buried at the bottom of the fourteenth page of the second section on June 9. That story, my good and patient friends, reports that the Central Intelligence Agency, in order to settle a lawsuit under the Freedom of Information Act, reluctantly disclosed—those are the words of the good gray lady herself—that journalists have been used in a variety of roles and missions. Among other duties, journalists provided cover or served as a funding mechanism, some provided nonattributable material for use by the CIA, some collaborated in or worked on CIA-produced materials or were used for the placement of CIA-prepared materials in the foreign media. Some journalists had even served as couriers and as case officers who secretly supervised other agents. And some—oh, it's been a long time a-coming—provided **assistance in suppressing what the CIA termed a media item, such as a news story.***[174] [This last allegation is supported by an article in the Boston Globe.*[175]*]*

We have been primed for this, like cattle for slaughter. Since the end of World War II, Americans have been transformed from the world's most productive, up-and-coming nation to one of its most helplessly passive. Rather than offering everyone an enlightening education in true democratic tradition, the more transparent of state governments ensure the dumbing down of the public by prohibiting the teaching of evolution unless it's "democratically" accompanied by its opponent, "intelligent design." (The apparently "stupid design" of developing species from vast numbers of trial and error "experiments" involves crunching numbers with lots of zeros in them. But in the field of mathematics, we are heading towards the mindset of those tribes whose numerical system goes no further than, "One, two, many.")

Americans are being "feminized," at least according to a common notion of women; what a teacher of mine used to call, "fat, dumb and happy." From "virile" producers, we have become passive consumers.

The young men in this scenario are the developing nations, the ones with a lean and hungry look, poised and working to take over. But they will not do a better job; they are simply more energized versions of their aging parents, the corporations.

Tactic 5,860: While Holding Innumerable Hearings to Show What a Good Job You're Doing, Make Sure the Press Doesn't Hear the People Who Are Telling the Truth

2005

Those of us who have been struggling for the last three and a half years to publicize the environmental disaster of 9/11 can attest to the truth of Bill Moyers' speech to the National Conference for Media Reform: The mainstream media often take the party line for gospel at the expense of the truth.

The trouble in our case is the vice-like hold that government agencies have over official inquiries. At almost every hearing on the environmental disaster of 9/11, whether local, state or federal, government agencies have testified first. Their monopoly over the proceedings has lasted until noon at which point most of the press have rushed out to edit their stories.

The rest of us, whether independent scientists, experts or unwashed masses, have testified after lunch or even after 5 PM. Since many elected officials leave as soon as they've delivered their own statements, often we've been reduced to delivering impassioned speeches to a lone City Council member or State Assemblyperson who has nodded sympathetically in between taking calls on his cell-phone.

One of the few exceptions to this disheartening picture was the EPA Ombudsman's hearing which made a point of having scientists such as Dr. Thomas Cahill of the University of California, then considered a maverick, testify first. The EPA Administrator at the time, Christie Todd Whitman, soon pulled the Ombudsman's authority out from under him, which effectively did away with the office.   (Ombudsman Robert Martin resigned in protest, as Whitman had known he would.)

From the get-go in the environmental disaster of 9/11, Dr. Marjorie Clarke of Hunter College testified that the air was "equivalent to dozens of asbestos factories, incinerators and crematoria—as well as a volcano." And Paul Bartlett of the Queens Center for the Biology of Natural Systems warned government officials of the way these contaminants would disperse and of the particular dangers of inside air. Apartments are dust collectors, he pointed out. The rain won't wash and the wind won't blow away the toxic contaminants.

But unlike the government accounts—"Nothing to worry about; we're doing a great job"—these truthful depictions, which were critical for residents to know in order to protect themselves and their families, didn't make it into the press.

A hearing without the press or most of the elected officials is like a tree falling in the forest: It doesn't make any sound or if it does, so what?

We the people objected to the way the hearings were organized.

"But," we were told, "the agency reps said if we don't let them go first, they won't testify at all."

I've never understood what would be so bad about that.

In response to a question from Dr. Marjorie Clarke at the New York Academy of Sciences, Andrew Revkin of the New York Times argued that it would have been "irresponsible" to report what non-government witnesses had testified. But the environmental disaster of 9/11 is an eloquent if catastrophic example of why the opposite is true: It's irresponsible to report only one side of a story, particularly when the other side is so powerfully supported.

"Look Over There!" or Leave Us Alone; China Pollutes Too

The press has learned the Magician's Rule Number One: Make sure the audience is looking somewhere else; hence, this morning's front page article in the New York Times about the pollution resulting from burning coal in China.[176]

I'm not saying it's not a God-awful mess over there or that the mess won't spread itself around the globe. But when, as the article asserts about nine-tenths of the way in, **"the average American still consumes more energy and is responsible for the release of 10 times as much carbon dioxide as the average Chinese,"** isn't our focus on China a case of the pot calling the kettle black?

Not to sound like a fortune cookie but in long articles, it pays to check out the last line:

> *China is using subsidies to make its energy even cheaper, a strategy that is not unfamiliar to Americans, Kenneth Lieberthal, a China specialist at the University of Michigan, told the New York Times. "They have done in many ways," he said, "what we have done."*[177]

Which brings to mind the last scene of Washington Square (or was it The Heiress?) in which the heroine sits unmoved upstairs while the suitor who once rejected her bangs on the door begging to be forgiven and let in.

"How can you be so cruel?" her companion says.

She replies, "I have learned from masters."

China has learned from its master, which is the United States. We showed the rest of the world the "good life" and now we act affronted that they're going after it.

China's pollution is horrendous, as the many protests around the country attest. The point is, why are we focusing so much attention on that rather than on our own backyard?

The Message of the Media

(In part, a response to blog readers who complain that despite their impassioned efforts, their families are not heeding their warnings.)

December 13, 2008

A few years ago I had a phone conversation with a woman I'd known in high school. At the time of the conversation, she'd had a major portion of her gut and liver removed because of cancer which doctors retroactively determined had started fifteen years earlier. They had not diagnosed it sooner, despite persistent symptoms, because medical students are taught, "When you see hoofprints in the sand, think, 'horses,' not 'zebras.' " Apparently, no one felt it necessary to point out that when you also see black and white stripes flashing by, it may be time to think, "zebras."

Black Swans, zebras... The Experts have forgotten that when the chance of something happening as the result of a particular act is one in a million, then if you perform that act a million, or even a hundred times, the odds change significantly.

My high school acquaintance was about to embark on a treatment of thalidomide, a teratogenic drug that was taken off the market in England years ago when the children of women who had taken it for morning sickness were born with truncated limbs.

It was a long shot but she focused on the slim chance that it could cure her. It didn't.

The point is: People will grasp at straws before facing God-awful realities.

That is all the more true in the case of Peak Oil and its fallout. People are at least theoretically aware of their own eventual death whereas the scenario facing us now is one undreamed of by almost everyone, at least consciously.

Perhaps the hardest part of activism about life and death issues is having to keep one's cool. If you jump up and down as the situation merits, you look like a nut.

The person shouting, "Fire!" looks like a nut too, until the people he's shouting to see or smell the smoke. Besides, the notion of "fire" is not new to them.

But Peak Oil is orders of magnitude greater and more complex as well as being sui generis.

On top of that, CNN still shows that heart-warming series in which you get to vote for your favorite hero; the equivalent of crying, "Look over there!" while the fire burns down your house.

So unless you have a willing audience, which is nine-tenths of the battle, you'd be advised to continue to hold some of that pent up, urgent energy in reserve. It will still be there when the time is right.

That's my two cents for dealing with friends and family. But our job will be made infinitely easier if we can get the media and the pols on board. In the chicken/egg conundrum of whether or not they shape opinion or simply react to it, let's face the fact that they have a lot more control than they admit.

And since they also have more information, they may soon be willing to listen.

As the Frog Boils

On the bumbling, stumbling efforts of celebrities to shed light in dark places and how the bad guys working there deflect it back onto the celebrities' own foibles or genitalia.

September 11 2009

Just as every day is your child's birthday for he's always somewhere in your thoughts, for some of us here at MikeRuppertblogspot, every day is September 11. Yet the enormity of the memory is especially acute on this wet, gloomy anniversary.

The mainstream media do a deft job of ensuring that. While paying pious lip service to the dead and their survivors, they twist the knife in the wound left that day by prominently presenting Charlie Sheen: Bush ordered 9/11.[178] We admire Sheen's courage and intentions but shake our head at his naiveté.

Last time Sheen raised questions about 9/11, the mainstream media raised questions about Sheen, suggesting he'd engaged in child molestation. (Whether or not the allegation was true misses the point, which is, "Why now?")

This time, that bludgeon is unnecessary as Sheen has provided enough rope to hang himself: His allegations are of the all too familiar amateurish sort, mixing justifiable questions with misleading, unprovable or just plain silly speculation. This allows him to be laughed off the global stage as Marion Cotillard was, once she linked her questioning of 9/11 with transparently clumsy doubts about the moon landing. The innocent forge ahead where angels fear to tread, their false friends leading them on with sweet-sounding notions that end in disaster.

For one of the most effective techniques for putting the public off the scent is the tactic known to practitioners of the martial arts:

Use the enemy's own weight and drives against him. Find his vulnerable spot and exploit it.

In this respect, Charlie Sheen is a GOP's fantasy nemesis with enough foibles to keep the tabloids salivating for more.

But instead of outrage, we succumb to the inevitable, at least for now. The frog is being boiled slowly. It might seem odd that he doesn't jump out for in fact, he does understand what's happening. He stays anyway because Hell is where your friends are and where, for the time being, they are determined to remain.

But don't be fooled. The water is still but warm, as the frog notes warily. His strength does not ebb... It merely waits.

The Father of the Terrorist

January 1, 2010

The latest Christmas horror movie—sorry, "news item"—concerning yet another Islamic fundamentalist planning to attack the West on one of its holiest of holidays, is concocted of tried and true ingredients: A threat at the height of a travel season, thereby easing the oil squeeze; a familiar "explosive" in familiar negligible quantities, smuggled in a private crevice. And if the shoe bomber led to all of us having to pad through the last lap of the airport in our stockinged feet, what's the logical conclusion to the underwear bomber? I guess the naked scanner's a reasonable compromise, huh?

Then there are the back stories.

Like Osama Bin Laden in the years leading up to 9/11, prior to his alleged attempt at a Christmas massacre (nice East v. West touch there, if a little heavy-handed) Umar Farouk Abdulmutallab had supposedly broken ranks with the rest of his family. The well brought up, Westernized Muslim turned into a Radical Fundamentalist, another family black sheep.

But unlike Osama, Umar is no mastermind; he's 23. In this (as well as in the muffed outcome of his alleged attempt) he harks back to John Hinckley Jr. of Reagan assassination-attempt fame.

The similarities of the three Threats to Our Way of Life do not end there for all their backgrounds reach into the highest echelons of the societies and even the administrations they sought to destroy.

The links of Osama's family to the Bushes are by now well known and won't be rehashed here.

But Hinckley was also no mere garden variety nut-job. His family, too, was connected to the Bushes:

Neil Bush, a landman for Amoco Oil, told Denver reporters he had met Scott Hinckley at a surprise party at the Bush home

January 23, 1981, which was approximately three weeks after the U.S. Department of Energy had begun what was termed a "routine audit" of the books of the Vanderbilt Energy Corporation, the Hinckley oil company. In an incredible coincidence, on the morning of March 30, three representatives of the U.S. Department of Energy told Scott Hinckley, Vanderbilt's vice president of operations, that auditors had uncovered evidence of pricing violations on crude oil sold by the company from 1977 through 1980. The auditors announced that the federal government was considering a penalty of two million dollars. Scott Hinckley reportedly requested "several hours to come up with an explanation" of the serious overcharges. The meeting ended a little more than an hour before John Hinckley Jr. shot President Reagan.[179]

Similarly, the father of Umar—who purportedly warned the CIA of his son's worrisome beliefs six weeks before they came to fruition in the alleged terrorist attempt—is not only the prominent banker who has been portrayed in the media; assuming that his name is not the Nigerian equivalent of Bob Johnson, he has also held powerful positions in energy (both electricity and oil,) communications and defense.

"Dr. Umaru Abdul Mutallab has held senior management positions in the Defense Industries Corporation of Nigeria (DIC)... has also served as chairman of the National Electrical Power Authority (NEPA)... and is on the board... of the Nigerian Communication Commission."[180]

The Defense Industries Corporation of Nigeria has been involved mainly in manufacturing AK-47's not only for Nigeria but also for neighboring countries.[181]

The New Nigeria Development Company of which Dr. Mutallab was General Manager, has a deal with Gazprom to analyze three oil blocks in the Northern part of the country (the Muslim part, where the rifles are being manufactured.)[182]

The Nigerian Communication Commission saw its Vice Chairman arrested in May for illegally withdrawing a license.[183]

The National Electric Power Authority, or NEPA, is so prone to power outages that the acronym is sometimes said to stand, somewhat clumsily, for, "Never Expect Power Always."

But it is as a banker that Mutallab Sr. is mainly known, most recently as Chairman of the First Bank of Nigeria about which Wikipedia says:

"The Bank traces its history back to 1894 and the Bank for British West Africa..."[184]

According to its founder, without a bank, economies were reduced to using barter and "a wide variety of mediums of exchange..." (Can't have that, can we?)

"The bank primarily financed foreign trade, but did little lending to indigenous Nigerians, who had little to offer as collateral for loans..."

After fixing all that, in 2008, the bank was rated by JP Morgan as one of the two "least preferred" of Nigerian banks.[185] And this was before it reported N7r4 billion bad loans in 2009 (a year in which they were in good company, however.)

Busy guy, Mutallub Sr. Maybe he should have spent more Sunday afternoons kicking around a soccer ball with Umar.

Orwell v. Huxley

July 27, 2009

The horizontal position in which I've spent most of the last week affords a new perspective, particularly given the guidance of whatever blog reader it was who recommended Neil Postman's classic work, Amusing Ourselves to Death.[186]

The thesis of said slim but nonetheless magnum opus is that we are not, in fact, marching into oblivion to the tune of Orwell's 1984; rather, we are dancing there to the tune of Huxley's Brave New World. Going out neither with a bang nor even a whimper, we exit jiving to a jingle. We have opted for euthanasia via television. Big Brother, to paraphrase Postman, turns out to be Howdy Doody.

And this was written in 1985, the good old days. It would be interesting to know what Postman had to say regarding 9/11. Though he died in 2003, offhand, I can't find anything.

While the basic tenet of the core members of this blog is that this is the time to cultivate one's garden in a more literal sense than Voltaire ever intended, one can't help pondering how we painted ourselves into this corner.

"It's the economy, Stupid." True, the economy is at the apex of our particular pyramid but right under it, along with the Congressional/military/ industrial complex, are the media. And Postman is the go-to guy for that angle.

When the renowned Shakespeare scholar, Dame Helen Gardner, was a student at Oxford, she was once chastised, by a friend who was studying medicine, for embarking on the frivolous study of English literature.

"But my dear Margaret," Helen replied, "What will your patients do when they get better?"

We are not confident we ever *will* "get better" since another tenet here is that things are going to get a whole lot worse first. But perspective is still illuminating and Postman offers it in spades, to continue the gardening theme.   From the seven hour long Lincoln/Douglas debates to the literacy rate of seventeenth century America (over 90% for free white men, 60% for unenslaved white women) to the impressive tidbit about where Americans learned the technique for making wheels out of a single piece of wood: from Homer.

Almost makes you proud until you remember that the point is the opposite.

Department of Bread and Circuses, Minus the Bread

Exhibit A: Eliot Spitzer

Oscar Wilde said that the hallmark of a first rate intelligence was the ability to hold two opposing ideas in mind at the same time while remaining sane.

This is what many of us are unable to do. One minute Eliot Spitzer is the savior brandishing his sword in the face of Wall Street; the next, he's the perp in a scandal rendered only more ignominious by being banal.

At once, we forget the opposing side of the coin. Or we remember but dismiss it as though a guy who sees call girls is unable to see the economy straight.

Spitzer, We Hardly Knew Ye But Don't Let That Stop Us from Opining
March 23, 2008

Thank God for Eliot Spitzer. Not only did the White Knight/Client 9 rescue us from the siege of CNN by Britney Spears; he also cleverly timed his fall from his high horse (in German, "Spitze" means "top") to camouflage the far greater implosion of the street whose own dirty tricks he'd investigated.[187]

For the Spitzer scandal broke shortly after an article he'd written was published on Valentine's Day in the Washington Post warning of the financial collapse we're witnessing now.[188]

The egghead former Attorney General morphed into the anti-hero at whom the public could throw eggs while The Street continued picking that same public's pockets.

Such heroism comes at a price, of course. The knight's shining armor has gotten bloody in the process. So while the Ph.D.'s weigh in, from blame-the-wife Dr. Laura to "Go figure" Dr. Janet Taylor, with equal relish (if less censure), I leap into the fray not as a shrink but, in true New York tradition, as an ex-analyzed.

The titillating bit about this uniquely American scandal (uniquely American not because of the behavior, which was cliché, but because of our professed shock) is the abrasive prosecutor's self-destructiveness. He had powerful enemies but in the end, he was his own worst etc., etc. Like a criminal returning to the scene of the crime until the cops finally nab him; like a fireman who reveals his inner pyromania by setting a record-breaking auto da fe, Spitzer threw his career on the very sword with which he had won it.

For there can be little doubt that a piece of him wanted to get caught. Spitzer was not just any politician discovered red-handed, with his pants down. (Sex turns all metaphors into double entendres.) He was the former Attorney General who had ridden to fame investigating prostitution rings.

While this conundrum has elicited outraged cries of, "Hypocrite!" such epithets don't get us very far. ("Karma" is another one that's been going and coming around.) What was said "hypocrisy" made of? The scourge of money-laundering schemes knew how to follow the money. And therefore, better than anyone, he knew how to leave a trail of breadcrumbs.

So far, at least eight breadcrumbs have been discovered, possibly amounting to $80,000. They were left in a pattern known as "smurfing" which, as Spitzer certainly knew, raises red flags with banks' compliance officers.

But why did he do it? Was it guilt? Exhibitionism? Was the governorship less fun than he'd hoped?

Such questions are beyond the reach of at least this idle speculator. But throw out a few more details. The sharks' appetites have only been whetted.

Lies, Videotape and Insanity

June, 2010

With infuriating predictability, the BP disaster is being used to discredit Peak Oil. I won't honor that effort by referring to its authors by name or linking to their articles. But needless to say, they are using the vastness of the spill to show that the end of oil resources is nowhere in sight.

Of course, the Peak Oil movement didn't say it was. It is the simplistic, kneejerk definition of Peak Oil by those who distort its message that is at work. The BP oil disaster confirms what the Peak Oil movement has always alleged: That we were at the end of *easy* oil; what was left would be more difficult and expensive to extract (implicit in "more difficult" is "more dangerous") until finally, it wouldn't be worth it. That there might be oceans of oil left (why did that image come to mind?) would be irrelevant since it would be left locked up in its natural habitat forever.

Doesn't the BP disaster confirm that the oil is indeed too difficult to extract? Not worth it?

The tactics of those who would discredit Peak Oil evoke those of the "fanatical-Muslims-attacked-the-World-Trade-Center" school of thought: Misstate your opponent's position; then ridicule the straw man argument.

The only surprising factor in this worn out scenario is that the public remains clueless. They have been knocked down, ripped off and screwed over in every possible area of their lives yet they still turn on the news and the internet and next thing you know, you're hearing Pentagon-speak out of the mouths of earnest youth.

It must be confusing for a people who are desperate for something real to hold onto, that isn't part of the great hall of mirrors reflecting each other which so much of life turns out to be. The news gets the weather right, more or less, most of the time.

And the talking heads seem sure of themselves, which the poor slob watching isn't, so why not believe them?

Thus does disinfo spread like a parasite riding its host to the next victim.

The process is reminiscent of a psychological experiment conducted years ago to study the reactions of pigeons to rewards and deprivation:

One group of pigeons was regularly fed adequate amounts of food and thrived.

The second group was regularly fed less food. They lost weight but adjusted.

The third group, however, was fed irregularly. Sometimes they got enough but sometimes they didn't; and sometimes they got nothing and wondered when they would eat next. Then the experimenters would overcompensate.

These pigeons went mad.

This last group is us: Told to get and spend for we are the world's consumers; maxed out as a result; working if we're lucky, encouraged then laid off; all while, like the White Queen in Alice in Wonderland, believing six impossible things before breakfast.

When the facade of this absurdity begins to crack, the rupture will spread and the structure collapse until centuries' worth of lies have been released.

Seize the Day for Tomorrow You Die; I'll See to It

First the good news: Congratulations! You were right! Now the bad news: The thing you were right about? We're screwed.

A day of humdrum grim news (unemployment increasing, a dire report from the UN about a time an unimaginable thirty years hence) has turned into one of leapfrogging headlines. "China's Monster Three Gorges Dam Is About to Slow the Rotation of the Earth" was superseded by, "Oil Spill on Track to Reach Atlantic No Later Than October."[189]   But then both were overshadowed by the acknowledgment of Peak Oil by Jim Chanos shorting the majors based on none other than diminished reserves.

It doesn't matter that in his speech the other night, Obama refrained from uttering the magic words "Peak Oil;" he acknowledged the fact.   But acknowledging the implications? That'll be a real milestone.

And on that score, don't hold your breath. We knew after 9/11 that the mainstream press would only pay attention to the health issues "when the bodies started falling." We were right.

The same principle still holds. This country looks only at the present, at what they can see happening. They don't extrapolate so that the same tragedy doesn't repeat itself *in a different context.* The press focuses on the sensational and warnings from experts just aren't sexy.

It's true that you can't tell the people more than they can take in; they'll simply spit out the message. What you need to do is prepare them for it so that after years of feeding them intellectual cotton candy, you're not suddenly expecting them to absorb and make sense of truth.

This is happening per force but at a pathetic level.

Let Us Now Praise Famous Men
and Our Fathers That Begat Us

June 20, 2010 (Father's Day)

Sometimes I think about my father in that pointless way one thinks of the dead: "What would he say about what I'm doing now?" He had a strong journalistic streak himself; like many in his writing circle, revering the profilist Joseph Mitchell, who was known as much for the exquisiteness of his prose as for the paucity of his output. (Out of deference, the *New Yorker* set aside an office for him for many unproductive years.)

It's a pointless question because our parents, at least mine, were children of their era. They knew that and would not have had it otherwise, any more than a fish would choose to move to Central Park South, even though it's some of the most sought-after real estate in the world. Having lived through the Depression and the War, and having seen segregation disintegrate, they relished what Francis Fukuyama notoriously called the "end of history." The prejudices and superstitions of their parents' countries seemed to belong to a less evolved consciousness. Who could imagine turning back?

A few years ago, I attempted to contact two of my father's friends to let them know what I'd learned since 9/11 as it had bearing on what was to come. These were influential, well-connected men who, if they wished, could convey the message further in the spheres of movies and letters. I also felt these two men were the most likely among my parents' old friends to be open to what I had to say.

The first, Walter Bernstein, might be receptive, I thought, because he'd written the screenplays, *Fail Safe*, about "an accidental sortie" of nuclear bombers to the USSR, and *The Front*, about the blacklist during the McCarthy era (of which Bernstein had first-hand experience). He was what used to be called "a lefty from way back" and was no stranger to the notion of corruption in high places. *Fail Safe* is particularly memorable for a rare foray by Walter Matthau into serious drama, playing an advisor who's itching for an opportunity to unleash a nuke.

Bernstein was as kind and cordial as one might wish but his gentle assessment was, "I hope you're wrong." "So do I," I said.

The second friend, whom I attempted to contact at an address which had worked years before, was Edgar Doctorow, the author of the novels *Ragtime*, about the twenties, and *The Book of Daniel*, about the trial of Julius and Ethel Rosenberg. But most intriguing was his role as editor at Dial Press when they published *Report from Iron Mountain*, a book that professes to be a spoof but which luminaries such as John Kenneth Galbraith swore was an actual government report. Galbraith said he knew this first hand because he'd been asked to work on it himself though he felt certain the final product was the work of either Dean Rusk or Clare Booth Luce.

Report from Iron Mountain concerns what would happen "if peace broke out." Since war is an essential part of the economy, phoney foes would have to be concocted. Slavery might have to be re-instituted.

Writing for the *Washington Post* under the pseudonym Herschel McLandress (a Jewish Scot?), Galbraith said he agreed with the book's conclusions. He was familiar with Keynes' Post-World War I work, *The Economic Consequences of Peace*, which discusses the inevitable "rapid depression of the standard of life of the European populations to a point which will mean actual starvation for some (a point already reached in Russia and approximately reached in Austria). Men will not always die quietly. For starvation, which brings to some lethargy and a helpless despair, drives other temperaments to the nervous instability of hysteria and to a mad despair."[190] Galbraith/McLandress only questioned the wisdom of releasing the report to "an obviously unconditioned public," (thus supporting this blog's admonition a couple of days ago that people have to be educated over time; you can't feed them soccer and Lady Gaga, then expect them to accept the notion of die-off.)

Doctorow did not respond to my letter though he'd been helpful in the past when I wrote fiction.

These non-responses were to be expected. Doctorow is almost eighty; Bernstein, over ninety. They may have felt that even if they'd "spread the word," their efforts would have led to a dead end; the only question was when.

At the same time, things are moving under the carpet. We at Collapsenet know this because we are under the carpet too, watching them. But also we are actors as well as observers, a circumstance as inevitable in life as it is in quantum mechanics.

"Let us now praise famous men, and our fathers that begat us."

The minimal response from my father's old buddies, as well as a far more enthusiastic response, several years ago, from a musician friend of mine, the late Rosalyn Tureck, who was of the same generation, confirmed my sense that the older generation wishes us well but feels relieved their time is up.

In terms of culture, our fathers' era may indeed have been the best of times; but in terms of environment, it was the worst of times. It's up to us to turn the ship around. It won't be smooth sailing after that but at least our children will have been set on the right course.

SOLUTIONS

**An introduction to some of the issues that need to be addressed
in an open global dialogue.**

Questioning Our Assumptions

April 12, 2009

The belief in spiritual Resurrection and related phenomena has done wonders for a whole lot of people. Who knows if they're right? One day, we'll all find out but then it'll be too late.

The belief in more mundane resurrections, such as for the economy and Life as We Know It, has also done wonders for a whole lot of people. But these days, some are questioning that belief. In fact, they seem to be sloughing it off as the snake sheds its old skin. For once you start questioning your belief in your representatives, you soon move on to your belief in the system as a whole; finally, to belief itself.

Whatever comes next, it's not going to be rooted in the same blind faith in Authority, Power and supposed Expertise, which has gotten us into this mess. It's not going to have much to do with blind faith in anything. Like the old guy at the end of *The Magnificent Ambersons*, people are going to stare into the fire and ask themselves the real questions they've spent their whole lives running away from. And that's the beginning of real knowledge.

Who's Up, Who's Down?

The great transvestite wit, Quentin Crisp, once said, "If you describe things as better than they are, you will be called an optimist; worse than they are and you will be called a realist; but if you describe things exactly as they are, you will be called a cynic."

They called us cynics and doomer-gloomers but look who is getting the last laugh.

Those who find this sentiment off-putting should be aware that no one gets the last laugh; like rock-climbers bound together, we fall together.

This is the most important lesson outside of a really useful one such as what crop to grow in your backyard: It is as wrong-headed to revere as to despise; in fact, it's just the opposite side of the same coin. The hero, if you have one, will disappoint, and far sooner than the meek will inherit.

My students, who hail from the most recondite reaches of the earth, may believe that So-and-so is a witch or that the bribery and corruption they came here to escape was the result of "Jewish influence," thus exonerating their own countrymen who were engaging in said bribery and corruption; but they are more open than Americans to the knowledge that we are not the world's saviours. We are fat, spoiled and laughably clueless about the rest of the world.

Then why did you come here? I ask them.

No answer; or one that quickly leads them to understand they came here in order to become as fat and spoiled as we are.

This is my purpose in teaching: To upend their assumptions; the more cherished, the more in need of upheaval or at least examination.

I have a student from somewhere in the Middle East/Central Asia who a year ago said that when he saw homosexuals, he wanted to kill them. (That is not an uncommon view among the students, regardless of where they're from.) One of the reasons he is here is that his family was afraid that if he stayed in his country, he would kill someone or be killed himself. (Homosexuals weren't his only enemies.) That, too, is not an uncommon reason for the students to be here; it is almost a rite of passage in certain countries.

When the question arose of what attribute the students were most proud of in themselves, this man said he was most proud of his loyalty to his beliefs.

Several weeks ago, we were discussing a court case concerning the custody of a child. The mother was a lesbian; the father, a convicted murderer.

The student from the Middle East/Central Asia said, "Give the child to the lesbians."

We all looked at him.

He shrugged. "I changed my mind."

Il Hamdul' illah. ("Thanks be to God.") There is hope.

Other Questions We Need To Ask:
The Triage of Remaining Oil Resources

Most Peak Oil experts agree we're facing times that try men's souls, not to mention their resources. Now that oil production is entering what Science Applications International Corporation Advisor Robert Hirsch has warned could be a precipitous decline, it makes sense to ask how we should triage the oil that remains: What per cent should be used for growing food? What per cent for developing renewables? Etc.

The necessity for thinking in these terms is heightened by galloping demand in those U.S. wannabes, China and India. As the late Matthew Simmons, author of Twilight in the Desert: The Coming Saudi Oil Shock and the World Economy, said:

> *"[W]e need a global economic cooperative framework for how we allocate oil use and in this framework we need to give India and China, for instance, an incremental use of another 50% more oil while we go on out [sic] diet to have any sense of equality. If we don't do this then we will basically end up playing musical chairs and musical chairs can get violent very fast."*[191]

So I asked several Peak Oil experts how they would allocate our remaining oil.

Jan Lundberg of www.Culturechange.org responded:

> "[Y]our points are crucial. A whole conference should be held on them. There's not much planning going on for a post-peak world, but if sanity somehow broke out and there was a little time to rework budget priorities, there would have to be funds put into the simplest, decentralized solutions for problems with growing food, providing minimal essential electrical power, and improving some transportation systems.

'Although old freeway-construction foe Mark Robinowitz is one of several Peak Oilists who feel that remaining oil ought to go to renewable energy development and implementation, I want to put a plug in for a probably more crucial and competing priority: removing roads and restoring the land. Without this -- requiring earth moving equipment using petrofuels -- we will have many decades of continuing erosion that kill salmon spawning streams and rivers. This is bigger than just salmon: it's about clean water and many species.

'For our Pedal Power Produce farm we opted for gasoline tractor-work to jumpstart crop growing for our organic produce. Nevertheless, seven years later now, I would say that greenhouse gas emissions have to basically stop, and the poisoning of the land from petrochemicals has to stop too. The unpleasant reality is that we feed ourselves thus. Putting efforts into real alternatives, instead of perpetuating the status quo, should be our clear goal."

I responded in a way that showed Jan I thought he was talking about taking a pick ax to Midtown Manhattan.
He clarified:

"On my position regarding roads, please use my original language because the greater amount of road decommissioning and removal and restoration is actually unpaved roads in rural hilly areas (mainly logging roads). Depaving is vital but even with flat areas there is more to it than just depaving if deep roadbeds are to be made agriculturally useful places. There simply will not be the energy and other resources to properly take out many paved roads: they will become bike paths, and trees will eventually do away with roads via root action."

In a phone conversation, Julian Darley of Post Carbon Institute in Vancouver said:

J.D: This is a huge question. That's why I didn't get back to you at first. My first thought is that we should be using almost none of [the remaining oil.]

But the first thing for any animal to think about is its food. Then we have to talk about what percent goes to renewables vs. what percent to developing vital chemicals. And what *are* those vital chemicals?

About half of the 21 million barrels that the U.S. uses daily goes to gas. A further percent goes to diesel. So this is some of what we use for food growth, tractors and freight.

Then there's a certain percent that goes into personal transportation. We certainly need to reduce our use of jet fuel and spend almost none on that.

We also need to move into more car co-ops. We could reduce oil use by a factor of ten or more if we did that.

And we have to shorten the supply chain and move to a biointensive agricultural system that uses no gas or diesel.

The U.S. should be working towards relying only on our native oil production, which would mean cutting our use by 80%. You have to cut your suit according to the cloth.

We also need to cut our heating and electricity demand. This will contract the economy, which is going to happen anyway.

You see, I have to turn your question around to: What do we need to do? Which bits are the easiest to cut?

Another big question is: How fast is the oil supply declining?

The only thing that interests me is being practical. Not using engineering solutions; they're coming ten to thirty years too late. I don't think they can be rolled out on the scale necessary. For instance, converting coal to liquids will make no difference. We have to cut demand.

This is a Heaven-sent opportunity to stop destroying the planet. The less damage we do, the better our oceans and the rest of the planet will be. We've been acting like a heroin addict.

I thought of the picture on the cover of a local newspaper that ambivalently denounced Petrocollapse, the Peak Oil conference in New York City that I moderated. The illustration was of a slumped Uncle Sam injecting black fluid into his arm.
Darley continued:

J.D: Let's not do what the Easter Islanders did. We're a cross between Easter Island and the Titanic. We've already hit the iceberg so we should fill the hole in the hulk.

We got into a tangled metaphor that mixed the Titanic with the canoes the Easter Islanders could no longer build once the last tree on the island had been destroyed (by rats rather than, as is commonly believed, by short-sighted Easter Islanders.)

J.O: Do you feel safe in Vancouver?

J.D: What do you mean?

J.O: Aren't you there because you think it'll weather the storm well?

J.D: What makes you say that?

J.O: I assume it.

J.D: Please don't assume that. I'm not doing this work for myself. People have to stop being selfish if we're to survive.

I didn't start out as a specialist in gas. I wrote *High Noon for Natural Gas* because I think it's an important subject. I used to write screenplays. [*Interesting, in light of the fact that Darley's M.A. from the University of Texas "culminat[ed] in a thesis about the elimination of television."*][192]

J.O: I know. I used to write fun stuff, too.

J.D: Anyway, Vancouver is a dangerous place.

J.O: With what?

J.D: Shootings. It's regarded as a glorious pearl but it has a lot of social and planning problems. If there were a place in

North America without problems, everyone would go there and it wouldn't be so wonderful anymore.

There are many places in North America without much rain. But it's not my fault.

J.O: Why do you say that? Did someone say it was?

J.D: Well people aren't happy when I talk about these things, but I didn't do it.

Australia, too. I didn't tell Great Britain where to put the five main cities in Australia. Instead of putting them where they could grow food, they founded them according to where it was convenient to send convicts.

We need a Plan R. What can we Retrofit? We need to use lower energy and make it fit. We need to use what I call "radical moderation." There's no revolution here.

They're putting a trillion solar panels in the desert. Who lives there? A lot of scorpions, so that's a bad idea.

J.O: Instead, those who know what's going on and are in a position to do something about it are just figuring out how to save themselves. They see it as a kind of Darwinism.

J.D: It's not Darwin. Social Darwinism has nothing to do with actual Darwinism, which I admire. The problem is Spencer and a few other Brits... Jeremy Bentham's another one.

I remember the sole story I've heard about Jeremy Bentham: He bequeathed a portion of his estate to London University on condition that they bring out his skeleton to attend meetings. They complied until the head fell off at which point only the head attended. Google provides a different version of this "memory."

J.D: I denounce both capitalism and communism. But there's also a deep, dark problem with liberalism at work here as well.

J.O: So what's your solution?

J.D: Global relocalization is the antidote to globalization. And shorten the supply chains.

J.O: That sounds like a version of the Communist rallying cry.

J.D: Ah, yes! "Villages of the world unite and shorten your supply chains!"

We can't run a small, model city with six and a half billion people. The rich will have to give up a lot. We can either plan or we can let it happen naturally. The question is how to do it without chaos.

Post Carbon should have an institute on every campus and in every town. We're interested in advising groups of all sizes.

It would also be better if we ate plants.

J.O: But you're not in favor of agriculture.

J.D: I wasn't in favor of agriculture ten thousand years ago. But we did it. What I said was "Biointensive agriculture."

We also made a terrible mistake ten million years ago when we came down out of the trees.

If we lived near the equator we'd be naked and we wouldn't have to worry about heat. Anywhere else, we'll freeze. But we made some big mistakes. Agriculture was a bad idea. It's no fun for billions of people who are poor and malnourished. I see people trawling the bins in Vancouver. Now it's going to become no fun for even more people.

Mike Ruppert says in his book, Confronting Collapse, and in the movie, Collapse, that we need complete transparency concerning oil reserves to improve the availability of those reserves to local governments.

Clearly, this discussion concerning triage is one that cries out to be continued.

Addendum May 12, 2011: The Fukushima disaster underscores the critical necessity of reserving sufficient oil resources to safely shut down nuclear power plants in order to avert more such catastrophes.

The Cow from One End to the Udder

March 28, 2006

The New York City Peak Oil Meet-up forged ahead last Thursday with its campaign to educate the public in basic farming skills, undeterred by the fact that the meeting was held in the belly of that most unnatural beast, Midtown Manhattan. As part of its series, "Bringing the Farm to You," Thursday's guests spoke about, "The Cow from One End to the Udder."

Deb Tyler, a dairy farmer from Cornwall Bridge in Connecticut, talked about growing up in Wisconsin and moving to New England where she came to appreciate the cow's ability to transform sparse grass in a rocky landscape into protein-rich sustenance. Adolescent rebellion took the form of eschewing meat, milk, grapes and an assortment of other foods on idealistic grounds that in the end seemed ungrateful and were anyway driving her crazy.

She returned to cows after getting her teacher's license and tried to come up with ways to bring cows to the classroom or vice versa. She now owns a herd of ten Jersey cows which, unlike the Holsteins most of us get our milk from, have normal pituitary glands that don't overdose us with hormones. Through the non-profit http://www.motherhouse.us/, she teaches classes in how to milk, "Eggs-perience Chickens," and "Get Your Goat" as well as master a host of other Old Style Life Skills. She also boards other people's cows from which they can get their own supply of unadulterated raw milk.

The herd is all female. Male Jerseys aren't so gentle and when they get to be a year old, Deb and her family eat them. Most of the cows in the herd are artificially inseminated by Deb herself since her arm is smaller than a man's and doesn't hurt the cow as much. The semen is injected into the unanaesthetized cow's cervix but the cows don't seem to mind.

A woman and her daughter who board a cow with Deb come every day, always in the same dresses or overalls. They also have one dress "for good."

"I thought I lived simply," said Deb, alluding to her Quaker philosophy, "but they've got it down."

Following Deb, Melanie Ferreira, a gourmet organic chef who recently founded the Academy of Healing Nutrition, http://www.academyhealingnutrition.com/, talked about the health-giving properties of raw milk. Although pasteurization was instituted to stop the spread of TB in the twenties, the TB was more the result of the unclean manufacturing processes used at the time rather than a risk from the milk itself. Pasteurization and homogenization rob raw milk of its health-giving properties, Melanie said, going on to warn the audience to beware the word "organic" which does not always mean what it implies.

She had brought a dozen eggs from "pastured" hens that eat bugs and worms and are therefore more nutritious. The eggs we buy often come from chickens that have been debeaked since the conditions in which they're raised are so "cooped up" in the original sense, they would otherwise peck each other mercilessly.

The eggs were a range of colors and sizes including one that was tinged with blue. Melanie cracked one egg open. The yolk was an orange mound, larger than what we're accustomed to, like a dilated pupil. The amniotic fluid was distinct from the rest of the white.

A piece of shell fell in. Saying, "The egg loves the egg," Melanie used half a shell to scoop it up. The shell-piece virtually leapt into the scoop of familiar substance, a marvel to those of us who remembered pursuing elusive bits with a spoon.

By way of a grand finale in showing nature's versatility, Melanie separated the film that clings to the inside of the shell and placed it on the arm of a volunteer saying, "Nature's band-aid."

Then Deb broke open a bottle of raw milk and, since it's illegal to sell it in New York State, passed around free samples.

Revolution and Victory Gardens

October 12, 2008

The New York Times is sounding a radical note, albeit muted by reasonably-cadenced prose.

In an article entitled "Farmer in Chief" in the Sunday Magazine, journalist Michael Pollan lays out a presidential policy plan for growing food during the next administration.[193]

It is filled with points which will sound familiar to Peak Oilists and Permaculturalists everywhere, denouncing monocultures which depend so heavily on pesticides and fertilizers and calling for a return to solar- rather than fossil fuel-based agriculture.

Pointing out the Dale Allen Pfeiffer nugget which Mike Ruppert has repeated in countless lectures, that it takes ten calories of fossil-fuel energy to produce one calorie of food as well as other equally galvanizing tidbits (it takes five thousand gallons of water to produce a pound of feedlot beef)—the article also provides some history of our current food-growing practices:

"After World War II, the government encouraged the conversion of the munitions industry to fertilizer—ammonium nitrate being the main ingredient of both bombs and chemical fertilizer—and the conversion of nerve-gas research to pesticides."

How many Americans, furrowing their brows as they read that passage over their morning coffee, are going to sit bolt upright in bed eighteen hours later at 3 AM? Probably not many, but otherwise Pollan would never have gotten away with it. It's a loaded sentence couched in a multi-thousand word article, like a landmine in an idyllic pastorale.

Pollan advocates regional food economies both in America and around the world and recommends setting up a Strategic Grain Reserve modeled on the current Strategic Petroleum Reserve.

He also points out:

"Right now, most of the conservation programs run by the USDA are designed on the zero-sum principle: land is either locked up in 'conservation' or it is farmed intensively. This either-or approach reflects an outdated belief that modern farming and ranching are inherently destructive, so that the best thing for the environment is to leave land untouched."

Some of his proposals are creatively sensible:

To qualify as "food," he recommends that an edible substance contain a minimum ratio of micronutrients per calorie of energy. He also suggests that "the White House [should] observe one meatless day a week—a step that, if all Americans followed suit, would be the equivalent, in carbon saved, of taking 20 million midsize sedans off the road for a year."

And while he doesn't use the phrase, "Food, not lawns" he proposes that the White House lawn should be a paragon for the rest of the country.

"[T]ear out five prime south-facing acres of the White House lawn and plant in their place an organic fruit and vegetable garden.

"When Eleanor Roosevelt did something similar in 1943, she helped start a Victory Garden movement that ended up making a substantial contribution to feeding the nation in wartime. (Less well known is the fact that Roosevelt planted this garden over the objections of the USDA which feared home gardening would hurt the American food industry.)"

Shortly after the publication of Pollan's article, Michelle Obama invited some students for a groundbreaking at the White House vegetable garden, the first since Eleanor Roosevelt's.

LEADERSHIP

The Moses of a Post Peak Oil World

June 18, 2008

> *The trouble with the world is that the stupid are cocksure and the intelligent are full of doubt.*
>
> *Bertrand Russell*

When the shit finally hits the fan, who will be the leaders who will carry us kicking and screaming towards the sustainable way of life that we should have been leading all along?

Will he be a Clint Eastwood type, far-seeing (you can tell from his squint), a man of few words? Or will he be possessed of that elusive quality, charisma, an Obama type to whom people naturally turn because of his easy, loose-limbed command of the facts combined with that facility that Joe Biden kicked himself around the block for noting, "articulateness?" Will he be tall? Will he be a woman?

What is "leadership," anyway?

As Justice Potter might have said, you know it when you see it (or hear it). As in the old E.F. Hutton commercial, when The Leader speaks, the rest of the room falls silent and listens.

Sometimes this is because he's making sense. Sometimes it's because he's wearing a suit. Sometimes it's because he's the loudest.

Whatever the reason, people accord him authority. He's the closest thing around to Daddy. While everyone else is scared clueless about what to do, The Leader seems sure of himself so they figure his confidence must be based on something.

Maybe he'll be an actor who played a leader in a movie. Knowing how to act the part, he will bark instructions.

"Finally we're getting somewhere," the others will think, regardless of where somewhere is.

❧   ❧

A few years ago, a band of New York City Peak Oil activists were discussing suitable crops to plant when they finally moved to their respective sustainable communities. Since New York City is in the Dark Ages when it comes to Peak Oil, these activists were, by default, leaders in the field.

But—and the activists were acutely aware of this—they were not farmers. They were novices, trying to scrape together what knowledge they could from the internet and the occasional bank-breaking weekend at an intensive Permaculture course.

So the conversation, while earnest and, by New York City standards, enlightened, fell short of providing useful information.

Until a young woman called Debbie spoke.

"Potatoes."

Her voice lacked the high-pitched excitement (the charisma factor) of the others, leaders all. And they seemed not to hear her.

But then a man who was sitting next to her proposed, "Potatoes! We forgot about potatoes!"

"Yeah, potatoes!" agreed another.

And so, by subliminal suggestion, Debbie's idea took over the conversation.

(A by-product of that evening is that I planted two potatoes on my windowsill in the hope of later writing an article called, "A Potato Grows in Brooklyn." One turned into a slimy mess; the other disappeared which perhaps means it morphed into soil. But that's another story.)

However, Debbie is not considered a leader either by the Meet-up or by herself. She just happens, time and again, to have the information everyone's looking for.

The others know this. Sometimes they ask her for advice and she provides it, as when an adolescent ventures out on his own, only to turn back to ask Mom for money. Then the Peak Oil Leaders boldly go forth proclaiming Debbie's information, having incorporated it into their rhetoric and made it their own.

৯ ৵

"We must change the paradigm!" goes the cry of the few brave souls who have for a long time seen what's coming and tried to warn those bits of the world to which they had access.

They're talking about infrastructure and the economy and other vital issues. But so far no one's addressed the assumptions on which we base our decisions, the notion that for the sake of simplicity and streamlined organization, there must be one person to whom we all look for instruction.

So it seems that when the world goes belly-up and the meek, if they know how to farm, shall inherit the earth, one thing shall emerge unscathed: that citadel, the grand social pyramid with drones at the base, some knowledgeable folk in the middle and on top, the One, True Sun to whom all others turn for enlightenment; He or She who in Ancient Greece was a god, in 20th century America was a movie star and in the 21st century will be a Peak Oil activist—the Leader.

Addendum, October, 2011: With its leaderless, myceliumlike structure, the Occupy Wall Street movement seems to have arrived at the same conclusion as is advocated here.

Gagging on Gurus

May 24, 2009

Mike Ruppert and I are on the same wavelength only going in opposite directions at the moment. As he was writing his review of Carolyn Baker's book, Sacred Demise: Walking the Spiritual Path of Industrial Civilization's Collapse,[194] I was writing this dyspeptic article on the same general subject of "spirituality."

It would appear we have different points of view on the matter, but I suspect that a glance beneath the surface would reveal a deeper convergence and harmony.

Let me also say straight out that I haven't read Carolyn's book yet. Plan to, as I greatly admire her work at From the Wilderness and on her website. From all that I know about Carolyn, she's solidly grounded in reality and is a bona fide shrink to boot so none of the comments below refer to anything like the work she does.

That said, I gotta tell you that spirituality makes me gag. Not the thing, which I wouldn't know if it fell on me, but the word. It is amorphous, vague, indulgent, meaningless and vapid. It gets us nowhere unless uttered in the company of a joint which gets some people somewhere—high, so they say—but that's another thing that doesn't work for me although I will grant that it's very real for some people.

As a word, it reeks of the West Coast.

I love the West Coast. Malibu's beautiful. Venice is a carnival. And the West Coast can't be beat for movies.

But when they start waxing spiritual on you, well... climate change can't swallow up that Venice fast enough.

What is this "spirituality" we keep hearing about in more-spiritual-than-thou tones? Is it like wealth? Legend has it that when asked how much his yacht cost, J.P. Morgan replied that if you have to ask, you can't afford it. If you have to ask what people are talking about when they talk about spirituality, you ain't got that either?

No, I ain't. I live in the real, dog-eat-dog world (a misnomer of course since dogs—faithful, good-natured creatures that they are except when nasty humans mistreat them—intuitively understand spirituality). People do things for reasons, whether they're conscious of those reasons or not. The reasons may be telic which is to say, purposeful. Or they may be etiological, driven by prior events. In other words, the reasons can lie in the past or the future or there can be a combination of both. But there are reasons and uncovering them can be helpful, if you need help.

But spirituality is a cop-out. It introduces a deus ex machina that has nothing to do with the plot. And that's cheating; doesn't work. You can't get there from here.

Herein lays the true continental divide between LA and NY. We New Yorkers are lifelong analysands. Even when we leave therapy, it doesn't leave us. We think like pseudo-shrinks. We talk like pseudo-shrinks. This is our particular way of driving each other crazy (in addition to standing in the doorway of the subway car so no one else can get on) and getting each other out of the craziness that the other pseudo-shrinks have driven us into.

It is our local "national pastime." When the emphasis is on "pseudo" you get psychobabble, which is as nauseating as any other quack remedy. But when the analysand has absorbed at least some of the lessons of therapy, you get something real.

Not Enlightenment. You don't become a Spiritual Person, one who's simply risen above the pettiness and moral squalor of this fucked up world. You get insight so that instead of levitating to the next plane, you can walk there (or at least out of your quagmire,) step by step. (It sounds as though Carolyn's book can actually help with that process.)

This rant is probably going to invite a slew of outraged, pseudo-calm "reflections" in defense of spirituality along with patient explanations and kindly guidance. Some will be published because some of you enjoy this sort of thing. Then I'll gag and that'll be that.

I know. I asked for it. Take a deep breath and count to ten. One... two.... Oh fuck it.

Everyman Mantra for the New Paradigm:
Le Roi, C'est Moi, Whether I like It or Not

October 12, 2008

Revolution is in the air. Even <u>Ben Stein</u> says so.[195]

The former Nixon speechwriter who crafted a whole persona out of a professorial drone (in the field of Economics, the "deadly science," no less) is sounding a little bewildered these days. If the old saying is true that a radical is a conservative who's been arrested, Ben's acting like a Wall Street hotshot who wakes up to find himself in a jail cell with a bunch of weirdo Peak-Oil salesmen.

Politics makes strange bedfellows. Like so many other things these days (Putin, for one), human commonality is rearing its head in the oddest places.

Which means that so is enmity.

My former enemy is now my ally so who is now my enemy? Oh, right: I am.

The head-scratching, "expert"-addicted American is going, perhaps for the first time, to have to do some independent thinking. Not grabbing the nearest sound bite and repeating it to his buddies as though it were sage counsel; not summing people up with the snappiest stereotype, but real research, uprooting all his fondest, most comforting assumptions.

Once that process begins, there is no end. The rabbit-hole of inquiry is one in which question leads only to bigger, more fundamental question. No longer can we automatically endow the older or even the more expert with authority. Like the earliest victims of AIDS who, for lack of knowledge among the medical profession, were forced to do their own research and come up with far-flung solutions which their doctors then adopted for their other patients as well, we must become the experts.

At least, expert enough to make rational decisions about our own lives. And in a world in which nothing can any longer be taken for granted, that is going to take some effort.

Where to start?

From scratch; seeking knowledge not just from the "suits," but from anyone who seems to have a handle on whatever the given problem is. The off-hand dismissal of people who lack credentials can be suicidal.

True sustainability must come hand in hand with equality. Our deeply-rooted pyramid notion of society stems from the days when pyramids were erected on the backs of slaves. It is going to have to crumble.

Ideally, what will grow in its place will follow the inherently more stable model of mushrooms. Via the intelligent design of evolution, mycelia have learned the lesson of fourth year ballet: It's easier to stand on two feet than on one toe. Thus they rely on a widespread network rather than a cynosure of unique importance.

"I am still an oak," said Jean Anouilh's magnificent hero as it died while the humble but pliable reed survived the storm. "Evolve or perish," says Mike Ruppert, referring to the human race in the face of Peak Oil. It's a bitter pill that evolution in this case may resemble, more, backpedaling in history and civilization. But people have been known to do what they needed to in order to survive. The pity in this instance is that the people who most need to compromise are the powerful who have the most to lose.

In an Infinite Cycle, Follower Becomes Leader

December 5, 2008

Below is a slightly edited email to a person important to me; otherwise I wouldn't have bothered trying to convince someone who so obviously wishes to remain HUA: (That one's hard to get by googling but you can guess. I did, when Mike first used it. It's a cops' term for a distracted driver.) This Person Important to Me had challenged the track record of FromtheWilderness.com as well as the significance of certain current events which FTW maintains are evidence of the collapse of which we had warned.

FTW, the blog and other writers correctly foresaw the Balkanization of Iraq, the disintegration of poorer countries such as Zimbabwe, the "Recession," the heightened tension between India and Pakistan and the steep and inexorable decline in oil production reported by the International Energy Agency last month, among other symptoms of global disaster too numerous to go into.

What do you think collapse looks like in the beginning? People on Madison Avenue looting Ralph Lauren? It first hits more fragile countries (think, "Latvia") before working its way up the food chain as it gathers momentum.

The U.S. has a financial situation that even the mainstream media are now comparing to the Great Depression and worse. The Peak Oilists warned of this years ago, remember?

To compare us to apocalyptic cults is superficial, arrogant bait. It derives from a wish to be cool by being a wiseass. Mark Twain said words to the effect of: "When I was fourteen, I thought my father was an idiot. When I was twenty-one, I found it remarkable how much wisdom the old man had acquired in seven years."

Instead of being an armchair critic who dismisses with a snarky soundbite, read and find out actual facts. If you're going to opt to be an Indian rather than a chief, at least choose your chief on the basis of concrete knowledge.

Hystericalmothers.com

Ever tell your son the story of the boy who didn't eat his broccoli? When he grew up, he couldn't be a soccer player and became an accountant instead. Does your daughter ignore your warnings that she might catch cold and have to miss the class play? Even though when you warned her to wear her kneepads skateboarding and she didn't, she scraped her knee so badly she had to get a shot? Do you think fear the underrated emotion and tell yourself it's what keeps rabbits alive?

Hysterical mothers, nags and anyone else who has railed against the force of will (*"I hate seatbelts!"*), you are not alone.

When a huge horse showed up at the gates of Troy, Cassandra prophesied, "No good will come of this." The Trojans branded Cassandra nuts and what happened? The horse was full of *Greeks*! Who destroyed Troy!

When Lois Gibbs told her neighbors that their homes and school were contaminated, the government said, "Everything's fine." What neighborhood was that? Love Canal!

When industrial hygienist Monona Rossol and Drs. Cate Jenkins and Marjorie Clarke warned of the toxic soup which was the air of Lower Manhattan following 9/11, did people sit up and listen? Right.

But not all the doomsayers are hysterical mothers. Few are hysterical and some aren't mothers or even women. Joel Kupferman, Hugh Kaufman, Congressman Jerrold Nadler and men on the staff of the New York Committee on Occupational Safety and Health also led the hue and cry following 9/11.

And many of the guys on the other side of the fence aren't men. Witness Whitman herself, the Darth Vader of Lower Manhattan who a few days after September 11, said, "I'm glad to reassure the people of New York that their air is safe to breathe."

So if not womanhood, what is it that distinguishes the hysterical mothers from the guys in suits?

That's right: It's the suits.

Juan Gonzalez may have been the first major journalist to cry, "Toxic!" after 9/11 but he's not a bureaucrat; hence, he doesn't wear a suit.

Joel Kupferman may be a lawyer but as he mostly hangs out at firehouses which are still contaminated from 9/11, again, no suit.

As my high school friend Elinor said: "The world is made in such a way that my mother always turns out to have been right."

So don't lose heart. Have the courage of your cautious convictions and remember the old adage: Just because you're paranoid doesn't mean they're not following you.

A Modern Variation on an Old Tale

May, 2010

Once upon a time, there was a young boy who lived in the town of Anywhere. One day his mother sent him to the woods to pick berries. On the way, he saw a wolf.

"Wolf!" cried the boy, as he ran back to the town.

"The child has an overactive imagination," said the townspeople and resumed building a road to the city where they could sell their berries.

A few days later, the same thing happened again.

"Be off!" said the townspeople to the boy whose concerns were becoming less funny by the moment, as well as more irksome.

The following week, the scene repeated itself a third time.

While the townspeople were throwing crateloads of rotten berries at the boy, the wolf bounded out of the woods and ate them all.

Occupy Wall Street

October 5, 2011

Immediate impression is of Union Square South, to whit: a throwback to the peace-and-love crowds of the sixties.

The sidewalk is arrayed with quotes from Lincoln, MLK, John Lennon, et al. Next to them lies a swirling, perhaps chemically induced, depiction of two sleeping figures in Yin/Yang arrangement or a chaste 69, if that's your turn of mind.

Down the stairs, a bazaar of characters intermingles with the press who are more laid back than usual since the event has a festive air. One coed wears a polar bear hat which may or may be intended to evoke global warming; a cheerleader from Louisiana rides a bicycle with a pink unicorn on the handlebars.

A guy in a green wig leans against a pole next to an American geezer of about sixty in the saffron robes of a Buddhist monk who talks at length to a reporter. Other media surround a guy in a beat-up hat (like Mike Ruppert's, come to think of it) who, in Lower Manhattan, comes off as a crusty eccentric. Normally the press don't give such people the time of day, much less ten minutes of tape but at Occupy Wall Street, oddity seems a desired commodity. A guy in a business suit walks around with a sign that reads: Harvard Man for Economic Justice. Another, as if to ensure the sabotaging of the whole affair, stands with a sign that reads Fart Smeller Movement.

The thing about hand-written signs is that unless you go out of your way, they end up looking like the scrawl of the Unabomber.

At the opposite end of the square, an obligatory drum and tambourine play ceaselessly. In between, a few people sleep on mattresses wrapped in plastic (a reporter says it was a rough night) but a lean, shirtless guy does some impressive yoga moves.

Amidst the circus, however, pressing issues assert themselves. The Ban Fracking movement has a strong presence with petitions circulating. Other people hold signs about student loans, taxing the wealthy or the pointlessness of elections. Among them, a woman with an intent expression weaves, bearing a flag which reads, Debt Is Slavery.

I have come with a press release which I give to the Daily News, Laura Flanders, Scottish, Spanish and Greek reporters as well as a guy from credit.com. (The major countries' media have left for the day; I'll try earlier tomorrow.) One blogger who won't divulge the website she works for, upon hearing that I'm with Collapsenet, asks if I know Max. Apparently, he's friended them on Facebook.

Some press are interested in interviews: Brazilian globo.com, a Dutch freelancer and two Chinese stations. One of the latter is represented by a reporter who has a hard time understanding the message. Predictably (since the press always veer towards "human interest") she asks, "What's your personal story?" but I don't provide one since if I did, that's the soundbite that would be chosen over the economic points.

However, she and her producer do understand English well enough to seize onto the phrase, "fiat currency." They ask if I think the root of our problem is China's manipulations of the yuan. I say, Emphatically not; it's *all* our fault. Their eyes light up. Perhaps they think that "our" means the US as opposed to China. The tape could easily be cut to make it look that way.

The other Chinese station, which is the equivalent of Bloomberg, is represented by an American stringer. This reporter understands the message perfectly and seems suitably alarmed.

Here's the press release:

Infinite Growth Is Not Possible on a Finite Planet

We are all guilty.
Our economic paradigm depends on infinite growth.
The system of interest on which banking rests demands this growth but compounding the problem (no pun intended) is

our reliance on fiat currency; that is, currency which is not related to a finite substance such as gold but currency which derives its value from the government's good word.

This is faith-based economics; it works only as long as the faith of the populace in that government. How is that faith doing these days?

As if these problems weren't enough, our economic paradigm also relies on fractional reserve banking which allows banks to have on hand only a fraction of their deposits. In the event of a run on the bank, everyone finds out exactly how much—or how little—that fraction is.

Finally, the control over money is not, as the founding fathers intended, in the hands of the people through their Congress. It was given to the Federal Reserve—despite the name, a private entity—over Christmas vacation on the eve of World War 1. The Fed has the power to create money out of thin air. This eventually finds its way into the hands of borrowers who then have to work to pay it back as well as work to pay back the interest which the Fed is then obliged to create out of some more thin air. Fortunately, there is no shortage of thin air.

All this must change. We are at a point in history which requires us to face these issues and the profound paradigm shift they call for. Our survival depends on it.

Wall Street must pay. But that does not mean that then we can go back to business as usual. The earth will not allow us to do that. Over the past century and a half we have used approximately half the oil ever created over the last four billion years. The second half is far more difficult to produce. Remember what happened when BP tried to extract it from the Gulf of Mexico.

How are we going to use the oil that remains? For pesticides to help feed the global population of 6.9 billion people? To fuel our factories to put people back to work?

Or to maintain our nuclear facilities so we don't have more Fukushimas erupting around the world?

Whatever our decision, we will not be able to continue as we have been, eating food which has traveled an average of 1500 miles before it is consumed.

These are issues that need to be faced squarely and understood in relation to each other and to the big picture. Our leaders, including "experts" in various disciplines, have been telling us lies or half-truths (which are more insidious.) We must educate ourselves or else we will be in the position of the blind man trying to describe the elephant by holding its trunk. And these days, that's a dangerous position to be in.

October 6, 2011

There was a marked "morning after" feeling at Occupy Wall Street yesterday; inevitable, given the conflagration on Wednesday. Organizer Victoria Sobel who, according to reports, is recognizable by her hair which is blond on one side and brunette on the other, was nowhere to be found. The press trucks were lined up across the street but their occupants also not around.

More than the usual number of people still slept on their air mattresses. Under a plastic sheet suspended two feet above the ground, a figure rustled; getting dressed? Hey, have these guys taken showers in the last three weeks?

Leaflets lay arrayed on the sidewalk with a notice that passersby should help themselves. The ones I was able to reach included Occupy Wall Street—FAQ ("Are you guys like the Tea Party?") Voting Vs. Direct Action, The Young Lords (if they're the same ones who were around three decades ago, they're no longer young,) Cointelpro—The Danger We Face, Shake Before Using and

Listening to the Land—An Interview by Derrick Jensen with Ward Churchill (the latter, of 9/11 notoriety.)

I walked around carrying a neon pink sign that read, "Infinite Growth Is Not Possible on a Finite Planet." A Unitarian minister said he'd just given a sermon on that very theme.

A middle-aged guy asked what the sign meant; then, what all these people were doing here. Since the movement has occupied headlines at least as much as it has Wall Street, I walked away. "You're not getting your message across," he taunted. Disruptive mole or are some people really that stupid?

The cleanup crew swept industriously since Brookfield Properties, which owns the site, has been making ominous noises about the "dangerous" unsanitary conditions that they say are mounting.

Then I walk straight into a familiar face... Greg Greene of End of Suburbia! We met when he taped the Peak Oil Conference Jan Lundberg suggested and I mc'ed in 2005.

With him was.... Jim Kunstler! He was a star speaker at that conference (as was Mike; it's where they first met.)

Jim was watching two twenty-somethings perform their morning Yoga routine; the girl, balancing on the boy's feet. Jim's just written another book and was going to speak at an event of Manhattan developers. Did they have any idea what they were in for?

"What do you think of the criticism that Occupy Wall Street hasn't unified their message?" he asked.

"The movement's been sabotaged."

"I heard there was Wall Street money getting in there."
"Same thing that happened at 9/11 Truth."

"I didn't have much sympathy for them," he replied.

"I know you didn't; and that's *why* you didn't."

"Let me ask you another metaphysical question," he went on, after a pause. "What's going to happen to Lloyd Blankfein's cappuccino machine?"

"Is there a problem with it?"

"It's taking over the world."

"But what'll happen when he runs out of coffee to fuel it?" I sobbed. No, that last line's made up. Too bad.

Telesur, a Venezuelan TV station, ask for an interview at 12:30 so I spend the intervening time practising the soundbite which the reporter has translated into Spanish for me. Then a ventriloquist's dummy from "The Daily" (as distinguished from The Daily Show) also asks for an interview. He has doleful eyes which helps his guests overcome a natural disinclination to converse with plastic.

ೞ ೮

October 7, 2011

Yesterday, OWS was back in gear after their hangover of the day before. Fresh murals (for want of a better word) lay spread out on the Broadway sidewalk, packed with figures and symbolism as in a Brueghel painting, but executed in the style of a comicbook.

Down the stairs, thousands milled or squatted on the sidewalk with chalk so that it was impossible not to step on someone's artwork.

A guy walked around with a sign on a flattened out cardboard box: Let Them Eat Twinkies.

I raised my neon pink sign aloft—Infinite Growth Is Not Possible on a Finite Planet—when a man with a videocamera on his shoulder pointed it out to his friend.

"I like your sign," said the friend. "I've been working on this issue for years. What do you do?"

"I write about these issues. How about you?"

"I write about these issues."

Pause. "What's your name?" I asked.

"Chris Martenson."

!

I introduced myself.

"I was one of the cameramen on Collapse," said the guy holding the videocamera, Livio Sanchez.

"What do you think of this event?" asked Chris.

"It's been sabotaged."

At this, a Wall Street Occupier manning a stand next to us perked up, remaining alert to the rest of our conversation.

"There's lots of real substance here," I went on, "but plenty of lunacy as well."

"That way the media can choose what to focus on," Chris elaborated.

"Can you stay later?" I asked. "They have a general assembly where you could speak."

The OWS guy chimed in now, enthused at the notion of Chris' maybe joining Danny Schechter who's been talking about his new film.

Introducing himself as Eco or Devon or several other names, he explained the protocol for speaking. It was the third time I'd heard the rundown and each time has been different but I'm going to try to go some night that I'm not working.

Since the group doesn't want to disturb the neighborhood with applause, they wiggle their fingers instead. Hand (not arm) raised means agreement; down, disagreement; held out evenly in front, on the fence.

All decisions are arrived at by consensus.

"When you're thoroughly infiltrated, that'll sabotage you," I said.

Eco or Devon then explained the sign to block irrelevant comments and the sign to protest the block. Makes you think: All that signing must help keep the community peaceful. Do the deaf who opt for sign language get into as many fights as other people?

We didn't need all that information but Eco's enthusiasm was endearing. The movement has the gush of youth and the grownups, via the media, who encourage them with their attention. What will happen when either side decides to move on?

ڡ   ڡ

October 8, 2011

Tonight I went to Zucotti Park via the West Side subway line which meant getting out at the Stock Exchange.

A small but intense demonstration was taking place across the street. A poster condemning Bank of America had been stuck in the door of the building on the corner underneath a silhouette of what was probably Lenin. On the steps, a topless woman stood with her back to the public. She was covered in body paint which a guy who was the envy of a hefty per cent of the crowd refreshed periodically. On the corner, the blackrobed death figure denouncing nuclear power did his slow-mo moves. Three cops sat atop motionless horses in the middle of the street, their mere presence keeping the crowd subdued.

A few blocks up, the park was hopping, with thousands of people packed in and spilling onto the street, possibly because of the warm weather, possibly because it's Saturday night. "Still Think This Is a Fringe Movement?" read one sign. Another offered to explain OWS to any "rich dummies" who didn't get it. I picked up a flier on Anarchist Basics and noted a few Ron Paul T-shirts on various lonely-looking middle-aged men.

"Is that a Confederate flag?" I asked a guy carrying a furled, full-size flag with few visible stars. "Puerto Rico," he answered in an appropriate accent. "And Cuba."

I'd gone with the thought of speaking to the General Assembly which takes place at seven, according to most accounts. One is advised to arrive a few minutes earlier however, since you have to sign up first with the facilitator and the floor opens only after Working Group reports and other items of business, all of which can take three hours. You get priority if you belong to a minority group, which includes women, but it's still a long haul.

"Who's going to be leading the General Assembly?" I asked a young man wearing a sticker that said Sanitation.

He put his hand on my shoulder, as when a child commits a faux pas and you want to correct her gently but firmly.

"There are no leaders," he explained. "You'll see who's facilitating."

Having nothing to do but wait, I eavesdropped on a conversation to my left.

"Are they Jewish people?" an oldish man asked an Occupier, who didn't have a clue as to the answer.

He was talking about the Koch brothers, he explained when I asked. Since Mayor Koch was Jewish, were they? He was not American but he knew enough English to understand that his question would have sounded even more uncouth had he said, "Are they Jews?"

You pick your battles so I refrained from saying, "Why is it that when Bush, Rockefeller, Carnegie, Mellon, Morgan, Chase, Cheney or Rumsfeld killed and stole, nobody mentioned their ethnicity?"

Sanitation buttonholed a guy who was on his way somewhere. "I need fifty people for full-time Sanitation duty," he said. "Read my lips: Fifty people. Full time."

"Read his finger," I said. He was holding the last bite of a muffin between his thumb and index finger so he was pointing for emphasis with the middle one.

Twenty past seven and still no sign of the General Assembly, nor an explanation as to why it was delayed. Sanitation called someone to find out. Since 1500 Occupiers had marched to Washington Square, they'd had a General Assembly there so that might be it for the day.

But no! Wait! someone else shouted. They're on their way back! Those sirens must be their police escort!

The General Assembly would take place at eight.

Back to waiting.

Sanitation stood on a table and shouted: Mike check!

No response.

Sanitation (not shouting, which constitutes sotto voce for this crowd:) Fuck all of you; let's try it again: (shouting) Mike check!

Chorus: Mike check! Sanitation: Mike check! Chorus: Mike check!

Sanitation (interspersed with Chorus): I need a staff! Of fifty people! For full-time sanitation duty! We're a massive! Group of people! And we create! A massive amount! Of waste! Sanitation! Is the bottom line!

Snappy but literally true. Sanitation is the movement's Achilles heel at the moment, the weakness that could get them thrown out by Brookfield Properties.

Guy in front of the main flower bed in the park: Mike check! Chorus: Mike check! Guy: Mike check! Chorus: Mike check!

Guy: (interspersed with repetitions from Chorus) I want! To read a poem! By Langston Hughes!

He read the poem, the chorus throwing the message to people further back.

"Or you can do that," reflected a guy called Rick, who knew what I was waiting for.

He was sitting at a marble table of which there are many scattered throughout the park. The kids manning the press area use them for laptops. This evening, other kids were using them for chess.

I stood on the table and shouted, to the responses of the chorus: Mike check! Mike check! We must change! Our economic! Paradigm! Etc.

The crowd repeated the phrases with their usual good-humored gusto. It's impassioning, if that's a word, to shout your lungs out. The North Koreans are onto something.

               ஒ   ல

October 11

If anyone was expecting a Columbus Day lull at OWS today, they were soon put straight. The place only gets more packed. The signs have tripled overnight. One, "Vive la Revolution!" is written with the trademark V of Anonymous and in the middle of Zucotti Park (Liberty Park, to some,) shapeless bundles are piled to the first branches of the fledgling trees. You pick your way to the other side of the park by stepping over plastic sheets which may or may not have someone buried underneath. These are people of infinite faith as well as fatigue lying here. How many times have they been awakened by someone stepping on their head?

The scene evokes the streets of New Delhi; the only thing missing, the hibachis on which the inhabitants—if that's an appropriate word—cook dinner.

The protesters have changed complexion since Saturday; a smaller percentage of enthusiastic twenty-somethings since the arrival of more bedraggled, ageless types. A familiar smoke chokes the air.

Where have all these Hippies been for the last thirty years? A pink-haired wraith of notable inarticulateness proves popular with the press.

Some people have brought their dogs who are presumably living off the scraps of the wholesome buffet laid out in the middle of the park.

The drums have multiplied too; one set, a shiny red of the sort not seen since the days of Lawrence Welk. A donation from a nightclub in the Catskills?

Guy serving lunch: "Mike check!" Chorus: "Mike check!"

The familiar refrain, like a call to prayer. "We're moving! This table! Over! To that tree!" Like the phrases, the pointing gesture is mirrored by the chorus.

Sanitation seems to have gotten their fifty full-time staff members in addition to some twelve-year-old volunteers who had the day off from school. The afternoon shift is in evidence industriously transferring garbage with gloved hands into black trash bags. But one of them confirms my suspicion that there's no way they can clean under the mountains of stuff—including indoor (rather than air-) mattresses—strewn around the park.

All it would take to sabotage this whole movement is two mice.

I ask a sober-looking kid a nagging question: A few of the local restaurants have been hospitable about the use of the bathroom but how is everyone taking a shower?

Some people have friends in New York, she says, and Sanitation is working on getting access to "public showers," a facility which I've never seen or heard evidence of though my mother used public baths in her childhood. But the girl herself hasn't had a shower since she got here. She washes her hair in whatever sink she can and for the rest, uses handi-wipes.

I offer her the use of my shower though tell her not to tell her friends as I'd like to meet them first. She hugs me in gratitude but so far there's no message from her.

Oggi, the Italian newspaper, does an interview, as do Telemundo and Purple (i.e., both blue and red) America. NBC has been consistently snooty once they've gotten the gist of the press release but a reporter at CBS reads it all the way through; probably, she is set straight as soon as she gets back to the studio.

෨   ෬

October 12, 12:30 P.M.
59th Street and Fifth Avenue

Three hundred marchers; almost as many cameras and notepads.

This crowd seems more locally based than OWS regulars; some signs are in Spanish and there's an infusion of African Americans.

Sign on a cardboard box: I'll Show You What Trickles Down.

A rumor goes out that there's a naked woman among us. No, just topless. Where? The blond woman at the top of the steps where one of the organizers is talking to reporters.

When the march starts and I find myself next to this woman I ask her, "Why are you wearing a mustache?" A pencil line of the sort people used to draw on the Mona Lisa adorns her upper lip.

"It's part of a drag queen character I do," she replies. Her answer seems to be true as she's wearing the pants of a man's business suit, but it only raises more questions along the lines of, What the hell does that have to do with this march?

The anti-fracking contingent hand out fliers for a demo at Cuomo's office. Website: www.unitedforaction.org.

Another upcoming event is to take place Saturday: A march to a Chase Branch where OWS will "support customers" who are closing their accounts. Perhaps this is the sort of event Chase had in mind when they donated $4 million to NYPD.

Off we go, chanting with determination which at times veers into bloodthirstiness: "Eat the rich! Take another bite out of that sonofabitch" followed by, "We're coming over for dinner." A conversation nearby muses on whether eating the rich would raise your cholesterol.

Every so often the topless woman calls out, "Titties are for entertainment, not protest." The marchers ignore her but she gets two radio interviews. Is this deliberate disinfo, simple exhibitionism or both? Will listeners understand she represents the antithesis of what the march is about?

First stop, an imposing building about a block up. Rumor goes out this is "J.P. Dimon's" residence, an understandable conflation of Jamie Dimon's name and the bank he runs. Someone else says it's Murdoch's; not everyone got the menu of residences where we're dropping by.

On to the next Fifth Avenue residence before heading down "Consulate Row" where employees of the Pakistani and Congolese consulates watch uncertainly from the front steps.

Two reporters stand on a low wall in front of one of the townhouses, snapping photos.

"Get down!" the cops order.

"The reporters could get us in trouble," a marcher notes.

Over to Park Avenue for the next three ports of call.

"This is better than at Foley Square," a reporter observes. "There, the cops had us penned in; here, they have less control."

They do seem a little worried about that and compensate by becoming more aggressive.

This is not a venue to get across the message of infinite growth not being possible on a finite planet; the press are totally focused on the march itself. But CBS does an interview to store for a lull in OWS activities. Ditto, the Guardian and a reporter from a financial website who has never heard of fractional reserve banking.

A few people from the neighborhood join us (not everyone here is super-rich). But our loudest support comes from administrative workers and possibly some clergy who cheer us on from the second storey windows of Park Avenue Christian Church where some of the world's fattest cat bankers attend every Sunday.

$\wp$ $\wp$

October 13, 2011

OWS is hard at work cleaning up in preparation for tomorrow's showdown, the motto of the day having apparently become, "We are all Sanitation now." A guy mops the tiles with sudsy water that smells benign although others are taking no chances, using toxic-smelling cleansers. A coed scrapes away at one of those ubiquitous mounds of dirty gum ground into the pavement that besmirch the city everywhere as though it has been raining mud. This is not OWS garbage; it's probably been there for decades. (When was the last time you saw someone chewing gum in New York?) Even the piles of clothes, mattresses and unidentifiable Stuff have been moved to clean underneath.

"Where will you go when the cops show up?" I ask a woman in an eighteenth century dress and wig.

"Who said we're leaving?" she replies archly.

"What's the plan?"

A guy with a gleam in his eye chimes in, "We're going to hold hands in a circle around the park. Come at 6:30 A.M."

"Are you Marie Antoinette?" I ask the courtier.

"Yes."

"You know she never really said that about cake; it's just a way to deflect the attention onto a woman."

"I know."

One regular of the protests is a young man who has no arms, though he does have hands. He uses them to play drums on an overturned plastic bucket which makes a lot more noise than you'd guess. Other days he may be found dancing, shirtless, on the park wall or engaged in some other highly visible activity which bears no obvious relationship to OWS grievances.

Today, shirtless again, he carries a sign which offers a kiss to any "ladies" who might find him cute.

"Has anyone taken you up on your offer?" I ask him.

"Three ladies," he replies with a grin.

The cleaning goes on in spite of the rain and the thousands of visitors criss-crossing the park, dirtying the ground as soon as it's been mopped. This movement is high on will and energy, shorter on understanding. People prefer to think in concrete images rather than abstractions, in terms of right now rather than any point in the supposedly uncertain future. Graphs of declining resources are no fun; they bring back memories of high school math class. Focusing on the super-rich provides a target for our rage and frustration. Not crunching the numbers enables us to think that toppling the bastard in charge of JP Morgan Chase or Goldman Sachs will be like breaking the piñata, allowing the goodies to fall among the unjustly deprived and deserving poor—problem solved.

People are angry and want to express it; they do not want to think, particularly when the conclusion is unpleasant. A Blood, Sweat and Tears speech will work only when they see that there is no alternative.

ൠ   ൠ

October 19

In between actions, as the last few days have been, Occupy never has less than a bustling air; part flea market, part Renaissance fair.

The occupiers have been using their down time to set up house. Along with the usual Information and Media areas as well as the buffet of veggies, rolls and unidentifiable but intriguing dishes in the middle (as always, the kitchen is the heart of the home), there's now a "comfort station" with racks of jackets and boxes of shoes to function as a communal closet. And against the Liberty Street wall, the library grows daily.

The Sanitation Team is sweeping industriously and the drums are more subdued today, perhaps the result of another bargain struck with Brookfield Properties as a condition of staying.

At the entrance to the park, activists stand holding their hand-wrought signs, whether earnest or irrelevant ("I [heart] you") while in the middle of the camp, bloated guys lie on their makeshift beds, not all of them looking tired. Is resentment growing towards the layabouts? For that matter, why haven't the homeless figured out this is a place to get free food? [Note from several months later: They soon do.]

A small crowd is snapping photos of two topless young women having their torsos painted with black lines against a pink "background" for one, purple for the other. A couple of days ago a young man stood on the sidewalk in his skivvies but it'll probably be a while before we arrive to find a guy getting his butt painted.

There are fewer press around at times like these but those who are may be more receptive to talking about fundamental problems with the economy. Yesterday, I talked to the Japanese. The journalist, whose English was limited, asked about "99%" but I didn't answer because that would ensure that the main point would never get aired.

        ❧   ☙

October 24, 2011

The large orange sculpture at the south east corner of the park is barricaded off; apparently, someone tried to climb it.

Down the steps, in the belly of the park itself, tents have sprouted overnight like mushrooms. I comment on this to a guy standing in front of his blue one. The rules have relaxed, he says, but it sounds more like a surmise than a fact.

"What are you going to do when winter comes?" I ask him.

"I don't know; do you have any ideas?"

"I haven't thought about it; do you?"

"Well, I don't know how it'll go over but I think we should all go to the pound and everyone get a dog."

Several hundred dogs... Unlikely to sit well with Community Board One which is complaining that occupiers themselves are defecating on their doorsteps. (How can I sabotage thee? Let me count the ways.) The businesses nearby that have been hospitable with their bathroom facilities do, after all, close for the night.

The drumming is more subdued than usual because the perennial band at the west end of the park has vanished. Another result of negotiations with Brookfield Properties? A sign written on a flattened cardboard box sets me straight: No, the drums were stolen.   ·

While the 500 inhabitants of the park were looking the other way? (The next day, the drums are back.)

A nerdy, middle-aged guy stands next to a banner with the CNBC logo on it beneath which is written, "Speaker's Corner." The guy is clearly not a reporter, at least, not of the usual stripe; he's camera-, tape recorder- and notepad-free as well as utterly passive but his shirt, also embossed with the CNBC logo, confirms this is not a hoax.

"Would you like a press release on our economic paradigm of infinite growth?" I ask him.

"All right. Would you like to speak?"

Turns out, this is the equivalent of a soap box in Hyde Park, only CNBC is enhancing the effect a thousand-fold by running a live stream.

Like me, the people swarming by are oblivious to the opportunity; thus the camera, perched on the roof of a van across the street, is recording minutes, if not hours on end, of the crowd passing before its fixed eye. Anyone seeing this at home would instantly change the channel.

"OK." What the hell.

"Stand here." He indicates a platform big enough for one person.

I do my spiel. For anyone who gives a rat's ass, scroll down to the 17th video, 1:50 in. The accompanying paragraph begins, "A man in a hat."[196]

You can't see it on the tape because the unmanned camera is stationary but some people do gather and stay to listen. One of them turns out to be a reporter from China Daily who afterwards asks for an interview. So maybe this wasn't a total farce after all.

ço   ළ

November 13, 2011

Took the day off work today to go down to Occupy Wall Street where I'd been invited to lead a Teach-In as part of their Peak Planet Conference. A panel including a woman from the Bolivian water wars met from 2-4 in the atrium of 60 Wall, the Deutsche Bank building, a few doors down from the Museum of American Finance. This being OWS, they left it to me to decide at the moment the Teach-In was to begin whether it would remain indoors or move back to Zucotti. An audience member pointed emphatically at the floor so I said, "Here."

Ben Zolno of New Message Media led a simultaneous Teach-In on Peak Resources and asked if we should combine groups, which we ended up doing.

Our smallish assembly was extremely well informed so the challenge was to tell them something they didn't already know. I had decided on the topic of The Big Picture which, if you've been reading these pages faithfully, you know is our economic paradigm of infinite growth. I said that if you don't bear that in mind at all times, you might gain a victory here or there but collapse will overtake you anyway; you'll win the battle but lose the war.

OWS has cornered the media market for the time being so to project these messages to the world at large, I suggested several future events:

1. Occupy the Suburbs. Get the message, "Food, Not Lawns" into the mainstream.

2. Occupy the Schools. Bring practical skills back into good repute and the education system.

3. Occupy the Military/Industrial Complex. That one's a gargantuan project but it represents a step for OWS in the direction of connecting the dots between the banks and the corporations.

The Only Thing We Have to Fear Is the Fear of Being Uncool

April 19, 2009

From revelers at a rock concert in Colombia to European farmers to Indian engineering students; from the redundant "unrest" at prisons to the oxymoronic "patient riots" at a hospital in South Africa, the natives are restless. Some, like 1,500 farmers in India, the birthplace of passive resistance, have turned that unrest on themselves by committing suicide.

Whether it's over the economic crisis, water, food, jobs, bonuses, Bernie Madoff, octuplets or perverts keeping young girls—offspring or otherwise—in a dungeon for years on end, people are outraged.

We may all be Madoffs as Nouriel Roubini maintains, but some are a deeper shade than others. Even Madoff himself pales in comparison to the economic system in which most of us have colluded, with whatever degree of understanding or willful ignorance. And some of those who have least benefited, like my students from the most far-reaching corners of the earth, are Madoff wannabes, pursuing the American dream of sipping the Kool-Aid at the last banquet of civilization-as-we-have-known-it.

What makes Madoff so mesmerizing is the way in which he resembles us, like a grotesque reflection in a funhouse mirror. In his recent isolation he has even managed to twist his self-image into a heroic one. God help us if he's justified for that will mean he's taking the fall for some even worse monsters who remain at large.

The Security and Exchange Commission, for instance. Like the idiot in the old saw which maintains that intelligent people talk about ideas; average folk, about events and idiots about people, the public fixates on Madoff because he's a human being they can see; even, at some level, identify with. The SEC is a deliberately low-key, boring institution, not the stuff on which the tabloid mentality thrives.

"But who could have foreseen this crisis?" goes the hackneyed refrain. (Echoes of, "9/11 was unprecedented.")

"Anyone who looked," shoots back the retort.

That is, anyone who did more than go through the motions of looking. Real looking means asking the basic questions.

Like Bethany McClean who started the unraveling of Enron by asking, "What does Enron actually *do* to make money?" Like Nobel Laureate Richard Feynman whose wife prodded him to join the team investigating the Challenger disaster by saying, "There will be lots of intelligent people asking intelligent questions. You will be the one to ask the *stupid* questions."

Rather than becoming more suspect over time, the scenario of bumbling, Keystone Cop-like agencies gets reinforced. If it could happen on 9/11, it could happen in the EPA afterwards and later, with foreclosures. If it could happen in those three cases, well, that just proves how susceptible oversight agencies can be. So why should we be surprised it happened at the SEC? But rather than focus on the sorry past, let us learn from our mistakes and pass legislation to ensure that it Never Happens Again.

The one thing people are unwilling to do is probe. To do so is to strike out on your own, estrange yourself from your fellow man. To question the status quo is by definition uncool. In the minds of your friends, you find yourself keeping company with those kids on the retard bus, the conspiracy theorists. This attitude is a holdover from the Middle Ages when you either went to church with everyone else or, if you dared question the prevailing wisdom, got excommunicated. It was part of the genius of the church to recognize that to hold onto its power, it had to entwine itself with the here and now. The hereafter is an abstraction but alienation from one's immediate fellows is hard for anyone to take. Thus do *mores* (customs) pass themselves off as morals and ethics emerge out of the ethos of the time.

But just in case a "heretic" was willing to take his lumps and head off to the woods to cultivate his "garden," God-fearing folk threw in torture and death as well.

We think we're past all that but it's only that the religion has changed. No longer do we object to Commies, queers or atheists (at least in New York.) If we believe in God, it's a merciful one, so we can afford to forget about him except when we need him.

The God we aspire to is Success with its accoutrements: money, power and fame. In its pursuit we worship myriad lesser gods like Hindu idols: Alec Baldwin, Tom Cruise, et al. Having achieved success, they have proved they're "smart" and thus find themselves opining on the war in Afghanistan or what to do about the black bile currently disgorging itself into the Gulf of Mexico. If they decide to run for office, they have the head start of name recognition.

So ingrained is our worship of anyone who appears on a screen that people who consider themselves cosmopolitan, open-minded liberals now get the heebie jeebies when it comes to questioning the major media whose genius is that it gives the illusion of choice, a smorgasbord of ideas. You can have the red candidate or the blue. They argue so they can't be two sides of the same coin.

Anyway, if it's all a big conspiracy, how come no one's blown the whistle?

I will answer from the issue of which I have the most detailed, first-hand experience as it is as good an example as any of how the authorities get away with it.

After 9/11, countless legislative hearings as well as three scientific panels were held to investigate the extent of the contamination resulting from the disaster and to come up with solutions.

The EPA was present at all these events to answer the questions of the visiting scientists. To my knowledge, none of those scientists was paid for his or her services although most received their agency or university salary. To have been called to serve in this capacity was an honor or at least a civic obligation, the thinking man's jury duty.

Also present were members of the Community whose function was to point out to those same scientists where the EPA were...uh, leaving out some critically pertinent facts.

"You underestimate the capacity of people to be stupid," I was told by friends concerning the government's actions following 9/11.

Not one of these friends was at any of the hearings; nor had they read From the Wilderness or other reputable 9/11 websites.

But having attended and testified at every meeting of every scientific panel and most legislative hearings held through c. 2005, I can assure you that whistles were blown, and loudly; and that not only the government agency being assailed but also some professors at august universities and some scientists whose hallmark is supposedly objectivity, persistently responded to the whistles by putting metaphorical cotton in their ears or by blowing an even louder, if equally metaphorical, tuba.

As with certain jokes, you had to be there. Every weapon in the arsenal of skullduggery was brought to bear, some of which have been described in this book.

By way of recapitulation: They lied outright; but more often they were a model of passive aggression, burying incriminating data in thousands of irrelevant pages, testing for the wrong substance or, if the right one, performing the wrong test with the wrong equipment in the wrong place, the wrong way.

The vast majority of people roll over for this because, outraged though they be, they do not feel up to the task of educating themselves.

The resurgence of religion is happy to step in with the antidote it has always offered: In place of knowledge, faith. In fact, so highly regarded is "faith" that to question it by the pursuit of knowledge is an insult to God.

Welcome back, Dark Ages; when the rise of the Church squelched the mathematical and geometric discoveries of Classical Greece which had been on its way to recognizing the heliocentricity of the solar system.

This, in the age of the Internet when knowledge is more equitably available than ever before.

Life copies high school. The football hero and the prom queen are the Jungian archetypes of our time. (All right, *my* time; amend accordingly.) What people haven't figured out is that the football hero and the prom queen may not remain on top of the heap and that what seems gauche today may be the ultracool of tomorrow.

To question the EPA in 2001 or Madoff in 2006 was geeky. Now it's cliché. To be truly cool, you can't be a member of the crowd; you have to lead it.

Links

http://www.chrismartenson.com ⊕ (Especially the Crash Course and its links page)

http://cluborlov.blogspot.com ⊕ Website for Dmitri Orlov, best known for his explication of the difference between the collapse of the former Soviet Union and the soon to be former United States. Guess which empire comes out ahead.

www.CollapseNet.com ⊕ Site for World News Desk and Mike Ruppert's analysis

www.dailyreckoning.com ⊕ Witty articles on the economy by Bill Bonner and Co.

http://www.energybulletin.net/primer.php ⊕ Peak Oil primer

www.fromthewilderness.com ⊕ Founded by Mike Ruppert and chronicling the CIA/drug connection, the involvement of the United States in 9/11, etc.

www.futurescenarios.org ⊕ Analysis of Peak Oil & Climate Change by Permaculture founder David Holmgren.

www.historycommons.org ⊕ A source for history that has been suppressed in the mainstream news

http://homebiome.com/index.php?top=resources ⊕ Excellent source for Permaculture links

http://kunstler.com ⊕ Website for James Howard Kunstler, author of The Long Emergency

www.lifeaftertheoilcrash.net ⊕ Seminal Peak Oil website with vital links

www.mikeruppert.blogspot.com ⊕ Former blog for me and Mike Ruppert www.oilempire.us   ✢ Treasure trove on 9/11, the Kennedy assassination and other scars on US history

http://www.peakoil.net/   ✢ Website for Colin Campbell who coined the term "Peak Oil"

http://permaculture.org.au/   ✢ Website for Geoff Lawton, key figure in foundation of Permaculture

http://ranprieur.com   ✢ Absorbing, original, personal essays on Permaculture, living off the grid, etc.

http://www.ricefarmer.blogspot.com   ✢ Website of key contributor to Collapsenet.com

http://www.thomhartmann.com   ✢ Author of Unequal Protection

www.webofdebt.com   ✢ Excellent economic analysis for the layperson.

www.wtceo.org   ✢ World Trade Center Environmental Organization. This website is still up in cyberspace but may require more than one effort involving various permutations of "http" and "www".

Films and Books

The Ascent of Money: Niall Ferguson

Crossing the Rubicon: Michael C. Ruppert

Confronting Collapse: Michael C. Ruppert

The Century of the Self: Adam Curtis' illuminating history of advertising.

The Power of Nightmares: Adam Curtis' history of the other side of the coin of advertising, war propaganda.

My Voice Will Go With You: The Teaching Tales of Milton H. Erickson, edited by Sidney Rosen.

CoLLapse: Chris Smith's documentary on Mike Ruppert's world-view.

Talks and books by Karen Armstrong, ex-nun and iconoclastic religious historian and memoirist; Richard Dawkins, biologist and Leonard Susskind, physicist; Derren Brown, hypnotist.

Endnotes

Note: A few links are no longer accessible.

1   CNN Wire Staff, "Radioactive Water leak from Reactor Stopped," http://webcache.googleusercontent.com/search?q=cache:iT9MHV8 CtFgJ:articles.cnn.com/2011-04-05/world/japan.nuclear.reactors_ 1_radioactive-water-fukushima-daiichi-nuclear-plant-tokyo-electric %3F_s%3DPM:WORLD+japan+%22hundred+thousand+times%2 2+%22radioactive%22&cd=1&hl=en&ct=clnk&gl=us&source=w ww.google.com.

2   Jack Mirkinson, "Paul Krugman: Fake Alien Invasion Would End Economic Slump," *The Huffington Post*, first posted on August 15, 2011, http://www.huffingtonpost.com/2011/08/15/paul-krugman-fake-alien-invasion_n_926995.html.

3   Lecture from series on the future of energy sponsored by the University of Wyoming's Ruckelshaus Institute of Environment and Natural Resources, http://webcache.googleusercontent.com/se arch?q=cache:v1fe1M4Pv5YJ:www.copvcia.com/free/ww3/09300 5_world_stories.shtml+%22future+of+energy+sponsored+by+the+ University+of+Wyoming's+Ruckelshaus+Institute+of+Environme nt+and+Natural+Resources%22&cd=1&hl=en&ct=clnk&gl=us&s ource=www.google.com.

4   M. King Hubbert, "Nuclear Energy and the Fossil Fuel," Shell Development Company Source Drilling and Production Practice (American Petroleum Institute, 1956).

    Kenneth S. Deffeyes, *Hubbert's Peak: The Impending World Oil Crisis* (Princeton NJ, Princeton University Press, 2001).

5   Cutler Cleveland and Robert Costanza, "Energy Return on Investment" (EROI). In *Encyclopedia of Earth* (Washington, D.C.: Environmental Information Coalition, National Council for Science and the Environment), first published in the Encyclopedia of Earth, September 18, 2006, last revised April 16, 2008, accessed

September 16, 2008, http://www.eoearth.org/article/Energy_return _on_investment_(EROI).

[6]   M. King Hubbert, "Exponential Growth as a Transient Phenomenon in Human History," in *Valuing the Earth*, eds. Herman Daley and Kenneth Townsend (Cambridge, Mass: MIT University Press, 1993).

[7]   Marcella S. Kreiter, "What's the Real Answer to Replacing Oil?" United Press International, May 29, 2011, http://www.upi.com/Bu siness_News/Consumer-Corner/2011/05/29/Consumer-Corner-Wh ats-the-real-answer-to-replacing-oil/UPI-63841306657800/#ixzz1i WPmUizS.

[8]   Chris Martenson, Ph.D., *The Crash Course: The Unsustainable Future of Our Economy, Energy and Environment* (John Wiley and Sons, Inc., 2011), 160.

[9]   Ben Aris and Duncan Campbell, "How Bush's Grandfather Helped Hitler's Rise to Power," *The Guardian*, September 25, 2004, http://www.guardian.co.uk/world/2004/sep/25/usa.secondworldwar.

John Loftus and Mark Aarons, *The Secret War Against the Jews* (New York: St Martin's Press, 1994), 44–67.

"The pharmaceutical industry and the German National Socialist Regime: I.G.   Farben   and   pharmacological   research," http://www.biomedsearch.com/nih/pharmaceutical-industry-Germa n-National-Socialist/19125905.html.

[10]   Jonathan Charles, "Former Zyklon-B maker goes bust," November 10, 2003, http://news.bbc.co.uk/2/hi/business/3257403.stm.

[11]   Robert L. Hirsch, "The Inevitable Peaking of World Oil Production," *Atlantic Council of the United States*, Bulletin, Vol. XVI, No. 5, October. 2005, 1-9, http://www.acus.org/docs/051007-Hirsch_World_Oil_Production.pdf; http://www.acus.org/docs/0510 07-Hirsch_World_Oil_Production.pdSenior.

[12]   Robert L. Hirsch (SAIC), Roger Bezdek, Robert Wendling, "Peaking of World Oil Production: Impacts, Mitigation and Risk Management," Washington, DC, US Department of Energy, 2005, accessed June 21, 2011, http://www.netl.doe.gov/publications/othe rs/pdf/oil_peaking_netl.pdf.

[13]   "Good-bye American Dreamland," www.Culturechange.org, May 20, 2005, Jan Lundberg, quoted by Congressman Roscoe Bartlett.

[14]   Dimitry Orlov, *Reinventing Collapse: The Soviet Example and American Prospects* (New Society Publishers, 2008).

[15]   Dimitry Orlov, "The Five Stages of Collapse," *ClubOrlov* (blog), February 22, 2008, http://cluborlov.blogspot.com/2008/02/five-stages-of-collapse.html.

[16]   WKYC-TV, "Ashtabula County: Judge tells residents to 'Arm themselves,' " April 9, 2010, http://www.wkyc.com/news/local/news _article.aspx?storyid=133951&catid=3.

[17]   Tony Galli, "Police stand down to gun-toters on Madison's State Street," WKOW, Madison, Wisc, April 8, 2010, accessed June 21, 2011, http://www.wkow.com/Global/story.asp?S=12280761.

[18]   Robert L. Hirsch, et al., "Peaking of World Oil Production: Impacts, Mitigation, & Risk Management," Washington, DC, US Department of Energy, 2005, accessed June 21, 2011, http://www. netl.doe.gov/publications/others/pdf/oil_peaking_netl.pdf.

[19]   "Court Backs Quick Permits for Mountain Coal Mines," *New York Times*, November 24, 2005, accessed June 21, 2011, http://query.nytimes.com/gst/fullpage.html?res=9D05E7D81631F9 37A15752C1A9639C8B63&scp=1&sq=Courts%20Back%20Quic k%20Permits%20for%20Mountain%20Coal%20Mines&st=cse.

[20]   Kenneth S. Deffeyes, *Hubbert's Peak: The Impending World Oil Crisis* (Princeton NJ: Princeton University Press, 2001).

[21]   David Pimentel, "Effects of Population Explosion on Environment and Food Production," Carrying Capacity Network, accessed June 21, 2011, http://www.carryingcapacity.org/alerts/pimentel.html.

[22] "Stevens v. Food," accessed June 21, 2011, http://populationmatte rs.org/wp-content/uploads/D5Food.pdf.

[23] Horace Herring, Richard York, Cutler Cleveland, "Jevons paradox" in *Encyclopedia of Earth* (Washington, D.C.: Environmental Information Coalition, National Council for Science and the Environment). First published in the *Encyclopedia of Earth* October 8, 2006; last revised date January 4, 2011, accessed June 21, 2011, http://www.eoearth.org/article/Jevons_paradox>.

[24] Oil Empire, "Peak Grain," accessed June 21, 2011, http://www.oil empire.us/peak-grain.html.

[25] Beverly Spicer, "Population and exponential growth with Dr. Albert Bartlett," *EarthSky* (blog), September 18, 2008, http://earth sky.org/human-world/population-and-exponential-growth-dr-alber t-bartlett.

[26] Karl Denninger, "The Ugly Side Of Exponents: Weekend Edition," posted October 1, 2011, http://market-ticker.org/akcs-www?post=1 95213.

[27] John Kenneth Galbraith (former Professor of Economics at Harvard), writing in *Money: Whence it Came, Where it Went* (1975).

[28] George Soros (interview), "You Need This Dirty Word, Euro Bonds," *Der Spiegel*, August 15, 2011, http://www.spiegel.de/inter national/europe/0,1518,780189-2,00.html.

[29] Tyler E. Bagwell, "The Jekyll Island duck hunt that created the Federal Reserve," Jekyll Island History, accessed June 21, 2011, http://www.jekyllislandhistory.com/federalreserve.shtml.

[30] David Feldman, "Notes: Duck Hunting, Deliberating, and Disqualification: Cheney v. U.S. District Court and the Flaws of 28 U.S.C. § 455(A)," *Public Interest Law Journal*, accessed June 21, 2011, http://www.bu.edu/law/central/jd/organizations/journals/pilj/ vol15no2/documents/15-2FeldmanNote.pdf.

[31] E. H. Brown, *Web of Debt* (Baton Rouge, LA.: Third Millennium Press, 2007).

[32] Nicholas Wapshott, *Keynes Hayek: The Clash that Defined Modern Economics* (New York: W.W. Norton, 2011), 281.

[33] Molly Grovak, "Long-Term Capital Management: An Introduction," *Bailouts* (blog), February 24, 2009 (07:39 p.m.), accessed June 21, 2011, http://picker.typepad.com/bailouts/2009/02/longterm-capital-management-an-introduction.html.

[34] Sheridan Bartlett, "$600,000,000,000,000?" *Newsweek*, October 18, 2008, accessed June 21, 2011, http://www.newsweek.com/2008/10/1 7/600-000-000-000-000.html.

[35] Bill Bonner, "Into the Wild," *The Daily Reckoning*, November 19, 2008, accessed June 21, 2011, http://www.dailyreckoning.co.uk/E conomic-Forecasts/wealth-disappears-rapid-deleveraging-continue s-35019.aspx.

[36] Vikas Bajaj and Michael M. Grynbaum, "Investors Buy U.S. Debt at Zero Yield," *New York Times*, December 9, 2008, accessed June 21, 2011, http://www.nytimes.com/2008/12/10/business/10market s.html?scp=1&sq=US+Treasuries+and+%22the+world%27s+safest %22&st=nyt.

[37] Georges Polti, *Thirty-six Dramatic Situations* (Book Jungle, 2007).

[38] Jeffrey Ball, "Peak Oil: Prominent Peaker Tells Allies to (Temporarily) Pipe Down," *Environmental Capital: Wall Street Journal Blogs*, November 14, 2008, http://blogs.wsj.com/environm entalcapital/2008/11/14/peak-oil-prominent-peaker-tells-allies-to-te mporarily-pipe-down/.

[39] http://www.threemonkeysonline.com/als/_peak_oil_production_us _energy_ department_robert_hirsch.html

[40] Stephen O'Brien, "Ireland 'will not survive fuel crisis,'" *Times Online,* February 1, 2009, http://www.timesonline.co.uk/tol/news/ world/ireland/article5627926.ece.

[41] Representative Jerrold Nadler, "Nadler, Clinton, Congressional Delegation and NYCOSH Demand that EPA 'Do its Job' on 3rd Anniversary of Damning Internal Report," press release, August 21, 2006, http://www.house.gov/list/press/ny08_nadler/NYCOSH3 rdannivEPA082106.html.

[42] Jenna Orkin, "9/11's Disastrous Precedent: The E.P.A. and a Dirty Bomb," *CounterPunch*, January 6, 2005, http://www.counterpunch .org/orkin01062005.html.

[43] http://www.projecttahs.org/tahsjsp/newscontent.jsp?newstype=4& filename= 041005112320.

[44] "RADIATION EXPOSURE DEBATE RAGES INSIDE EPA—Plan to Radically Hike Post-Accident Radiation in Food & Water Sparks Hot Dissent" (news release), Public Employees for Environmental Responsibility, April 5, 2010, http://www.peer.org/news/news_id.p hp?row_id=1325.

[45] Jerome a Paris, "Countdown to $200 Oil: International Energy Agency Says Current Prices Justified," *European Tribune*, July 1, 2008, http://www.eurotrib.com/story/2008/7/1/17430/07446.

[46] Brian O'Keefe, "Here comes $500 oil," CNN, September 22, 2008, http://money.cnn.com/2008/09/15/news/economy/500dollaroil_oke efe.fortune/index.htm. (The quote originally used for this article was for $300 oil.)

[47] Deborah Solomon, "Math is Hard: Questions for Harry Markopolos," *New York Times Magazine*, February 25, 2010, http://www.nytimes.com/2010/02/28/magazine/28fob-q4-t.html?sc p=1&sq=Math%20is%20Hard:%20Questions%20for%20Harry%2 0Markopolous&st=cse.

[48] Theodore Roscoe, *The Lincoln Assassination, April 14, 1865, Investigation of a President's Murder Uncovers a Web of Conspiracy* (New York City: Franklin Watts, Inc., 1970).

49 L. Fletcher Prouty, *JFK: The CIA, Vietnam, and the Plot to Assassinate John F. Kennedy* (New York, NY: Skyhorse Publishing, 2011).

50 L. Fletcher Prouty, "The Guns Of Dallas," http://www.john-f-kennedy.net/thegunsofdallas.htm.

"The Christchurch Star 23 November 1963," Christchurch City Libraries, http://christchurchcitylibraries.com/heritage/newspapers/star23nov1963/.

51 L. Fletcher Prouty, *The Secret: The CIA and Its Allies in Control of the United States and the World*, http://www.bilderberg.org/st/index.htm.

52 L. Fletcher Prouty, "The Guns of Dallas," http://www.ratical.com/ratville/JFK/GoD.html.

53 Jim Hershberg, "Anatomy of a Controversy, Anatoly F. Dobrynin's Meeting With Robert F. Kennedy, Saturday, 27 October 1962," reproduced with permission from The Cold War International History Project Bulletin, Issue 5, Spring 1995, http://www.gwu.edu/~nsarchiv/nsa/cuba_mis_cri/moment.htm.

54 John Judge, "Not All Conspiracies Are Created Equal," ratical.com, October 30, 2002, http://www.ratical.com/ratville/JFK/JohnJudge/notAllCequal.html.

55 James Douglass, "The Hope of Confronting the Unspeakable," speech delivered to Coalition on Political Assassinations, Dallas, Texas, November 2009, http://www.oilempire.us/jfk-unspeakable.html.

56 John Judge, "Assassination as a Tool of Fascism," speech delivered at The Fourth Reich in America, http://www.ratical.org/ratville/JFK/JohnJudge/ATF.html. A transcript of the entire conference, "The Fourth Reich in America," is available from Flatland Books, P.O. Box 2420, Fort Bragg, CA 95437.

[57] Paul Volcker (interview), "Commanding Heights," PBS, September 26, 2000, http://www.pbs.org/wgbh/commandingheight s/shared/minitext/int_paulvolcker.html#2.

[58] William Clark, "Revisited—The Real Reasons for the Upcoming War With Iraq: A Macroeconomic and Geostrategic Analysis of the Unspoken Truth," original essay, 2003, http://www.ratical.org/rat ville/CAH/RRiraqWar.html.

[59] Nathaniel Blumberg, *The Afternoon of March 30: A Contemporary Historical Novel* (Big Fork, MT: Wood Fire Ashes Press, 1984), 25.

[60] John Judge, Part II of interview, David Ratcliffe, November 18, 2000, http://www.ratical.org/ratville/JFK/JohnJudge/112600.html.

[61] Nathaniel Blumberg, *The Afternoon of March 30: A Contemporary Historical Novel* (Big Fork, MT: Wood Fire Ashes Press, 1984), 154-155.

[62] Benazir Bhutto interview by David Frost, Frost over the World, Al Jazeera English, November 02, 2007, available at http://www.youtube.com/watch?v=f1uLdmct8_E.

[63] Ewen MacAskill, "Bhutto assassination could have been prevented, says UN report: Pakistan officials condemned for failing to protect Benazir Bhutto or investigate her death properly," *The Guardian* (U.K.), April 16, 2010, http://www.guardian.co.uk/world/2010/apr/ 16/benazir-bhutto-assassination-un-report.

[64] Michael C. Ruppert, *Crossing the Rubicon: The Decline of the American Empire at the End of the Age of Oil* (Gabriola Island, Canada: New Society Publishers, 2004).

[65] Nicholas Wapshott, *Keynes Hayek: The Clash that Defined Modern Economics* (New York: W.W. Norton, 2011), 263.

[66] Ibid.

[67] Andrea Vogt, "Italian court rules men convicted of gang rape do not have to be jailed: Supreme court triggers outrage by upholding

decision to annul jail sentence of two 19-year-olds who raped 16-year-old," guardian.co.uk, February 3, 2012 http://www.guardian.co.uk/world/2012/feb/03/italian-court-gang-rape-jailed.

68 Thom Hartmann, *Unequal Protection: The Rise of Corporate Dominance and the Theft of Human Rights* (San Francisco, CA: Berrett-Koehler Publishers, 2010.)

69 Helen Ellerbe, *The Dark Side of Christian History* (Orlando, FL: Morningstar and Lark, 1995), 20.

70 John Simkin, "Military Industrial Congressional Intelligence Complex," *The Education Forum* (blog), February 13, 2006, http://educationforum.ipbhost.com/index.php?showtopic=6116&st=0.

71 Dick Cheney, speech at the Institute of Petroleum Autumn lunch, 1999, http://www.energybulletin.net/node/559.

72 Henry R. Kranzler, M.D., and Ting-Kai Li, M.D., "What Is Addiction?" National Institute on Alcohol Abuse and Alcoholism Publications Washington, DC: National Institutes of Health, accessed June 24, 2011, http://pubs.niaaa.nih.gov/publications/arh 312/93-95.htm. (An advisor has pointed out that George Bush's use of the term "addiction" in connection with oil should be a clue that actually something else is going on. The advisor maintains, correctly, I think, that our situation is more fundamentally dire than the term "addiction" implies for you can kick an addiction.)

73 Steven Kuhn, "Prisoner's Dilemma," *The Stanford Encyclopedia of Philosophy* (Spring 2009 Edition), ed. Edward N. Zalta, http://plato.stanford.edu/archives/spr2009/entries/prisoner-dilemma/.

74 "Iran says tests 'flying boat' in Gulf War Games," Reuters, April 4, 2006 (9:20 AM BST), http://wtceo.org/wtcenvironmentalorganizat ioniranflyingboat.htm.

75 "Venezuela Says U.S. Preparing For Invasion," KMBC.com, Kansas City, April 11, 2006, http://wtceo.org/wtcenvironmentalorg anizationvenezuelau.s.navalexercisescaribbean.htm.

[76] Sandeep Kikshit, "India Transfers Ship to Maldives," *The Hindu*, April 17, 2006, http://www.hindu.com/2006/04/17/stories/2006041 706371200.htm.

[77] "NZ to Sign Trade Deal In Beijing", 9MSN, April 6, 2008, http://news.ninemsn.com.au/article.aspx?id=94006.

[77] "China Pledges Millions to Pacific Multi-Million Dollar Mining Deal Signed with PNG," CNN, April 4, 2006, http://wtceo.org/wtc environmentalorganizationchinapacificislandstaiwan.htm

[78] http://edition.cnn.com/2006/WORLD/asiapcf/04/04/china.pacific.ap/.

[79] "Turkmen president to talk gas in China," RIA Novosti, April 2, 2006, http://en.rian.ru/world/20060402/45083555.html.

"Kazakhstan, China to jointly build large-scale power plant," Xinhua/*People's Daily Online*, April 1, 2006, http://english.peopl e.com.cn/200604/01/eng20060401_255104.htm

"Russia to supply electricity to China on large scale," Xinhua/*People's Daily Online*, March 30, 2006, http://english.peo ple.com.cn/200603/30/eng20060330_254683.html.

"China president Hu to discuss energy cooperation with Saudi Arabia, Nigeria," *AFX News Limited*, April 14, 2006, http://www.forbes.com/feeds/afx/2006/04/14/afx2670631.html.

[80] "Vietnam wants deepened ties with China," Xinhua/*China View*, April 7, 2006, http://news.xinhuanet.com/english/2006-04/07/cont ent_4398192.htm.

Yin Soeum, "China grants $6 mln in aid, loans to Cambodia," Reuters/*The Star Online*, April 8, 2006, http://thestar.com.my/new s/story.asp?file=/2006/4/8/worldupdates/2006-04-08T112625Z_01 _NOOTR_RTRJONC_0_-244042-1&sec=Worldupdates.

[81] "China explores new oil shipping route with neighbors," Xinhua/*China View*, April 4, 2006, http://news.xinhuanet.com/eng lish/2006-04/05/content_4387855.htm.

[82] "New railway ferry proposed," Xinhua/*China View*, April 1, 2006, http://news.xinhuanet.com/english/2006-04/01/content_4373266.htm.

[83] Elizabeth Rosenthal, "Migrating Birds Didn't Carry Flu," *New York Times*, May 11, 2006, http://www.nytimes.com/2006/05/11/world/europe/11birdflu.html?_r=1&oref=slogin.

[84] "China calls for joint efforts to curb emerging infectious diseases in Asia," Xinhua/*China View*, April 4, 2006, http://news.xinhuanet.com/english/2006-04/04/content_4384589.htm.

[85] Luan Shanglin, ed., "China Endeavors to Build Harmonious Environment," *China View*, March 30, 2006, http://news.xinhuanet.com/english/2006-03/30/content_4365869.htm.

[86] "Sudan Oil and Human Rights," Human Rights Watch, November 24, 2003, http://www.hrw.org/en/node/12243/section/10.

[87] "India, Russia to Sign Trade Agreement," *Express News Service*, February 7, 2006, http://www.indianexpress.com/storyOld.php?storyId=87420.

Pallavi Aiyar, "Indian Firm Taps China's Appetite for Green Energy," *The Hindu*, March 16, 2006, http://www.hindu.com/2006/03/16/stories/2006031604881600.htm.

Press Trust of India, "Government Eyes Free Trade Agreements with China, Indonesia, Japan, and Korea," *Financial Express*, March 21, 2006, http://www.financialexpress.com/news/govt-eyes-ftas-with-china-indonesia-japan-korea/39651/0.

[88] "Myanmar to Sell Gas to India," Press Trust of India / New Delhi, May 13, 2006, http://wtceo.org/worldtradecenterenvironmentalorganizationindialinks.htm.

[89] "1,500 farmers commit mass suicide in India," The Independent, originally in the *Belfast Telegraph*, April 15, 2009, http://www.independent.co.uk/news/world/asia/1500-farmers-commit-mass-suicide-in-india-1669018.html.

90 http://news.monstersandcritics.com/asiapacific/article_1151544.php/China%60s_resource_challenge.

91 www.eia.doe.gov/emeu/cabs/chinaenv.html.

92 "China Furniture Destroys Forests," BBC News, March 24, 2006, http://news.bbc.co.uk/2/hi/business/4842808.stm.

93 "Carlyle to Invest $30 Million in China Flooring Firm," Reuters, March 29, 2006, http://wtceo.org/worldtradecenterenvironmentalorganizationcarlylegroupbuysflooringcompanyinchina.htm.

94 "Transcript of BBC Expose on Bush, bin Laden and the Carlyle Group," transcribed by Mario, November 28, 2001, http://911review.org/Wget/www.vanshardware.com/news/2001/november/011128_BBC_Carlyle/011128_BBC_Carlyle.htm.

95 "China Puts Chopsticks Tax on Menu," CBBC Newsround, March 22, 2006, http://news.bbc.co.uk/cbbcnews/hi/newsid_4830000/newsid_4832600/4832624.stm.

96 Associated Press, "Japan Fears Shortage of Wooden Chopsticks," Gulfnews.com, May 14, 2006, http://gulfnews.com/news/world/other-world/japan-fears-shortage-of-wooden-chopsticks-1.236856.

97 Joe McDonald, "China Turning to Artificial Rain to Clear Beijing Air After Coking Dust Storm," Associated Press and Oh My News, April 18, 2006, http://english.ohmynews.com/ArticleView/article_view.asp?no=286566&rel_no=1.

98 "China to Build World's First 'Artificial Sun' Experimental Device," Xinhua/People's Daily Online, January 21, 2006, http://english.people.com.cn/200601/21/eng20060121_237208.html.

99 Sergei Blagov, "Kazakhstan, Kyrgyzstan, Uzbekistan, and Tajikistan Sign Pact To Preserve Aral Sea," The Jamestown Foundation, *Eurasia Daily Monitor*, vol. 3:162, September 5, 2006, http://www.jamestown.org/single/?no_cache=1&tx_ttnews%5Btt_news%5D=32000.

[100] "Complete 9/11 Timeline," *History Commons* (blog), http://www.historycommons.org/timeline.jsp?timeline=complete_9 11_timeline&before_9/11=foreignIntelligence.

[101] "Rebuilding America's Defenses," Project for a New American Century, www.newamericancentury.org, quoted in www.oilempire .us, September 2000, http://www.newamericancentury.org/Rebuild ingAmericasDefenses.pdf.

[102] Coleen Rowley's Memo to FBI Director Robert Mueller, an edited version of the agent's 13-page letter, *Time*, May 21, 2002, http://www.time.com/time/covers/1101020603/memo.html.

[103] CBS News, September 26, 2001, as quoted in *Crossing the Rubicon*, Michael C. Ruppert, 238.

[104] "LIHOP, MIHOP and Hijacking the Hijackers," http://www.oilem pire.us/lihop-mihop.html.

[105] "NRO: National Reconnaissance Office: CIA's plane into building exercise during 9/11," http://www.oilempire.us/nro.html.

[106] "December 24, 1994: Al-Qaeda Connected Militants Attempt to Crash Passenger Jet into Eiffel Tower," *History Commons* (blog), http://www.historycommons.org/context.jsp?item=a112496ethiopia air.

[107] Michael Elliot, "How the U.S. Missed the Clues," *Time*, May 27, 2002, posted online May 19, 2002, http://www.time.com/time/cov ers/1101020527/story.html.

[108] Michael C. Ruppert, *Crossing the Rubicon: The Decline of the American Empire at the End of the Age of Oil* (Gabriola Island, Canada: New Society Publishers, 2004), 401.

[109] For a rich chronicle of the myriad evidence of Bush Administration involvement in the 911 attacks, see www.fromthewilderness.com, www.oilempire.us and Paul Thomson's 9/11 timeline.

[110] James L. Connaughton (Chairman, Council on Environmental Quality), United States Senate, "EPA's Response to 9-11 and

Lessons Learned for Future Emergency Preparedness," Senate hearing testimony, June 20, 2007, http://epw.senate.gov/public/ind ex.cfm?FuseAction=Files.View&FileStore_id=14f89321-ab27-4bc 4-a9ce-e56fee22a1ab.

[111] United States National Commission on Terrorist Attacks on the United States, *The 9/11 Commission Report* (Washington, DC: 2004), 555. Available at: http://www.9-11commission.gov/report/ 911Report.pdf.

[112] Unites States Environmental Protection Agency, Office of Inspector General, Evaluation Report, "EPA's Response to the World Trade Center Collapse: Challenge, Successes, Areas for Improvement" (Washington DC: August 21, 2003), 9-19. Available at: http://www.epa.gov/oig/reports/2003/WTC_report_2 0030821.pdf.

[113] Jenna Orkin, "The EPA and a Dirty Bomb," *CounterPunch*, January 6, 2005, http://www.counterpunch.org/orkin01062005.html.

[114] Jenna Orkin, "9/11's Disastrous Precedent: The EPA and A Dirty Bomb," January 6, 2005, http://www.counterpunch.org/orkin0106 2005.html; http://www.etf.energy.gov/pdfs/eo13212.pdf.

[115] Jo Becker, Barton Gellman, "Leaving No Tracks," *Angler: The Cheney Vice Presidency* (blog), *Washington Post*, June 27, 2007, http://blog.washingtonpost.com/cheney/chapters/leaving_no_tracks /index.html.

"Christine Todd Whitman," in "Cast of Characters" in *Angler: The Cheney Vice-Presidency* (blog), *Washington Post*, http://blog.wash ingtonpost.com/cheney/about/cast_of_characters/#Whitman.

[116] Ibid.

[117] "Sidley Austin Is Top Provider Of Legal Services To The Hedge Fund Industry, Says Alpha Magazine," *Global Custodian*, http://home.globalcustodian.com/news/Prime-Brokerage/Sidley-Au stin-Is-Top-Provider-Of-Legal-Services-To-The-Hedge-Fund-Indus try,-Says-Alpha-Magazine/20573.

[118] http://www.sidley.com/newsresources/highlights/.

[119] "Sidley & Austin Client G.D. Searle Cleared of Price Fixing in U.S. District Court," press release, December 1, 1998, http://www.sidley.com/newsresources/newsandpress/Detail.aspx?news=1482.

[120] "Sidley & Austin Clients Win Three Major Cases Decided by the Supreme Court on the Same Day," press release, June 26, 2000, http://www.sidley.com/newsresources/newsandpress/Detail.aspx?news=1465.

[121] Rick Weiss, "Bush Unveils Bioethics Council: Human Cloning, Tests on Cloned Embryos Will Top Agenda of Panel's 1st Meeting," *Washington Post*, January 17, 2002, http://www.washingtonpost.com/ac2/wp-dyn/A57155-2002Jan16?language=printer.

[122] James McManus, "Please Stand by While the Age of Miracles Is Briefly Suspended: How the president is trying to kill my daughter," *Esquire*, August 1, 2004, http://www.esquire.com/features/ESQ0804-AUG_STEM#ixzz1MOPD2T00.

[123] Bradford A. Berenson biography, Sidley Austin, LLP, http://www.sidley.com/berenson_bradford/.

[124] Don Van Natta, Jr., "Agency Files Suit For Cheney Papers on Energy Policy," *New York Times*, February 23, 2002, http://www.nytimes.com/2002/02/23/business/agency-files-suit-for-cheney-papers-on-energy-policy.

[125] "Detention and Interrogation of Captured 'Enemies': Do Law and National Security Clash?," Brookings Judicial Issues Forum No. 6, The Brookings Institution, Washington, DC, December 12, 2005, http://www.brookings.edu/events/2005/1212defense.aspx#transcript.

[126] Michael Abramowitz, "Bush Aides' Misuse of E-Mail Detailed by House Committee," *Washington Post*, June 19, 2007, http://www.washingtonpost.com/wp-dyn/content/article/2007/06/18/AR2007061800809.html.

"Detention and Interrogation of Captured 'Enemies': Do Law and National Security Clash?," Brookings Judicial Issues Forum No. 6, The Brookings Institution, Washington, DC, December 12, 2005, p. 55, http://www.brookings.edu/events/2005/1212defense.aspx#TRA NSCRIPT .

[127] Ibid., p. 17.

[128] Ibid., p. 18.

[129] "Detention and Interrogation of Captured 'Enemies:' Do Law and National Security Clash?," Brookings Judicial Issues Forum No. 6, The Brookings Institution, Washington, DC, December 12, 2005, p. 20, http://www.brookings.edu/events/2005/1212defense.aspx#TRA NSCRIPT .

[130] Jean Barr, "A disaster plan in action: How a law firm in the World Trade Center survived 9/11 with vital records and employees intact," http://findarticles.com/p/articles/mi_qa3937/is_200305/ai_ n9260326/.

[131] Ibid.

[132] Ibid.

[133] Ibid., http://findarticles.com/p/articles/mi_qa3937/is_200305/ai_n9 260326/pg_3/.

[134] Alex S. Perry Jr., "Adolf Hitler—An Overlooked Candidate for the Nobel Prize," *Barnes Review*, July/August 2004, http://www.barnes review.org/index.php?main_page=document_product_info&cPath= 89_111&products_id=502.

[135] "About Willis Carto," accessed December 2011, http://www.willis carto.net/html/about_willis.html.

[136] http://www.oilempire.us/parallels.html#pearl.

[137] David Ruppe, "U.S. Military Wanted to Provoke War with Cuba," ABC News, May 1, 2001, http://abcnews.go.com/US/story?id=92 662&page=1.

[138] William Shirer, *The Rise and Fall of the Third Reich: A History of Nazi Germany* (Simon and Schuster, 1960), http://911review.com/precedent/century/reichstag.html.

[139] "Late Justice for Nazi Scapegoat; Verdict Against 1933 Reichstag Arsonist Thrown Out," Spiegel Online International, January 11, 2008, http://www.spiegel.de/international/germany/0,1518,528050,00.html.

[140] David Derbyshire, "The Color of the Universe is Pale Turquoise," *The Daily Telegraph* (Britain), January 11, 2002, posted as "In 1991 David Icke Was Ridiculed Throughout The UK For Wearing Turquoise And Stressing It's Importance In The National Media. They Said He Was a Lunatic. Now a Scientist Has Revealed That Turquoise Is the Base Colour of the Universe," available at http://www.davidicke.com/articles/mysteries-mainmenu-40/24-in-1991-david-icke-was-ridiculed.

[141] Clifford Shack, "Hitler was a Rothschild," David Icke.com, http://forum.davidicke.com/showthread.php?t=147354.

Clifford Shack, *Hidden History* (blog), http://hidhist.wordpress.com/hitler/...-a-rothschild/.

[142] Jon Ronson, "Beset by lizards," *The Guardian*, March 17, 2001, http://www.guardian.co.uk/books/2001/mar/17/features.weekend.

[143] Jon Ronson, *Them: Adventures with Extremists*, (New York, NY: Simon and Schuster), December 31, 2002, http://books.google.com/books?id=XVJPQ2-aieMC&pg=PA165&lpg=PA165&dq=%22reptilian+races%22+%22crinklies%22+%22tall+blondes%22&source=bl&ots=aPCMbWjUkO&sig=st0Vpz0dGcKVxUwDt9ZKhQuz7Ew&hl=en&ei=KJ_mTcu2DcTa0QGrg9CICw&sa=X&oi=book_result&ct=result&resnum=3&ved=0CCMQ6AEwAg#v=onepage&q=%22reptilian%20races%22%20%22crinklies%22%20%22tall%20blondes%22&f=false.

[144] Nicholas D. Kristof, "Martyrs, Virgins and Grapes," *New York Times*, August 4, 2004, http://www.nytimes.com/2004/08/04/opinion/martyrs-virgins-and-grapes.html?scp=1&sq=Martyrs,%20Virgins

,%20and%20Grapes&st=cse&gwh=6D08C6257612DDC386F19E
23FDCCA35B.

[145] Andrew Berwick, "A European Declaration of Independence,"
(London, 2011), http://www.kevinislaughter.com/wp-content/uploa
ds/2083+-+A+European+Declaration+of+Independence.pdf.

[146] Raymond Pearl, *Studies in Human Biology* (Baltimore, MD:
Williams and Wilkins, 1924), http://docs.google.com/viewer?a=v&
q=cache:VmhkLDVchzMJ:phe.rockefeller.edu/carrying_capacity/cc
5.pdf+%22two+billion%22+%22carrying+capacity%22&hl=en&gl=
us&pid=bl&srcid=ADGEESg6591NTsJ2XgQIuENiCdadUqvN6Ex
n-KEkmfgyQQllB7MH9gFf9gVne3wJm6kokcnGn0Fx1YL0in6C
eqNrgd9PE4kCEekEEhngzPp5sSVNT6rbVXl26MxBnwkzX_EoCy
pAvG0I&sig=AHIEtbRnhg0JXG_OuhwcaMwO2dEd0c4RvQ.

[147] http://www.truthout.org/docs_2006/020206R.shtml.

[148] http://www.youtube.com/user/TheBigFixMovie?feature=mhee.

[149] Presentations to the Lifting the Fog Conference in San Francisco,
November 2006, written combination, http://911review.com/article
s/orkin/post911lies.html (of morning), http://www.archive.org/deta
ils/liftingthefog_2006_11_11_session4,   (and   evening)
http://www.archive.org/details/liftingthefog_2006_11_11_session4.

[150] Conference Summary, "Lifting the Fog: The Scientific Method
Applied to the World Trade Center Disaster," November 11, 2006,
Session   4,   Day,   Evening   (UC   Berkeley,   California),
http://www.archive.org/details/liftingthefog_2006_11_11_session4,
Orkin conference text at http://www.911review.com/articles/orkin
/post911lies.html.

[151] Robert S. Truesdale, Stephen M. Beaulieu, Terrence K. Pierson,
*Management of Used Fluorescent Bulbs: Preliminary Risk
Assessment*, final report submitted to David Layland of the US
EPA, October 1992, Research Triangle Institute, Research Triangle
Park, NC, p.5, available at http://www.p2pays.org/ref/23/22634.pdf.

[152] "Smoke Detectors and Americium," World Nuclear Association, accessed June 29, 2011, http://www.world-nuclear.org/info/inf57.html.

[153] EPA Report, September 20, quoted in *Fallout: The Environmental Consequences of the World Trade Center Collapse*, Juan González (The New Press, 2002).

[154] Andrew Schneider, "Public Was Never Told That Dust from Ruins Is Caustic," *St. Louis Post-Dispatch*, February 10, 2002, posted as "Air Today, Gone Tomorrow: Caustic Dust Blankets World Trade Center Area," on http://landofpuregold.com/truth15.htm.

[155] Delta Group for the Detection and Evaluation of the Long-Range Transport of Aerosols, "World Trade Center Debris Pile Was a Chemical Factory, Says New Study," September 10, 2003, http://delta.ucdavis.edu/WTC.htm.

[156] "Toxicological Genomics and *Daphnia*," Center for Research in Environmental Sciences, Indiana University http://www.indiana.edu/~cres1/daphnia.shtml.

[157] Rep. Jerrold Nadler, "Nadler Exposes Dramatic Double Standards and Mishandling of Hazardous Materials Testing and Removal in Downtown Residences," press release, January 16, 2002, http://nadler.house.gov/index.php?option=com_content&task=view&id=726&Itemid=88.

[158] Sam Smith, "Air Today... Gone Tomorrow, 9/11 Memo Reveals Asbestos Cover-Up," *New York Post*, July 16, 2004, http://landofpuregold.com/truth202.htm, also http://www.nypost.com/news/regionalnews/25149.htm.

[159] Hugh B. Kaufman v. United States Environmental Protection Agency, Complainant's First Amended and Supplemented Complaints, No. 2002-CAA-00022, United States Department of Labor, Office of Administrative Law Judges, https://docs.google.com/viewer?a=v&q=cache:-XltSQAA1uwJ:www.peer.org/docs/epa/08_1_8_amended_kaufman_complaint.pdf+whitman+%22shares%22+%22port+authority%22+%22stock%22+%22world+trade+cent

er%22+%22hugh+kaufman%22&hl=en&gl=us&pid=bl&srcid=AD
GEESjO9rsk6RHOElo3C7Kl5Ud_wB3V1hO0l45DmE6BZ0BToZ
JtaacJkhdcVSJyUpMPg7IhL4g98MEdnXaPrmwtD7VjEr8aVmgN
7XGJAh5k8-Af3AnYsAgLEWuIhnrImj0m1xjC4uSC&sig=AHIEt
bTe9KIAs12UL-ojIo6MybeeT79eQA.

[160] Laurie Kazan-Allen, "Asbestos Fallout From September 11,"
Ummah Forum, January 21, 2002, http://www.ummah.com/forum
/showthread.php?23022-Asbestos-Fallout-From-September-11.

[161] Cate Jenkins, Ph.D., memo to TERA COPC Committee, et al.,
"COMMENTS: TERA SEPTEMBER 2002 PEER REVIEW DRAFT,
World Trade Center Indoor Air Assessment," October 22, 2002,
http://www.scribd.com/doc/45070072/Jenkins-102202-Constiutent
s-Concern-TERA-Comments.

"Profile: William Muszynski," *History Commons* (blog),
http://www.historycommons.org/entity.jsp?entity=william_muszyn
ski.

[162] Francesca Lyman, "Criticisms of the EPA," in *Messages in the
Dust: What are the Lessons of the Environmental Health Response
to the Terrorist Attacks of September 11?* (Denver, CO: National
Environmental Health Association, 2003), http://www.neha.org/9-
11%20report/index-Criticis.html.

[163] Government Accountability Office, GAO-07-1091, "World Trade
Center: EPA's Most Recent Test and Clean Program Raises
Concerns That Need to Be Addressed to Better Prepare for Indoor
Contamination Following Disasters" (Washington, DC:
Government Accountability Office, September 5, 2007),
http://www.gao.gov/htext/d071091.html.

[164] Zachary A. Goldfarb, "SEC Investigator Raised Madoff Concerns
Years Ago, Was Asked to Look Elsewhere," *Washington Post*, July
2, 2009, http://www.washingtonpost.com/wp-dyn/content/article/20
09/07/01/AR2009070104223.html.

[165] Jenna Orkin, "EPA's Latest Betrayal at Ground Zero," December 1, 2005, *CounterPunch*, http://www.counterpunch.com/orkin12012005.html.

[166] Matthew Wald, "Pending US Advice on 'Dirty Bomb' Is Under Fire," *New York Times*, December 8, 2004, http://www.nytimes.com/2004/12/08/politics/08nuke.html?scp=1&sq=&st=nyt.

[167] Matthew Wald, "U.S. Plans to Offer Guidance for a Dirty-Bomb Aftermath," *New York Times*, September 27, 2004, http://www.nytimes.com/2004/09/27/politics/27nukes.html?scp=1&sq=&st=ny.

[168] Jenna Orkin, "The EPA and the Dirty Bomb," *CounterPunch*, January 6, 2005, http://www.counterpunch.org/orkin01062005.html.

[169] Jenna Orkin, "Repetition Instills False Belief in Parents," letter to the editor, *The Spectator: the Stuyvesant High School Newspaper*, September 25th, 2002, http://stuyspectator.com/spectator/display.cgi?id=1006.

[170] U.S. Environmental Protection Agency, U.S. Consumer Product Safety Commission, U.S. Department of Housing and Urban Development, *Protect Your Family From Lead In Your Home*, June 2003, accessed June 30, 2011, http://www.epa.gov/lead/pubs/pyfcamerabw.pdf.

[171] Kevin Ruffner, "CIA's Support to the Nazi War Criminal Investigations," April 14, 2007 (Washington, DC: Central Intelligence Agency), https://www.cia.gov/library/center-for-the-study-of-intelligence/csi-publications/csi-studies/studies/97unclass/naziwar.html.

[172] Dalya Alberge, "Red Cross and Vatican helped thousands of Nazis to escape: Research shows how travel documents ended up in hands of the likes of Adolf Eichmann, Josef Mengele and Klaus Barbie in the postwar chaos," *The Guardian*, May 25, 2011, http://www.guardian.co.uk/world/2011/may/25/nazis-escaped-on-red-cross-documents.

173 Monique Harden, Nathalie Walker, "#779—What the Chemical Industry Fears," *Rachel's Environment and Health News*, Environmental Research Foundation, October 30, 2003, accessed June 30, 2011, http://www.rachel.org/?q=en/node/5710.

174 Nathaniel Blumberg, *The Afternoon of March 30* (Big Fork, MT: Wood Fire Ashes Press, 1984), 346–347, http://www.nathanielblumberg.com/bush.htm.

175 Stephen Kurkjian and Jeff McConnell, "Restraining the Media at the CIA," *Boston Globe*, August 22, 1989, http://www.highbeam.com/doc/1P2-8134593.html.

176 Keith Bradsher and David Barboza, "Energy Challenge: Pollution From Chinese Coal Casts a Global Shadow," *New York Times*, June 11, 2006, http://www.nytimes.com/2006/06/11/business/worldbusiness/11chinacoal.html?pagewanted=1&_r=1 .

177 Ibid., http://www.nytimes.com/2006/06/11/business/worldbusiness/11chinacoal.html?pagewanted=all.

178 "Charlie Sheen claims US government was behind 9/11," *The Telegraph* (U.K.), September 11, 2009, http://www.telegraph.co.uk/news/celebritynews/6171714/Charlie-Sheen-claims-US-government-was-behind-911.html.

179 Nathaniel Blumberg, *The Afternoon of March 30: A Contemporary Historical Novel* (Big Fork, MT: Wood Fire Ashes Press, 1984), http://www.nathanielblumberg.com/bush.htm.

180 Finmal Finance Board of Directors, Finmal Finance Services Limited, accessed June 30, 2011, http://finmalfinance.com/.

181 "Nigeria to Mass-Produce Nigerian Version of AK-47 Rifles," *People's Daily Online*, October 2, 2006, accessed September 28, 2011, http://english.peopledaily.com.cn/200610/02/eng20061002_308128.html.

182 Randy Fabi, "Gazprom Signs North Nigeria Oil Search Deal," Reuters, April 1, 2009, accessed September 28, 2011,

http://www.reuters.com/article/2009/04/01/nigeria-gazprom-idUSL
193737520090401.

[183] Ayo Okulaja, Elizabeth Archibong and Ifedayo Adebayo, "EFCC arrests communications commission boss," May 18, 2009, http://234next.com/csp/cms/sites/Next/Home/5418598-146/EFCC_arrests_communications_commission_boss_.csp.

[184] First Bank of Nigeria, "Our History," accessed September 28, 2011, http://www.firstbanknigeria.com/InsideFirstBank/OurHistory/tabid/265/Default.aspx.

[185] Naija Lo Wa, "J.P. Morgan's Analysis of Nigeria Banks," July 11, 2008, accessed September 28, 2011, http://www.naijalowa.com/jp-morgans-analysis-of-nigerian-banks/.

[186] Neil Postman, *Amusing Ourselves to Death: Public Discourse in the Age of Show Business* (New York, NY: Penguin, 1985).

[187] Greg Palast, "Eliot's Mess," March 14, 2008, accessed September 28, 2011, http://www.gregpalast.com/elliot-spitzer-gets-nailed/.

[188] Eliot Spitzer, "Predatory Lenders' Partner in Crime," *Washington Post*, February 14, 2008, accessed September 28, 2011, http://www.washingtonpost.com/wp-dyn/content/article/2008/02/13/AR2008021302783.html.

[189] Cutler Cleveland, "China's Monster Three Gorges Dam Is About to Slow the Rotation of the Earth," *Business Insider*, June 18, 2010, accessed September 28, 2011, http://www.businessinsider.com/chinas-three-gorges-dam-really-will-slow-the-earths-rotation-2010-6.

Alexandra Weitze, "Oil Spill On Track to Reach Atlantic No Later Than October," *Wired Science*, June 17, 2010, accessed September 28, 2011, http://www.wired.com/wiredscience/2010/06/oil-spill-in-atlantic-by-october/.

[190] John Maynard Keynes, "The Economic Impact of the Treaty of Versailles," in *The Economic Consequences of the Peace*, edited extract, *The Guardian* (U.K.), September 5, 2009, accessed